3703405092

D1438745

Brigadoon, *Braveheart* and the Scots

Cinema and Society Series

General Editor: Jeffrey Richards

BRIGADOON, BRAVEHEART
AND THE SCOTS

Distortions of Scotland
in Hollywood Cinema

Colin McArthur

PARK LEARNING CENTRE
UNIVERSITY OF GLOUCESTERSHIRE
PO Box 220, The Park
Cheltenham GL50 2RH
Tel: 01242 714333

I.B. TAURIS
LONDON · NEW YORK

Published in 2003 by I.B.Tauris & Co Ltd
6 Salem Road, London W2 4BU
175 Fifth Avenue, New York NY 10010
www.ibtauris.com

In the United States of America and in Canada distributed by
Palgrave Macmillan, a division of St Martin's Press
175 Fifth Avenue, New York NY 10010

Copyright © Colin McArthur, 2003

The right of Colin McArthur to be identified as the author of this work
has been asserted by the author in accordance with the Copyright, Designs
and Patents Act 1988.

All rights reserved. Except for brief quotations in a review, this book, or
any part thereof, may not be reproduced, stored in or introduced into a
retrieval system, or transmitted, in any form or by any means, electronic,
mechanical, photocopying, recording or otherwise, without the prior
written permission of the publisher.

ISBN 1 86064 927 0

A full CIP record for this book is available from the British Library
A full CIP record for this book is available from the Library of Congress

Library of Congress catalog card: available

Typeset in 11/13.5 Adobe Garamond by Steve Tribe, Andover
Printed and bound in Great Britain by MPG Books Ltd, Bodmin

Contents

Illustrations

General Editor's Introduction

It is a commonplace that Hollywood has conquered and colonised the imagination of the rest of the world. In doing so, it has created celluloid images of other countries and other cultures filtered through its own ideological preoccupations and priorities. England, Scotland, Wales and Ireland all have Hollywoodised images that exist alongside and interrelate with their own self-generated images. In this deeply researched and passionately argued book, Colin McArthur analyses the two Hollywood films that have done most to define Scotland's image worldwide – *Brigadoon* and *Braveheart*.

He traces the genesis, production histories, promotion and reception of the two films, carefully relating them to their respective cultural contexts of the 1950s and 1990s. He explores the creation of the 1947 Broadway musical *Brigadoon* by a Central European émigré (Frederick Loewe) and a New York Jew (Alan Jay Lerner), drawing on tropes and themes in the tartanry and kailyard traditions of Scottish depiction that McArthur sees as part of the 'Scottish Discursive Unconscious', which constructs Scotland as a timeless melange of bagpipes, kilts, castles, clansmen, heather, whisky and mist. He follows it through its transposition to the screen in 1954 by the Arthur Freed unit at MGM. In a classic dream factory pronouncement, Freed declared that Scotland didn't 'look Scotch enough' for the film and had it shot at Metro's Culver City studio. After a thorough visual analysis of the film,

McArthur traces its afterlife and charts its continuing influence on perceptions of Scotland.

Braveheart was the product of a very different cultural climate, both in Scotland and in Hollywood. McArthur subjects the film to penetrating critical scrutiny, in particular showing how it is constructed from the conventions and tropes of classic Hollywood cinema, how it selects from history for its own ideological purposes and how it has been interpreted and appropriated by audiences in Scotland and elsewhere. This stimulating, insightful, multi-layered study makes a major contribution to our understanding of the mythmaking power of Hollywood, the creation and propagation of cultural identities and the diverse relationship of audiences, critics and intellectuals to key films.

Jeffrey Richards

Acknowledgements

Claire Mistry of Cameron Mackintosh Ltd; Jane Mann and Janice West of the RADA Library; Sir Ludovic and Lady Kennedy; Ned Comstock and the staff of the University of Southern California Library; Murray Grigor; Sandra Archer and the staff of the Margaret Herrick Library of the Academy of Motion Picture Arts and Sciences; Professor David McCrone; Professor Stephen Banfield; Ian Wallace OBE; Elena McArthur; Dr Jennifer Lynn Oates; Alistair Lawson; the staff of the British Film Institute Library; Professor Lisa Tickner and colleagues in the Visual Culture and Media department of Middlesex University; Professor Charles Withers; Jeremy Peyton-Jones; Euan Hague. Particular thanks to all my fellow Scots who – for an intended earlier version of a book solely on *Brigadoon* – submitted their views on that film and apologies that the changed conception of the book precluded the inclusion of all but a handful of these views. Substantial parts of Chapter 5 appeared in the *Journal for the Study of British Cultures*. My research on *Brigadoon* in the Freed and Minnelli papers in Los Angeles was facilitated by a travel grant from Glasgow Caledonian University during my period there as Visiting Professor. I am most grateful to that institution and, in particular, to Professor Bill Scott for facilitating this. Finally, Jeffrey Richards has, as ever, been a most supportive and perceptive editor, and, woven into this, and every other project I work on, is the life-stabilising presence of my wife, Tara.

To Tom Nairn, Malcolm Chapman
and Murray and Barbara Grigor,
who lit the way.

Introduction

J anet McBain, in her invaluable filmography of feature films of the period 1898 to 1990 in which Scotland and the Scots are represented, includes close to 350 titles. Many more have since been added. Of all these films, however, only two – *Brigadoon* and *Braveheart* – could be said to have continuing major resonance in Scottish culture and its diaspora. This book is about that resonance and what, within the films themselves and their audiences, might account for it.

Brigadoon and *Braveheart* have provoked sharp debate about how Scotland and the Scots (and in *Braveheart*'s case, Scottish history) should be represented on screen, some Scots being outraged by the way they, their country and their national history have been portrayed. The case of *The Satanic Verses* illustrates how lethal might be the response of a group which feels offended by a work of art. The history of cinema is not without its own, albeit less apocalyptic, examples. In the 1940s and the 1950s archiepiscopal letters were read from the pulpits of Roman Catholic churches warning the faithful that they should on no account see films such as *Forever Amber* and *Baby Doll*; in the 1950s British veterans of the war in the Western Desert picketed cinemas showing *Rommel: Desert Fox* on account of its allegedly too sympathetic portrayal of its subject. Later,

the John Wayne film *The Green Berets* was picketed by groups hostile
to its view of the war in Vietnam, as was *Cruising* by gay groups;
and some feminists demonstrated against *Dressed to Kill*. Perhaps
taking a leaf from the Islamic fundamentalist notebook, some radical
Protestant groups, particularly in the USA, threatened (and
sometimes delivered) violence against the makers, distributors and
exhibitors of Martin Scorsese's *The Last Temptation of Christ*; and,
most recently, the Disney film *Aladdin* provoked serious trouble in
Malaysia, Indonesia and elsewhere because of its insensitive portrayal
of Islam. It is not only confessional, gender and sexual orientation
groups which have been moved to outrage and sometimes action by
the way they have been represented on film. It is true also of *national*
groups. The Norwegians, it is said, were none too keen on their
portrayal in *Song of Norway* and the Chinese were certainly very angry
about Michelangelo Antonioni's documentary film *China*.

As far as is known, the Moderator of the General Assembly of the
Church of Scotland (or, perhaps more appropriately, the Chairman
of the Saltire Society, a prominent Scottish cultural body) has not
issued a *fatwa* against anyone connected with *Brigadoon* or
Braveheart. Nevertheless, both films are sources of 'trouble', though
of rather different orders. *Brigadoon* began its life on the Broadway
stage in 1947, but it is the 1954 film version round which the
turbulence swirls. Having been received in the 1950s as an engaging
divertissement containing some laughable howlers about Scotland, it
has since developed two separate intertextual lives. Its pleasing charm
has found its way into, for example, the naming of retirement homes,
certain species of flowers and certain domestic pets, mainly among
the petit-bourgeoisie. Its other, more rancid, intertextual life has
been within another fragment of the middle class – the Scots
intelligentsia. At a quickening pace since the 1950s, and accelerating
markedly in the context of the cultural self-analysis which attended
the failed devolution referendum of 1979, *Brigadoon* has come to be
seen, among those whom Tom Nairn described as 'pointy-heids', as
the very nadir of mawkish Tartanry and Kailyard, the latter anathema
to an earlier Scottish intellectual (also quoted by Nairn), who
described it as 'holding up our fellow-countrymen to the ridicule
and contempt of all sane and judicious human beings'. Surfacing
regularly in Scottish broadsheet journalism, often in contexts quite
unconnected with cinema, as shorthand for all that is twee and

regressive, 'Brigadoon' had gained such currency by the 1990s that the makers of *Four Weddings and a Funeral* – with complete certainty that the reference would be widely understood – could have the character played by Simon Callow, first sighting a Scots baronial interior, cry 'Christ! It's bloody Brigadoon!'.

But central as the argument over *Brigadoon*'s 'Scottishness' is to this book, it is not the whole story. *Brigadoon* has been successively a Broadway show and not just a Hollywood, but also an MGM, film, in each instance bearing the institutional, generic and stylistic marks of these forms. The book begins with the question 'Where did *Brigadoon* come from?'; more specifically, how did a fantasy about Scotland emerge from the heads of a New York Jew, Alan Jay Lerner, and an émigré from Central Europe, Frederick Loewe? It then explores the shaping of *Brigadoon* within the norms of the Broadway musical theatre of the 1940s, not least in terms of the recently established hegemony of the 'integrated musical', the kind of show in which book and music were interwoven with narrative. It then examines the filming of *Brigadoon* within two key structures: MGM's Arthur Freed unit – progenitor of the 'golden age' of the film musical – and the auteurist oeuvre of Vincente Minnelli as they negotiated the potentially repressive forces of the MGM bureaucracy and the major film censorship mechanism of the time, the Production Code Administration. The final chapter on *Brigadoon* deals with the often bizarre story of its marketing, how both theatre and film reviewers have responded to it and its use and abuse by diverse groups.

Much as *Brigadoon* has, from time to time, raised temperatures among Scots intellectuals, it seems small beer compared with *Braveheart*. From the moment of its announcement as a project to be made (partly, as it turned out) in Scotland, through the actual shooting to its delirious European premiere in Stirling, complete with *son et lumière* effects at Stirling Castle, *Braveheart* has been both lauded and traduced, on historical, ideological and aesthetic grounds, in Scotland and in the Scots diaspora and beyond. The examination of *Braveheart* begins with the concept of 'the *Braveheart* effect', how it has been appropriated by diverse 'official' politicians, tourism executives, sports personalities and journalists, and wider 'unofficial' political interests, and to what ends. What *Braveheart* is in itself, a late-twentieth-century, multi-generic Hollywood movie, has often been lost in its diverse appropriations. The next chapter, an application of the critical method of Roland Barthes in his book *S/Z,* analyses it as Hollywood artefact, challenging its appropriators to measure their claims against this evidence. Although the Barthesian mode of analysis is primarily descriptive, its purpose being to demonstrate how densely significatory even the smallest fragment of a text might be, applied to *Braveheart* it has the side effect of revealing just how aesthetically impoverished and uninflectedly derivative that film is. The novelist Allan Massie observed to the present writer the aptness to Randall Wallace and Mel Gibson (the writer and director respectively of the film) of Ambrose Silk's judgement on the paintings of Poppet Green: 'You can hear her imagination creak, like a pair of old, old corsets on a harridan.' Several elements of *Braveheart* have entered popular consciousness, none more so than the 'Gift of a Thistle' scene in which the child Wallace, at the graveside of his murdered father and brother, is handed a thistle by the child Murron, his future wife. Questions are raised about the aesthetics and morality of James Horner's music, the casting of the child William and the use of props in this scene. The 'Gift of a Thistle' chapter deploys a critical method now, regrettably, highly unfashionable – the close examination of filmic *mise-en-scène* as a way of revealing the filmmakers' moral attitudes to the narrative they have constructed and their filming of it. Although this method is deployed here in relation to one short scene only, it could profitably be applied to *Braveheart* as a whole. A variant of the method would be to compare any scene in that film with an analogous scene from another film. For instance, the scene of Wallace's and Isabelle's brief sexual liaison might be contrasted with the scene in Jean Renoir's *La Grande Illusion* (1936) in which a runaway French prisoner of war, befriended by a German widow, spends the night with her. The scenes are directly analogous in being about lonely people finding a fleeting closeness, but the delicacy of Renoir's *mise-en-scène* (the wider range of emotions, the discreetness of the camera placement, the restraint of the playing, the leaving of much unsaid and unseen) reveals the extent to which the *Braveheart* scene is a farrago of romantic clichés.

The 'historical' debate about *Braveheart* has generated much heat, but little light. An attempt is made to render this debate more nuanced by mobilising historian Robert Rosenstone's concepts of 'true invention' and 'false invention'. Following my own review of the film in *Sight and Sound*, I was savaged (unjustly in my view) in the letters column of that journal for discussing *Braveheart* as though it were primarily an act of historiography rather than a generic entertainment. Hopefully the attention given herein to the film as film will put that charge to rest. However, those journalists (and some academics) who put historiography and filmmaking in hermetically sealed boxes should not be let off the hook. (Multi-) generic Hollywood entertainment as it is, *Braveheart* nevertheless offers a view of (Scottish) history. The book closes with a chapter on what is by far the most worrying aspect of *Braveheart*, its appeal to (neo-)fascist groups and to what might be called the proto-fascist psyche. Deploying ideas drawn from Klaus Theweleit and Umberto Eco, this chapter suggests that *Braveheart* is the modern 'Ur-Fascist' text *par excellence*. This, I hasten to clarify, is not to accuse the film's makers of being fascists, rather of having delivered a film which is a godsend to the proto-fascist psyche.

As the final chapter indicates, this book is in part highly contestatory, but its writer's historical polemic against aspects of *Brigadoon* has eased to the point where he now better appreciates its charm and its far from negligible aesthetic qualities while still finding its representation of Scotland and the Scots problematic. *Braveheart* has few such ameliorating qualities. When it first appeared I described it, in an article in the broadsheet *Scotland on Sunday*, as 'aesthetically vulgar and ideologically contemptible' (McArthur 1996). I see no reason to alter that opinion. To reinsert the term 'vulgar' into contemporary critical discourse is to wave a red rag at a bull, so freighted is it with High Art elitism and so comprehensively have critical judgements been abandoned in the face of the popular (often defined crudely in terms of box-office returns). Sick of the kind of critical writing which celebrates mindlessly every manifestation of the popular, I use the term 'vulgar' consciously and polemically as a blunt instrument for making distinctions of quality between one instance of popular art and another. I assume that the kind of nuanced judgements made herein between *Brigadoon* and *Braveheart* (not to mention my other critical writings) will pre-empt the charge of unreconstructed Adornoesque elitism.

Some will query why so much fuss is being made about a couple of transient entertainments and will doubtless see the exercise as the stampeding hobbyhorses of a notoriously polemical critic. Whatever truth may lie in that, the issue goes far beyond the present writer's psychology. Scotland is currently at a watershed in two important ways. After a century of (almost all) cinematic representations of Scotland and the Scots having been produced furth of Scotland, mainly in Hollywood and the Home Counties of England, indigenous film production structures have emerged. There has been insufficient debate about the kinds of films such indigenous structures ought to prioritise with, in my view, too rapid a surrender to the 'Hollywood on the Clyde' position which would welcome virtually *any* kind of film production in Scotland, irrespective of aesthetic quality or ideological orientation, so long as it provides jobs, attracts outside finance and helps the tourist industry – desirable aims, needless to say, but not at *any* price. Hopefully this book will re-ignite that peremptorily foreclosed debate.

The other aspect of the watershed is, of course, the devolution of (certain limited) powers to Scotland and the setting up of the Scottish parliament. This has rightly provoked debate about the kind of society post-devolution Scotland should become. That will be shaped by diverse factors, but artistic representations, including films, are part of the picture. As the book argues, *Brigadoon* embodies the Scottish Discursive Unconscious – the core of which is an ensemble of images and stories about Scotland as a highland landscape of lochs, mists and castles inhabited by fey maidens and kilted men who may be both warlike and sensitive – which serves internationally to signify 'Scottishness'. Without in any way discounting the long-term ideological effects of *Brigadoon* and the Scottish Discursive Unconscious on, not least, Scots themselves, it is likely that *Braveheart* is having the most immediate and dramatic effects on post-devolution Scotland. It has already inflamed the *ressentiment* of anti-immigration groups such as Scottish Watch and Settler Watch and *seems* (a properly-mounted sociological study is urgently needed) to be having unpleasant effects on some young Scottish men, particularly in the way they relate to English people. On the other hand, *Braveheart* seems to have generated renewed interest in Scottish history and brought additional tourists to Scotland. The social costs and benefits of *Braveheart* need to be soberly assessed.

In the last analysis *Brigadoon* and *Braveheart* are too important to be left within the realm of entertainment.

1

Where Did *Brigadoon* Come From?

O wad some power the giftie gie us
To see oursels as ithers see us!
Robert Burns

Cultural historians love temporal coincidence and the less wary may be seduced into regarding it as an explanatory principle. Consider the following coincidence. On 13 March 1947, the Broadway musical *Brigadoon* opened at the Ziegfeld Theater, New York, ran for 581 performances, garnered many awards, including 'Best Musical of 1947' from the New York Drama Critics Circle, and proved to be the biggest hit of the 1947 Broadway season. Its impact on the theatrical and the wider community can be gauged by images generated by it forming the front cover of the prestigious drama journal *Theatre Arts*. *Brigadoon* is about two Americans who, on a trip to the Scottish highlands, stumble upon the village of the title, which emerges from a deep sleep for only one day every hundred years. One of the Americans is a cynical realist but the other, a yearning Romantic, falls in love with a village woman and opts to join her as Brigadoon recedes once more into its hundred-year sleep. The most *dramatic* action concerns the single malcontent, a rejected suitor, who tries to cross the bridge which is the portal into the 'real' world, a move which, if successful, would cause the village to vanish forever. Hunted down and (albeit accidentally) killed, his grieving father's words are less about his loss than his own shame at his son's apostasy. Tuneful Broadway musicals do not readily invite ideological analysis but, as the foregoing description makes clear, this part of the story is about conformity and the deadly consequences of failing to conform. It is this perception which caused critic Stephen Harvey to refer to *Brigadoon* as 'a closet horror story'.

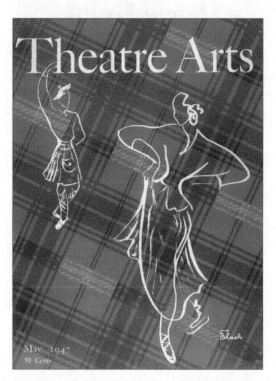

1. *Brigadoon* captures the attention of the American theatrical world of 1947. The cover of *Theatre Arts*.

The other half of the coincidence. On 27 October 1947, in a packed committee room in Washington DC, John Howard Lawson, a leftist screenwriter and founder and first president of the Screen Writers Guild, prepared to testify before a sub-committee of the House of Representatives Committee on Un-American Activities. The proceedings quickly became heated on account of Lawson's insistence that, like several 'friendly' witnesses, he too would read a prepared statement and the forbidding of this by the Chairman, Congressman J Parnell Thomas. Lawson's brush with Thomas concluded thus:

THOMAS   (pounding gavel) Are you a member of the Communist Party, or have you ever been a member of the Communist Party?

LAWSON   It is unfortunate and tragic that I have to teach this Committee the basic principles of American...

THOMAS   (pounding gavel) That is not the question. The question is. Have you ever been a member of the Communist Party?

LAWSON   I am framing my answer in the only way in which any American citizen can frame his answer to a question which absolutely invades his rights.

THOMAS   Then you refuse to answer the question; is that right?

LAWSON   I have told you that I will offer my beliefs, affiliations, and everything else to the American public, and they will know where I stand...

THOMAS   (pounding gavel) Excuse the witness.

LAWSON   ... as they do from what I have written.

THOMAS   (pounding gavel) Stand away from the stand.

LAWSON   I have written Americanism for many years and I will continue to fight for the Bill of Rights, which you are trying to destroy.

THOMAS   Officers, take this man away from the stand.

(cited in Fried 1997: 42–43)

Lawson (with nine other Hollywood personnel making up the Hollywood Ten) was sent to jail for contempt of Congress and by the early 1950s the process enacted in Lawson's case – known to us retrospectively as 'McCarthyism' after its most avid proponent, Senator Joseph McCarthy – was the order of the day in the United States of America. Loyalty oaths, blacklisting, dismissal: once again, failure to conform could be deadly.

It is tempting to take *Brigadoon* and the Lawson testimony – so close to each other in time – and to seek some simple one-to-one relationship between them, perhaps suggesting that the cultural artefact *reflects* what was happening (or about to happen) in the wider society. Much critical ink has been spilt in demonstrating the inadequacy of such a reductionist view of the relationship between a society and its art objects. Without, however, wholly losing sight of the 'conformity' connection, it is not going to take us very far in answering the question 'Where did *Brigadoon* come from?'

Let's approach the question more obliquely. I began with a vignette of Lawson being bullied by Thomas, himself soon to be incarcerated for taking bribes, in a Washington committee room in 1947. Here are three further vignettes, frozen in three photographs, which will begin to signal the diversity of the tributaries which flowed into *Brigadoon*. Wendy Smith, in her book *Real Life Drama: The Group Theater and America, 1931–1940*, includes a photograph of the entire Group Theater company, probably taken in 1931, at the Brookfield Center, the company's base in rural Connecticut. At the centre of the group stand a rather skinny young woman and a somewhat portly young man. They are Cheryl Crawford (co-founder, with Harold Clurman and Lee Strasberg, of the Group Theater) and Robert Lewis, at that time a raw actor with the company. They would go on to become respectively producer and director of *Brigadoon* in 1947. The intriguing question is by what route did these two stalwarts of perhaps the most prominent leftwing theatre group in America arrive on the seemingly depoliticised and 'frivolous' Broadway musical stage a decade and a half later? Several books on American dance include a photograph (also from the 1930s) of the trustees of the American Ballet Theater. As befits the High Art orientation of ballet at the time, the figures in this photograph (including the distinguished American composer, Aaron Copland) are posed more formally than the Group Theater people. The trustees include Agnes De Mille and Oliver Smith, who were to go on to become choreographer and set designer respectively on *Brigadoon* in 1947. The analogous question is by what route did these practitioners of High Art end up in what was widely seen as a low- (or at least middle-) brow form. The final photograph, much reproduced in books about the American musical theatre, is of two youngish men, one seated at a piano, the other leaning on its lid. The former is Frederick 'Fritz' Loewe, born into a middle-class, possibly half-Jewish family in Berlin, the latter Alan Jay Lerner, scion of a well-to-do New York Jewish family, the composer and librettist/lyricist respectively of *Brigadoon* who would go on to co-create some of the most memorable of musicals, including

Paint Your Wagon, My Fair Lady and *Camelot*. The most intriguing question relating to both is how – neither having been to or had any association with Scotland – they came to light on it and signify 'Scottishness' so iconically in their show. The careers of all six figures will contribute significantly to answering the question of where *Brigadoon* arrived from in 1947 and how it came to be precisely as it was. However, it is an important argument of this book that the conscious control and decisions of particular artists never tell the whole story of how art works signify. Equally, perhaps more, important are the unconscious traditions and discourses the artists inhabit, the kinds of ideas they take for granted about, for example, what constitutes a Broadway show or what 'Scotland' means. Nevertheless, the careers of these six figures – involving the complex melding of socially-conscious theatre, High Art ballet and popular musical entertainment – are useful initial routes to the opening of *Brigadoon* in March 1947.

2. Signifying Scotland. The cover of a 1947 programme
booklet for *Brigadoon*.

Alan Jay Lerner and Frederick Loewe

It would seem logical to begin with the librettist and composer of *Brigadoon*, since it is they who shaped the initial artefact which would then have had to be touted round possible producers and backers before it would arrive at the Ziegfeld Theater in March 1947. The most extensive account of the backgrounds and characters of both men is Gene Lees' *The Musical Worlds of Lerner and Loewe*. In terms of character, what emerges from Lees' account is both men's powerful impulse towards fantasy, and not just in their work. Indeed, Lees poses serious questions about the veracity of Loewe's version of his own biography: his having been trained as a concert pianist in Vienna and Berlin, his having studied with the composers Busoni, d'Albert and von Reznicek, his having been, at 13, the youngest soloist to have appeared with the Berlin Symphony Orchestra, his claim to have won the Hollander Medal in Berlin in 1923, his coming to America in the early 1920s, his frustrated attempts to build a concert career, and his having turned to disparate occupations for seven years, including cow-punching and boxing, the latter including a bout with the future World Featherweight Champion Tony Canzoneri. Geoffrey Block's entry on Loewe in the highly respected *The New Grove Dictionary of Music and Musicians* reads:

> His claim to have studied with Eugen d'Albert and Ferrucio Busoni before emigrating to the USA in 1924 remains unverified and questionable. Also, by his own account, Loewe worked in a series of unusual and sometimes improbable occupations that included boxing, gold prospecting, delivering mail on horseback and cowpunching.
>
> *(Block 2001: 73)*

Several critics have queried the likelihood of a putative concert pianist risking his hands in the boxing ring. Certainly, some of his earliest musical successes were in less elevated musical milieux than those he claimed had shaped him.

With regard to Lerner, Lees writes:

> There is no trace of religion in any of the writings of Alan Jay Lerner, but there is an immense amount of fantasy, a fascination with superstition and the occult that is surprising in a man of his background. When he was twelve and at the Bedales School in

England... [he heard that] Sir Arthur Conan Doyle was going to deliver a paper on the nature of the existence of God to the British Society for Psychic Research... Lerner said that from that time... 'nothing, outside of the theatre has intrigued me and sustained my unflagging interest more than the occult, extrasensory perception, reincarnation and all that is called metaphysical (until it is understood and becomes physical)' ... Lerner consulted an astrologer to set the opening date for *Camelot*... He had a fixation on the number thirteen... A yearning to believe that there is something beyond death infuses his work.

The Day Before Spring erases time barriers, with some of the characters coming from past eras. *Brigadoon* is about a town that returns to life every hundred years. *On a Clear Day You Can See Forever* deals with reincarnation. The lives of the protagonists of *Love Life* cover more than a century and a half. *Camelot* is drawn from a tale about early and half-pagan Christianity, filled with magic and a promise that this idealized kingdom will come again.

(Lees 1991: 29–30)

Important as this trait was in Lerner, we should be wary of seeing the otherworldly dimension in *Brigadoon* as arising solely from Lerner's predisposition, for there was, in the period of the show's gestation and opening, a more widely-shared *cultural* bias towards the very impulses Lees identifies as being so important to Lerner's makeup. Many Broadway shows and films of the time – for example, *All That Money Can Buy* (1941), *Here Comes Mr Jordan* (1941), *I Married a Witch* (1942), *The Human Comedy* (1943), *Yolanda and the Thief* (1945), *Angel on My Shoulder* (1946), *A Matter of Life and Death* (1946), *The Ghost and Mrs Muir* (1947), *Heaven Only Knows* (1947) – dealt with the supernatural, less in the characteristic modern form of the horror story than in tales of witchcraft, heaven and hell, the appearance of the Devil and the presence of guardian angels. Whatever form these tales of the supernatural took, what united them all was that the dead return to commune with the living, hardly a surprising theme during and immediately after the grievous loss of life of the Second World War and within a society which was, at that time, deeply Christian. The next chapter will develop the argument that certain Broadway musicals immediately preceding *Brigadoon* may have fashioned the particular mould from which it was cast. *Carousel* (1945), for instance, begins with its central protagonist in heaven and learning that he is permitted to return to earth for only one day. So then, the less than firm grip on reality of Lerner (and arguably Loewe) plus the strong thrust in American culture of the time towards the supernatural may partially explain that dimension of *Brigadoon*, but why the *Scottish* setting since, as has been indicated, neither Lerner or Loewe had any connection with Scotland? The matter of the Scottish dimension of Loewe's score will be dealt with presently. With regard to Lerner's story and libretto, however, Gene Lees tells us that:

> Lerner always claimed that *Brigadoon* was an original tale that grew out of his admiration for the books of J. M. Barrie, particularly those such as *Auld Licht Idylls* and *A Window in Thrums* set in the writer's native Scotland. He said the germ of the plot came to him from a muttered remark by Fritz Loewe to the effect that 'faith moves mountains'. Lerner said, 'For a while I had a play about faith moving mountains. From here we went to all sorts of miracles occurring through faith and eventually faith moved a town'.
>
> *(Lees 1991: 48)*

Certainly Lerner would have become familiar with the work of JM Barrie from two sources. It was a feature of the moneyed classes of the USA, particularly those on the eastern seaboard, that they became anglophile in their tastes. One of the manifestations of this was to send their offspring to English (usually) public schools. Thus Lerner spent some time at the Bedales School in Hampshire at a moment (the late 1920s and the early 1930s) when Barrie's reputation as both novelist and playwright was high and Lerner would almost certainly have encountered his work in both forms. However, even if Lerner had never left the USA he is likely to have acquired some exposure to Barrie's work on account of the remarkable success, in America and elsewhere, of the particular literary 'school' within which Barrie (with two other major practitioners, Ian Maclaren and SR Crockett) is usually included, the Kailyard (literally 'cabbage patch'). Anathema to most Scots intellectuals on account of its sentimentality and failure to connect with the modern, industrialising world, Kailyard is described, in *The New Companion to Scottish Culture*, thus:

> Certain features recur: a tendency to operate in a rural, agricultural community usually one or two generations in the

past... a restricted cast featuring one or more ministers; ... worthy dominies of village schools... [and] hard-working ordinary people drawn from a very narrow section of the population, tenant farmers or above, to the exclusion of the very rich and very poor. Another group excluded... is women... They support, they raise families, but the central role is given to the men... Narrow, too, are the range of plots and the permissible range of emotions. Situations recur. Death is a frequent visitor, and family feuds and rifts predominate also. Children run away from home to 'the City', that fearful off-stage Hell.

(Daiches 1993: 169)

A cursory glance at the story of *Brigadoon* will indicate the closeness of the world described above to that into which the two Americans stumble. The missing dimension of the supernatural is amply present in several of Barrie's dramatic works, most notably *Mary Rose* which, as described by David Hutchison:

focuses on the strange experiences of a girl whose life is arrested when she steps onto a remote Hebridean island. The first time her parents 'lose' her for a few days, but on the second occasion she disappears for twenty-five years, leaving behind her young husband and their baby son. When she returns she has not aged at all... At the end of the play she returns as a ghost [and] as the curtain falls she is summoned to her final rest and walks into the night.

(Hutchison 1987: 170)

The parallels with *Brigadoon* are too obvious to need spelling out and, indeed, both Barrie and *Mary Rose* were to be recurrent points of reference in the British press when *Brigadoon* opened on the London stage in 1949. Both *Mary Rose* and *Brigadoon* – and, for that matter, James Hilton's *Lost Horizon* – may have drawn on the Gaelic legend of *Tìr nan Og*, the land of perpetual youth. The fact that the Kailyard, however, dealt with lowland Scotland and *Brigadoon* with the highlands will be addressed below. The Kailyard novelists were themselves émigrés from Scotland whose work was perhaps aimed primarily at other émigrés, but which struck a chord with devotees of sentimental literature throughout the English-speaking world, particularly North America where the Kailyard novelists made lecture tours, were lionised and were widely read.

As Lerner himself has indicated, the work of JM Barrie (and possibly the Kailyard tradition more generally) is a Scottish influence of which he was entirely conscious. To be highly speculative, there is a sentence in one of Ian Maclaren's novels which runs 'A thocht... ye... wud send me back tae Jean wi' guid news in ma mooth.' Is it possible that this is the germ from which grew the song 'I'll Go Home with Bonnie Jean'? There were, of course, other Scottish influences – the terms 'Scottish discourses' or 'discourses about Scotland' would be rather better – at play in the world as a whole and perhaps particularly in the USA. In Neil Simon's uproarious comedy *The Sunshine Boys*, the rancorous old troupers (played in the film by Walter Matthau and George Burns) have a final rehearsal for the television programme which will reunite them in their most famous vaudeville sketch. A voiceover locates them in a roster of vaudeville greats, photographs of whom are montaged in the background. Although for the most part unnamed and indistinct, several of the vaudevillians are glimpsed as being in Scottish highland dress, among them Sir Harry Lauder. The filmmaker Murray Grigor persuaded the veteran Hollywood film director Sam Fuller to appear in his film *Scotch Myths*. Fuller wrote his own lines and spontaneously recalled how, as a child, he had been taken to see Lauder in Chicago and that the queues had stretched for several blocks around the theatre. Something of the enormous appeal of Lauder in the United States may be conveyed in the following newspaper account of his first visit there in 1907:

> The arrival of Mr Harry Lauder, the comedian, in New York tomorrow on a five weeks' engagement... will be made the occasion for a unique celebration by the English, Scotch and Irish inhabitants of the city. When the *Lucania*... arrives at quarantine today Lower Bay will resound with the national strains played by a band of Scotch Highlanders, which, with the chief members of the British colonies, will meet the great liner on a specially chartered tug. On the pier further demonstrations of welcome will be enacted. Mr Lauder will make his first appearance on Monday, and after his last song a band with fife and drum will again strike up national airs. The theatre will be crammed with sons of the British Isles, who have their residence in New York. Already the seats have been sold out for weeks ahead and the first five or six nights' audiences will be almost exclusively composed of people

of British descent. Mr Lauder [is] engaged at the largest salary
ever offered to a foreign music-hall artiste...

(Daily Mail, *2 Nov 1907: 5)*

3. The influence of Harry Lauder. Fred Astaire and
Ginger Rogers in *The Barkleys of Broadway*.

Lauder would return many times to the USA and if, like the
Kailyard novelists, his initial appeal was to émigré Britons, the
experience of Sam Fuller indicates that it spread rapidly through
other American communities until he would become – as in the
montage from *The Sunshine Boys* – among the most illustrious figures
in vaudeville's hall of fame. Lauder's influence can be gauged by the
extent to which mimicry of him became part of other artistes' acts,
as in Greer Garson's music-hall turn in *Random Harvest* (1942) and
the Astaire/Rogers number 'My One and Only Highland Fling' in
The Barkleys of Broadway (1949). Such was Lauder's status in America
that, with the exception of that other great British icon, Charlie
Chaplin, he would become the only non-American featured on a

United States savings stamp. Like the Kailyard novels, Lauder's stage persona (and indeed his 'real' life, since he did not distinguish between the two) causes Scots intellectuals to gnash their teeth, and for very much the same reasons. Cairns Craig has located Lauder in relation to Scottish culture as follows:

> [The] turning of the back on the actuality of modern Scottish life is emblematically conveyed in the figure of Harry Lauder – Kailyard consciousness in tartan exterior – who evacuates from his stage persona, indeed from his total identity, the world of the Lanarkshire miners from which he began...
>
> *(Craig 1982: 13)*

The key phrase for our purposes is 'Kailyard consciousness in tartan exterior'. It was Lauder's 'distinction' – and the source of his popular appeal – that he united the two main discourses whereby Scotland is 'recognised' in the modern world, the Kailyard, which I have already described, and Tartanry, which constructs Scotland as a mist-shrouded land of lochs, mountains, shaggy cattle and alternatively warlike or gentle natives clad in tartan and living 'close to Nature'. It is this latter quality which – the discourse runs – makes Scots particularly attuned to the supernatural. It is a discourse in which marginalised peoples throughout the world will recognise themselves. Tartanry has its origins in the Ossian poems of James Macpherson in the 1770s and the poems and novels of Sir Walter Scott in the first third of the nineteenth century, both being phenomena which gripped the consciousness of Europe and its outcrops in the New World and which brought Scotland right to the centre of imaginative life. It is difficult now to grasp the extent to which Ossianism and Scottism colonised consciousness at this time and, albeit less intensely, thereafter. The ostensibly ancient and anonymous bard Macpherson claimed to have translated from the Gaelic (most likely he composed the fragments himself) was hailed as a northern Homer (as befitted the neo-classicism of the time), Napoleon slept with a copy of the poems by his bedside and had David execute paintings of scenes from them on the roof of his bedchamber. Such was the extent of the prints, paintings and sculptures generated by the poems, that a major international exhibition on the theme of Ossianism could be mounted and toured throughout Europe (but, inexplicably, not the UK) in the 1970s. The reason for its failure to reach these shores is all too explicable. Decisions relating to what shows and tours in British galleries were (are?) made largely within the Home Counties of England and what had Ossianism to do with them. Nor was painting and sculpture the only site to be transformed by Ossianism and Scottism. Felix Mendelssohn's overture *Fingal's Cave* (*The Hebrides*) is perhaps the best-known piece in the musical Ossianic mode, which included at least two operas, and Scott's poems and novels were the starting points for up to 60 operas and numerous other shorter pieces. All of this helped create the nineteenth- (and to some extent twentieth-) century tidal wave of what Roger Fiske has called 'Scotland in music: a European enthusiasm', the title of his book on the subject. Individual works help swell this Tartanry tradition and may indeed – as in the case of *Brigadoon* – become emblematic of it. Certainly, by the turn of the nineteenth to the twentieth century, the twin discourses of Tartanry and Kailyard – often intertwined – had come to be hegemonic over the ways Scotland and the Scots were thought and written about, visualised and represented in music. Literature, historiography, ethnography, drama, the concert platform, painting, sculpture, photography, advertising, right down to film and television today, all have been colonised by Tartanry and Kailyard to the extent that other possible narratives about Scotland, for example as a centre of philosophical enquiry in the eighteenth century or as a source of industrial innovation in the nineteenth century, have largely been evacuated from popular memory. Tartanry and Kailyard, therefore, would have been the dominant (perhaps the only) discourses within which both Lerner and Loewe would have imagined Scotland. The implications of this for Loewe's score will be addressed below.

Four further realisations of Tartanry/Kailyard – more or less contemporary with the gestation of *Brigadoon* – are worth mentioning. One of the features of the world into which Lerner and Loewe (and indeed the other four figures I have identified as crucial to *Brigadoon*'s formation) were born was the relatively recently constituted international postal service, an important dimension of which was (and to some extent still is) the sending of picture postcards. Although the years 1900 to 1918 are spoken of as 'the Golden Age of Postcards', Austria, 1875 is usually cited as the place and date of the first recognisably modern picture postcard. The standard guide to the field, Tony Byatt's *Picture Postcards and Their Publishers*, lists almost 300 British publishers during the 'Golden Age', of whom about 15 per cent were Scottish, including some of the most distinguished names in the business. They, in particular, generated thousands of cards on Scottish subjects, most usually views and comic cards but also cards displaying clan tartans and highland dress but, because of the 'picturesque' nature of highland scenery, many British – and, indeed, continental European – publishers produced extensive series of Scottish views and depictions of Scottish military regiments and 'clansmen'. Such cards circulated extensively not only in the UK and Europe but in North America and British overseas possessions more generally. This was particularly true wherever there was a Scots community and could certainly have been an important source of knowledge – or, more accurately, myth and ideology – about Scotland. As will be seen when we come to consider the screen version of *Brigadoon*, several of its minor characters bear uncanny resemblances to figures on Scottish comic postcards.

Quite apart from British films about Scotland which may have been released in the USA – for example, *I Know Where I'm Going* (1945) – Hollywood itself, throughout the 1930s, regularly produced films either set in Scotland or with a Scottish dimension in which Tartanry and/or Kailyard are writ large. These included an adaptation of JM Barrie's *The Little Minister* (1934), *Mary of Scotland* (1936) and two accounts of Scottish regiments serving on the North West frontier of India, *Bonnie Scotland* (1935) and *Wee Willie Winkie* (1937). Also, as has been mentioned, vaudeville was well stocked with 'Scotch comics' and Scotland was thematised in the late 1930s in Tin Pan Alley. The context of this seems to have been the rise to dominance of swing at this time. One of the outcomes, in a series of 'novelty' numbers, was to bring swing into opposition with areas previously thought of as highbrow or decorous, as in Ella Fitzgerald's 'Mr Paganini' in which that staid master is urged to 'swing'. The determinants of this development seem to have worked in reverse order to that postulated in (Althusserian) Marxist theory. While there was undoubtedly a cultural determination in the *last* instance – the societal drift to middlebrow culture – there was an economic determinant in the *first* instance – the 'strike' of the American Society of Composers, Authors and Publishers (over radio royalties) which denied the broadcasting companies access to 90 per cent of their usual song fare. The 'classics' being out of copyright, were thus fair game for rearranging. 'Folk' material became similar fodder. Maxine Sullivan executed a very popular swing version of 'Loch Lomond', as did Martha Tilton, the Benny Goodman Band vocalist, at the famous 1938 Goodman concert at Carnegie Hall, while Ella Fitzgerald might include an extempore phrase from a Scottish song in an otherwise 'straight' swing number – for example, from 'Comin' Through the Rye' (which itself got the jazzed-up treatment as 'Swingin' through the Rye) in 'Sing Me a Swing Song' – and even recorded an entire 'Scottish' novelty number – 'Macpherson is Rehearsin'. It is worth quoting from this to demonstrate how close its Kailyardesque lyrics are to the kind of songs Lauder was purveying in vaudeville:

Oh, Macpherson is rehearsin'
And the bagpipes are affected
For Macpherson is rehearsin' to swing.
And from Edinburgh to Dundee
Every lad and every lassie
Knows Macpherson is rehearsin' to swing.
'Ach, I dinna care,' said Sandy
'If the elders no' approve,
I've a chick where plans are handy
And I'm in a mellow groove.'
Oh, the bonnie, bonnie lassies
With the kilties on their chassis
Have forgotten all about the highland fling.
Young and old folks get together
And there's truckin' in the heather
When Macpherson is rehearsin' to swing.

Apart from the words themselves, certain features of the orchestration and Fitzgerald's delivery are worth commenting on. The orchestral opening is preceded by what had become, or was to become, the popular structure for signifying 'Scottishness' in music, the same note repeated four times to give the impression of a bagpipe skirl. This was precisely the motif – with the addition of a grace note – which would introduce Loewe's Overture to *Brigadoon*. Also,

Fitzgerald alters her diction to roll her 'r's heavily, widely used to signify 'Scottishness' in speech.

The fourth 'channel' through which images of Scotland would have entered the consciousness of Lerner and Loewe was advertising. When, after the Second World War, the United States economy became the richest and most powerful in the world, one of the dimensions of that power was its becoming the cynosure for marketing campaigns from all over the world. Everyone wanted to soak up the surfeit of dollars, none more so than the luxury industries of the UK, such as automobiles like Rolls Royce and Jaguar, shipping lines such as Cunard and Blue Funnel and Saville Row tailoring. Scotland was represented in this scramble for dollars by two products in particular, tourism and whisky. Although this had been to some extent true of the inter-war period, sumptuous advertisements, especially for whisky since the Scottish tourist authorities could not match the funding of the whisky companies, increasingly suffused the pages of up- and middle-market American publications such as *Fortune, Collier's, Life, Saturday Evening Post* and the *New Yorker*, most usually drawing on Tartanry/Kailyard images of Scotland. Post-*Brigadoon* advertisements often draw upon *Brigadoon*-like landscapes and rustic bridges, opening up the likelihood that the show was both (to some extent) shaped by and shaping advertising. Additionally, the advertising of American products often had recourse to 'Scottish' themes, especially when thriftiness and value for money were the campaign themes. Thus, virtually every time Lerner or Loewe flicked through the pages of the main American magazines, they would have been confronted by (mainly Kailyard/Tartanry) images of Scotland and the Scots.

There is one further element in the initial writing of *Brigadoon* which reflects ironically not only on Lerner's often tangential relationship with reality, but evokes the shade of his discursive ancestor, James Macpherson. Like him, Lerner too was accused of plagiarism. Shortly after *Brigadoon*'s Broadway opening, there was a curious exchange of letters in the *New York Times* between a drama student and Lerner. The student pointed out that, apart from the 'happy' ending whereby the American remains for eternity in the village with his faery love, the incidents of *Brigadoon* are virtually identical with those of *Germelshausen*, a tale written in the early nineteenth century by the German Romantic Friedrich Wilhelm

Gerstäcker. Lerner, in his reply, conceded that *Germelshausen* had been drawn to his attention, but only after he had completed the first draft of *Brigadoon*. The charge of plagiarism was taken up by George Jean Nathan, theatre critic of the *New York Times*, and it obviously stung Lerner so deeply that, over 30 years later, in his memoirs, *The Street Where I Live*, he was to accuse Nathan of being motivated solely by sexual jealousy. The interest of these exchanges is in their symptomatic quality, their being of a piece with the unreality of *Brigadoon*'s world. That said, the discursive framework, dominated by Tartanry and Kailyard, within which Lerner and Loewe fashioned *Brigadoon*, has all too tangible results in the 'real' world.

4. Tartanry, pastoralism and sentimentality.
A characteristic advert for Scotch whisky from an
upmarket American magazine of the late 1930s.

Some decades after the appearance of *Brigadoon*, the Scottish Development Agency, anxious to further awareness of Scotland's scientific and engineering traditions with a view to attracting inward investment, questioned top German executives about the ideas of Scotland they held. Overwhelmingly, they described Scotland as a good place to fish and shoot in, but not to build factories in. Given that this discursive framework has been hegemonic for nearly two centuries – shaping the makers of Broadway shows in the 1940s and German executives in the 1990s – it would also have been the conduit whereby the other two pairs in our resonant photographs, Crawford/Lewis and De Mille/Smith, acquired their ideas about Scotland. However, while examination of historically-determined ideas about Scotland is a necessary element in the analysis of *Brigadoon*, it is not sufficient to explain its complexities. The other two pairs would bring their own discourses and practices to bear on the shaping of *Brigadoon*.

Cheryl Crawford and Robert Lewis

Looked at from the outside, institutions, particularly those motivated primarily by political ideology, appear tight-knit, even monolithic but there are invariably differences of temperament and political emphasis among the individuals comprising them. The Group Theater was no exception. The dust jacket of Wendy Smith's book carries a photograph from a performance of the Group's most famous play, Clifford Odets' *Waiting for Lefty*. Several of the actors give the clenched fist salute emblematic of communism, others mutate the salute into raised fist defiance and the young actor in the foreground has his arms raised in a 'we shall overcome' gesture. Nearly two decades later that same actor – better known as the theatre and film director Elia Kazan – would give the names of some of his erstwhile comrades to the House Committee on Un-American Activities. Different temperaments, different politics.

Of the trio who founded the Group Theater, Harold Clurman seems to have been the visionary who articulated the conception of a politically progressive theatre and Lee Strasberg seems to have been its principal theoretician with regard to acting. Unquestionably, however, it was Cheryl Crawford who held the operation together administratively. It was she, for example, who – as well as scouting for and locating the Brookfield Center – devised the Group's recruiting scheme of structured meetings of interested actors at which, Strasberg having explained the Stanislavskian technique on which the company's performances would be based, she would explain its organisational structure. As Wendy Smith describes it:

> The only Group director with any fund-raising experience was Crawford... She was conscientious and devoted: she studied the subscription plans and financial organisation of various European theatres in an attempt to devise a method whereby the Group could be permanently funded... Crawford also had the Group incorporated and issued a stock offering at $100 a share... Would-be shareholders didn't exactly come charging up the one hundred steps that led to the Group's offices... The spring of 1932, some two and a half years after the [Wall Street] Crash, was not a good time to be floating stocks. The subscription drive Crawford launched in mid-March was only slightly more successful. What the Group offered subscribers, in return for $2, was a twenty percent reduction in box-office prices and one free seat per season.
>
> *(Smith 1990: 72–79)*

Although the skills Crawford deployed were primarily managerial and financial, she was far from being a desiccated number-cruncher. Undoubtedly she was committed to the general aims of the Group and directed seven of its productions. It would be nice to record that she directed the two Group productions written by John Howard Lawson, with whom our story began, but since they were directed by Lee Strasberg that pleasing homology must be gainsaid. Clearly Cheryl Crawford had her own independent vision of theatre.

> The most interesting aspect of [Crawford's] subscription plan was its goal of drawing the audience into the life of the Group. In addition to their box-office reduction and free seat, subscribers were told, they would be asked to submit their criticisms on each play; the directors would respond to them in open meetings of the entire Group, including the audience, during the runs of the plays. Crawford in particular felt strongly that 'the audience is just as much a part of the theatre as the actor or the playwright. In order to create the sort of theatre we want, we have to have the right audience, just as we have to have the right actors and the right plays'.
>
> *(Smith 1990: 79)*

It was her respect for the audience and her perception of it as active which would ultimately take Crawford to the commercial Broadway musical theatre at one of its moments of greatest innovation and, arguably, artistic achievement. Always the most musically inclined of the Group personnel, she it was who, with Harold Clurman, brought Kurt Weill into the Group's orbit to do the score for Paul Green's play *Johnny Johnson*. During their early lean years in America, Weill and his actor/singer wife, Lotte Lenya, would 'camp out' in the home of Cheryl Crawford and her partner, Group actress Dorothy Patten, and in the late 1940s, after the success of *Brigadoon*, Crawford would bring together Weill and Lerner and produce on Broadway the result of their collaboration – *Love Life*.

Clearly more pragmatic than many others in the Group, Crawford was nevertheless very much of the left politically – she and Lee Strasberg were on the advisory board of the socialist Theater Collective – although Wendy Smith describes her as among 'the less political Group members'. It might be guessed that her political commitment would have had to be substantial to have coped with the recurring financial pressures and the inflated egos of some Group members. Crawford, along with Strasberg, was to resign from the Group in 1937, a contemporary news report outlining some of the contradictions, in addition to the recurrent financial pressures, which were splitting the company apart:

> Three factions have figured in recent manipulations. [The revolt of actors against directors was only] one fight. The actors themselves are divided between the 'stars', including members of the Group who went to Hollywood recently to make a picture for Walter Wanger, and the other players. The non-stars resented this 'desertion', feeling that if the Group aristocrats had stayed on it might have been possible to continue with another production… Another cause for complaint among the rank-and-file members of the company was the alleged practice of the Group's hierarchy in passing out choicer parts to a group-within-the-Group.
>
> *(cited in Smith 1990: 304)*

Thus it was that Cheryl Crawford became an independent producer in 1937, emerging from the Group with considerable administrative and financial experience and an impressive book of contacts ranging from theatre owners and backers through to the most accomplished writers, actors, directors, composers, set and costume designers and choreographers of her generation. These qualities and contacts would serve her well in the setting-up of *Brigadoon*.

Barely in his twenties when he joined the Group, Robert Lewis was, like Cheryl Crawford, musically inclined – his parents had been upset when he gave up his studies as a cellist to concentrate on the theatre – and a particular devotee of opera. While, also like Crawford, his commitment to the leftist political values of the Group should not be doubted, his interest in 'heightened theatricality' – a phrase which recurs in Wendy Smith's account of Lewis in the Group – was a source of tension with the politically more hard-nosed members. His enthusiasm in this regard, and the tension it engendered, is well summed-up in Wendy Smith's account of the Group actors' attempts to extend their technical capabilities by engaging the choreographer Helen Tamiris to give them classes in movement:

> Bobby Lewis was an especially ardent student; he strove always in his work for a stylised, heightened theatricality in which movement played an important part, along with music and visual effects. Lewis was something of a renegade in the Group, whose belief in emotional truthfulness and relevant contemporary drama meant that most of their productions were in the realistic tradition of nineteenth – and twentieth – century European and American theatre.
>
> *(Smith 1990: 90–91)*

This impulse to 'heightened theatricality' would take Lewis to places – geographically and emotionally – where many of his Group colleagues would not have wished to go, culminating in the directing of Cheryl Crawford's production of *Brigadoon* on Broadway in 1947. Certainly the impulse was visible in his actorial performances with the Group and in his studying with the Russian actor, dramatic theoretician and teacher Michael Chekhov (who had worked directly with Vakhtangov and Stanislavsky) at Dartington Hall in England in 1938. Predictably, what Lewis most admired about Chekhov (who, with his Sigmund Freud-like appearance, would play Ingrid Bergman's psychiatrist mentor in Hitchcock's *Spellbound* in 1945) was his commitment to movement and visual stylisation. Lewis' irritation at the Group's less than wholehearted endorsement of precisely these qualities was to erupt in a formal memo, part of which is quoted by Wendy Smith:

> Group productions lack colour, rhythm, movement – all those *other*
> things in the theatre besides psychology.
>
> *(cited in Smith 1990: 358)*

Lewis would embrace these qualities, in spades, in his direction of
Brigadoon. He would progressively abandon acting for directing and
teaching, founding – with Crawford and Kazan – the famous Actors
Studio in New York, the practice of which, popularly dubbed 'the
Method', would become more widely known through the film work
of 'graduates' of the Studio such as Marlon Brando, Montgomery
Clift and James Dean. Given that Lewis' involvement in *Brigadoon*
might be seen as the coming to fruition of all these qualities which
the Group inhibited, it is a pleasing coincidence that one of his
earliest muscle-flexings as director should have been the William
Saroyan play of 1939 – *My Heart's in the Highlands*.

Agnes De Mille and Oliver Smith

Of the three pairs in the photographs with which I began, Lerner
and Loewe already occupied the popular terrain of Broadway
(although Loewe would get there by way of the tradition of European
classical music), Cheryl Crawford and Robert Lewis would get there
by way of leftwing theatre and De Mille and Smith would arrive via
the High Art of classical ballet and 'legitimate' theatre. The
relationship between High and Popular Art was as complex in post-
Second World War America as elsewhere and the two areas were
nowhere near as hermetically sealed from each other as might be
supposed from their linguistic binarism. To indicate the informal
links which united cultural workers of diverse 'levels' in a metropolis
like New York, when Cheryl Crawford, for financial reasons
connected with the Group's ongoing penury, was forced to relinquish
her New York apartment, she rented it to the classical composer
Aaron Copland, the same Copland who would write the score for
the Agnes De Mille-choreographed ballet *Rodeo* in 1941/2. Equally
interestingly, De Mille choreographed *Rodeo* for the High Art Ballet
Russe de Monte Carlo, enforcedly sojourning in the USA as a result
of the Axis occupation of its European base. De Mille's description
of her triumph with *Rodeo* at that temple of High Art the
Metropolitan Opera House in New York, resonates with the journey

made by so many American choreographers, painters, composers and other artists between the wars:

> Ballet gesture up to now had always been based on the classic technique and whatever deviated from this occurred only in comedy caricatures. The style throughout, the body stance, the walk, the run, the dynamic attack, the tensions and controls, were balletic even when national folk dances were incorporated into the choreography. We were trying to diversify the root impulse and just as Gershwin impressed on the main line of musical development characteristics natural to his own unclassical environment, we were adding gestures and rhythms we had grown up with, using them seriously and without condescension for the first time. This is not a triviality: it is the seed and base of the whole choreographic organisation. If dance gesture means anything, it means the life behind the movement.
>
> *(De Mille 1952: 307)*

It was entirely appropriate that, in addition to the extravagant floral tributes showered on De Mille on the Met stage at the end of *Rodeo*, one 'bouquet' should have been made up of glowing American corn decked out in red, white and blue ribbons. A distinctively vernacularised American choreography had come into its own, driven by the beer-hall, barn dance and hoedown rhythms of Copland's score. However, the very popularity of *Rodeo* may sound a warning note. It is an oft-times troubling feature of popular art that it follows too closely the contours of popular ideology. We began our story with two attempts at enforced conformism – the runaway in *Brigadoon* and the screenwriter John Howard Lawson. It is awesomely coincidental that ideological conformism is precisely the charge that has been made against Agnes De Mille's choreography for *Rodeo*, though this time from the perspective of post-1960s feminism. In her book *The Shapes of Change: Images of American Dance*, Marcia Siegel wonders why *Rodeo* 'hasn't been denounced and picketed by women's liberationists'. She goes on:

> De Mille's community... is entirely homogeneous. In fact, the moral purpose of her ballet is to show the error of being a non-conformist... *Rodeo* personifies all the conventional ideas about courting. In trying to be like the men the Cowgirl loses their

respect; they want their girls to be mysterious, unpredictable, helpless, to wear bows in their hair and not smell of leather and horse sweat... [T]o be correct is to belong, and belonging is all.

(*Siegel 1979: 128–129*)

The danger of following through a trend in terms of the practice of a single artist is the implication that the single artist is the 'onlie begetter' of the trend. Nothing could be further from the truth. American art of the 1920s, and particularly the 1930s, was rooted in politics and history and, at the risk of considerable over-simplification, two main trends are discernible: an impulse to Americana and an impulse to (most usually) socialist politics, very often intertwining with each other. Painters and sculptors; theatre and film writers, directors and actors; musical performers and composers; and dancers and choreographers had, as individuals and in groups, increasingly come to define their arts as American and, particularly in the 1930s, socially-conscious, usually (but not exclusively) from a leftist perspective. Each art (and, indeed, each artist) has its own complex story but the twin impulses to slough off European influence and become American and to engage with society as a whole and not just elites, unquestionably pulled American art – and here this is a gross, if useful, oversimplification – towards the vernacular and away from High Art, towards realism and naturalism and away from modernism. This tendency would continue, indeed intensify, after the Japanese attack on Pearl Harbour in December 1941 and America's entry into the Second World War. The rubric under which these tendencies then operated was 'patriotism'. The sombre subtext to our story is the McCarthyite purges of the Cold War, which would drive underground this progressive conception of patriotism. Indeed, many of those on the left who had been most alert to the danger of fascism in the 1930s would be denounced during the Cold War as 'premature anti-fascists'. A full account of the turn to the socially-conscious vernacular would have to deal with the crucial influence of certain federal government mechanisms such as the Federal Arts Project, the Federal Music Project, the Federal Theater Project and the Federal Writers Project which boldly mobilised 'creative' personnel into publicly-funded work on much the same basis as plumbers, carpenters and bricklayers. All were part of Roosevelt's New Deal for kick-starting the American economy out of the depression which had followed the Wall Street Crash of 1929. Whether or not the artists in question received direct government funding – private sponsorship by rich individuals was also important – the turn to the American vernacular and to speaking to wide audiences is discernible in, for example, Copland's scores for the ballets *Rodeo*, *Billy the Kid* and *Appalachian Spring* and in the vernacularised movements the choreographers (Agnes De Mille, Eugene Loring and Martha Graham respectively) fashioned from the music; in Thomas Hart Benton's abandoning New York and modernism to return to his native Kansas City and a regional, realist style of painting (Benton would be perhaps the most dramatic example of social concern manifesting itself as rightwing populism rather than socialism); and in Orson Welles' directing *Cradle Will Rock* – a musical about organised labour – under the auspices of the Federal Theater Project. It would be wrong to see the embracing of the vernacular as a total turning of the back on modernism and formal complexity. Much of the interest of a remarkable artist like Copland lies in the extent to which the tradition of European art music, including post-Stravinsky modernism, is discernible in his apparently most simple vernacular compositions. Something of the same argument can be made about the choreography of Agnes De Mille and possibly the artwork of Oliver Smith. Coincidentally, the first theatre commission Smith received was to design the sets for *Rodeo*. Although Smith was a realist in the sense that his sets were always clearly locatable in specific times and places, they often had an austere, sometimes dreamlike quality with long vistas and low horizons very reminiscent of Surrealism. Clearly his work too reflected a tension between High Art and the vernacular.

Three photographs, three pairs of theatre workers and three different orientations to art: such were the diverse tributaries which would come together in *Brigadoon* – and which would be underpinned by the unconscious discourses about Scotland and the Scots which would have shaped all six artists. However, whatever the diverse origins of *Brigadoon*'s key personnel, whatever the strength of the unconscious shaping discourses, they all met on the terrain of the Broadway musical, a genre with its own diverse tributaries, characteristic forms and audience expectations. It is to the location of *Brigadoon* in that form we must now turn.

2

Brigadoon and the Broadway Musical

> The Broadway musical... thanks to certain fiercely competing
> groups composed of speculators, popular stars, good scene
> designers, bad composers, witty if second-rate song writers,
> inspired costumers, and truly modern dance directors, has
> become the authentic expression of all that is American.
>
> *Bertolt Brecht*

In *The Player*, Robert Altman's accomplished film about the
workings of Hollywood, Griffin Mill (Tim Robbins), the antihero
studio executive, explains to the erstwhile lover of the screenwriter
he has accidentally killed that, of the 50,000 scripts he receives each
year, he can green light only 12. Learning that her dead lover's script
was not among the 12 because 'it lacked certain elements that we
need to market a film successfully', the heroine enquires what these
elements are. Mill then recounts the key ingredients not just of the
classic Hollywood film, but of that form at a particular moment
(1992) of its development – 'suspense, laughter, violence, hope, heart,
nudity, sex, happy endings... mainly happy endings'. Mill evades
her next question, 'What about reality?'. With the replacement of
nudity and sex with singing, dancing and romance, Mill's list
amounts to a fair description of *Brigadoon* and of the Broadway
musical more generally. The fact, however, that we have had to erase

sex and nudity from Mill's list indicates that, although the form remains generically recognisable, it is far from static. It alters its form over time, partly in relation to changing social *mores* (sex and nudity are much less controversial in contemporary times than in the 1940s) but also in the relationship of its formal ingredients. Richard Kislan, in his exhaustive analysis of the form of the Broadway musical, articulates the Grand Narrative, the consensual view, of the development of the form by a telling anecdote:

> Oscar Hammerstein II had been engaged to collaborate with Jerome Kern and Otto Harbach on a musical for Marilyn Miller called *Sunny* (1925). The collaborators accepted the challenge and with the energy of mutual artistic stimulation marched headlong into the producer's office armed with the dramatic possibilities of the project. Management resisted: the show was to be an elaborate vehicle for the star. In desperation, the collaborators read a detailed outline of the plot. Marilyn Miller replied, 'When do I do my tap dance?' Two years later, Jerome Kern and Oscar Hammerstein II wrote *Show Boat*.
>
> *(Kislan 1980: 163)*

Kislan's account is itself a rhetorical piece of writing which, in its account of the mutually incompatible positions, deploys the dramatic binarism so beloved of popular art. It expresses in a nutshell what is now the orthodox view of the development of the Broadway musical that, up to the 1940s, it was in a state of adolescence characterised by disparate forms such as revue, vaudeville, burlesque and operetta, a state in which there was little if any integration among the elements – song, dance, comedy, spectacle – occupying the couple of hours of a show. According to this orthodox view (for a dissenting view see Williams 1992: 58–63), the 'maturity' to which the musical aspired was the integration of all these elements round a coherent narrative. Kislan's citing of *Show Boat* in the 'punch line' of his story reflects the consensus that it was a proto-integrated musical which brought all the elements into partial relationship. Kislan calls the long haul to the integrated musical 'the battle of the book' which would be 'won' in the 1940s and 1950s with a string of successful musicals taking their coherence from the strength of their *libretti*. One of the subtexts of this book is that the apparently hermetically sealed compartments of High Art and Popular Art are, in fact, extremely leaky, with personnel and ideas moving in two-way transit between them. The much-touted contemporary idea of 'crossover' (reflected in, for example, the Three Tenors phenomenon) is far from new. This is underlined in Geoffrey Block's account of the formation of what, referred to above as the consensus, he describes as the Broadway musical canon:

> [T]he criteria for Broadway musical canonization are strikingly similar to those established for the European musical canon. Just as Beethovenian ideals of thematic unity and organicism became increasingly applied to dramatic works (culminating in Wagner's musical dramas), Broadway musicals after Rogers and Hammerstein's *Oklahoma!* (1943) would be evaluated on how convincingly they realized a new 'ideal type', the integrated musical. Integrated Broadway musicals share with their European operatic counterparts the ideal of a musical drama in which the various parts – song, story and movement – form an interdependent and homogeneous whole. With the notable exceptions of *Show Boat* and *Porgy and Bess* (1935), the pre-Rogers and Hammerstein musical offers striking parallels with Baroque operas, where composers and librettists serve larger-than-life stars who arrest the action with their show-stopping arias. After *Oklahoma!*, canonical musicals frequently aspire to and often approach Joseph Kerman's standard of European operatic excellence and use music to define character, generate action and establish atmosphere.
>
> *(Block 1993: 527–528)*

So central has *Oklahoma!* become as the hinge on which the 'book' or 'integrated' musical pivots that Ethan Morrden, in his *Beautiful Mornin': The Broadway Musical in the 1940s*, takes his title from one of the lyrics of that show and discusses musicals as disparate as *Cabin in the Sky* (1940), *Pal Joey* (1940) and *Lady in the Dark* (1941) under the chapter heading 'The Road to *Oklahoma!*'. Morrden, whose position is echoed in every major account of the Broadway musical, goes on:

> The very title of the show has become a summoning term meaning 'The work that changed the form.' Well, it did. Its immediate and all-encompassing influence takes in: a cycle of shows with historical American subjects; a fascination with characterful rather than plot-

filled stories and with conversational lyrics, leading to a concomitant decline of the genre number [the kind of song with no connection with the surrounding action]; a proliferation of musical scenes, especially in the addition of a few spoken lines between the vocal choruses, thus to keep story tension vital; a layout of long first act and short second act (because the stronger stories need more exposition time and the act break must now arrive at a genuine dramatic climax and not because the candy counter is ready for business); and in a sudden emergence of atmospheric, personalized, narrative dance, not for prestige but to bridge the gap between the script and the score, that place where neither speech nor song quite expresses what we need to know.

(Morrden 1999: 78–79)

With the sole exception of its reference to 'a cycle of shows with historical American subjects' – which would indeed come to be discernible in Rodgers and Hammerstein's own *Carousel* (1945) and Irving Berlin's *Annie Get Your Gun* (1946), as well as reflecting the connection between what high and popular artists were doing at the time – Morrden's description could be a blueprint for *Brigadoon*. It might be argued, therefore, that while imaginings of Scotland and the Scots were the major *unconscious* discourses which wrote *Brigadoon*, Lerner and Loewe, at a conscious level, had the Broadway musical in general, and the integrated musical such as *Oklahoma!* in particular, as the template from which they fashioned their show. It would have been a model very much in the forefront of Cheryl Crawford's mind in assembling the production personnel. Writing about *Oklahoma!*'s choreography, Morrden observes:

No wonder *Oklahoma!*'s dance plot impressed Broadway so much. Here at last was the reason all those ballet people had been choreographing musicals: to do in dance what the script and score could not do in words and music. To consult a character's feelings. Surely one of the attractions of the forties classics was their choreography, exposing to an uninitiated public the excitement of high-maestro dance... [T]he once occasional dream ballet would become de rigueur: there were at least four others in the eighteen months after *Oklahoma!*'s premiere.

(Morrden 1999: 77–79)

As readers may already have guessed, the choreography of *Oklahoma!* was devised by Agnes De Mille and for good measure its sets were designed by Oliver Smith. In certain important respects, therefore, *Oklahoma!* was imprinted on *Brigadoon*.

The insistence of historians of the Broadway musical on the 'integrated' nature of post-*Oklahoma!* shows may be somewhat at odds with the account, in the last chapter, of the diverse cultural backgrounds of the key production personnel of *Brigadoon*. Whatever 'integration' was finally achieved, it is clear that Lewis, De Mille and Smith had substantial reservations about the material they had been hired to work on. As Robert Lewis tells it:

> The first thing I did after reading the script of *Brigadoon* was to sit down in a quiet bar with Agnes [De Mille], order a couple of martinis – it turned out to be a couple for each of us – and face up to the problem of how to neutralise the operettalike goo in the story. The question we asked ourselves was 'How do we set about killing Jeannette Macdonald?' Oliver Smith told me that he stopped reading the script when he came to the reply of the Scottish dominie to the American Tommy's question 'So you're all perfectly happy living here in this little town?' The old man answers: 'Of course, lad. After all, sunshine can peep through a small hole.' Said Oliver, 'If I had read any further I'd never have been able to design the show'. By the time Agnes and I had finished our analysis of the original script, the inherent whimsy in the story was alleviated by the addition of a violent chase, a stately sword dance and a powerful funeral. This last was always resented by the composer, Fritz Loewe, probably because the musical accompaniment was an existing, authentic Scottish funeral dirge played on bagpipes that emitted a sound offensive to his Viennese ears.
>
> *(Lewis 1980: 168)*

The question 'How do we set about killing Jeanette Macdonald?' and Lewis' reference to the 'operettalike goo' of Lerner's libretto reveal not only the different artistic agendas of the key players, but the perception that *Brigadoon* may not have been as far distant from one of the central strains in American musical theatre – operetta – as subsequent historians have claimed. Indeed, Richard Traubner, in his *Operetta: A Theatrical History*, is prepared to classify *Brigadoon, Oklahoma!* and many more of the great Broadway musical successes of the 1940s and 1950s as operettas, though clearly Lewis is applying a narrower definition more in accord with a popular understanding of the term. That understanding is of a melodically lush form, emerging in Vienna in 1905 with Franz Lehár's *The Merry Widow* and often, though not invariably, set in an imaginary Mitteleuropa, which the term 'Ruritania' evokes, with aristocrats in resplendent white uniforms. Clearly bearing some relationship to opera, but without that form's stringent vocal and musical demands, the genre became immensely popular throughout Europe and America where it was associated principally with the names of three Europeans: Victor Herbert, born in Dublin; Rudolf Friml, born in Hungary; and Sigmund Romberg, born in what is now the Czech Republic. The birthplaces of Friml and Romberg were, at the time, provinces of the Austro-Hungarian Empire – the sumptuous court of which was clearly the model for that in so many operettas – so they would have looked to Vienna as their cultural capital. Demonstrating once more the leakiness between High and Popular Art, Herbert was a composer of opera and concert music (his Second Cello Concerto is said to have influenced Dvořák) and was for a time conductor of the Pittsburgh Symphony; and Friml was a pupil of Dvořák and for many years an accompanist of the violin virtuoso Jan Kubelik. Lewis' invoking of Jeanette Macdonald's name calls to mind the film versions of the operettas of these men, such as *Naughty Marietta* (1935), *Rose Marie* (1936), *Maytime* (1937), *The Firefly* (1937) and *New Moon* (1940), and her on-screen partnership with Nelson Eddy. To illustrate the danger of pigeonholing any artist within a single dimension of the American musical theatre, the same Oscar Hammerstein II, whom future historians would celebrate as the 'co-inventor' with Richard Rodgers of the integrated musical, was associated with the books and lyrics of *Rose Marie* and *New Moon*. Although Macdonald's film career was in decline by the time *Brigadoon* was hitting Broadway, her name, genie-like, would still have produced all the associations of sentimental operetta which Lewis (with his political theatre background) and De Mille (with her High Art background) would have considered anathema. The operetta tradition was by no means defunct on Broadway by 1947. Oscar Straus' *The Chocolate Soldier* was revived the same week *Brigadoon* opened.

Before leaving the matter of the 'integrated musical', it is worthwhile putting a question mark against the virtually unanimous insistence of historians of the Broadway musical that the path to integration was somehow natural, as though integration were the Shangri-La to which the form had been aspiring since its inception. Steve Neale, discussing primarily the film musical, has written:

> Integration... became an ideal not only among those who wrote, directed and choreographed musical dramas, but also among critics, theorists and historians. It has tended to produce a canonic crest-line, a tradition of landmark films, shows and personnel. Although... there is no evident reason for preferring integration, and although there are significant differences between Broadway's crest-line and Hollywood's, both have resulted, on occasion, in partial or distorted accounts of the musical's history.
>
> *(Neale 2000: 106–107)*

This is a complex theoretical question which it would be out of place to pursue further here but, for example, the insistence on integration may be an important factor in the relative exclusion of Kurt Weill's musicals from the Broadway pantheon. Although the famed German-based collaboration between Weill and Bertolt Brecht lasted for little more than three years, it may be that, even in Weill's abandoning of his 'serious' German music for his 'light' American music, he still retained some of the Brechtian commitment to 'emphasising... the didactic at the expense of the culinary, thus converting luxury goods into vehicles for education and places of entertainment into media of communication' (Taylor 1991: 122). Such a commitment, most evident in, for example, the Brecht/Weill musical *Die Dreigroschenoper* (1928) which 'stood for the deliberate antithesis, not only of late Romanticism in general but also, pointedly, of the sentimental world of contemporary operetta' (Taylor 1991: 137) would have been profoundly suspicious of the rush to integration of the Broadway musical of the 1940s which, in a way quite contrary to Brechtian strategy, sought to engulf the audience emotionally.

It might be safely assumed that the majority of the New York theatregoers who filed into their seats in the Ziegfeld Theater on the evening of 13 March 1947 were animated less by the theory of the Broadway musical's form than by the prospect of a good night's entertainment which, whatever the degree of integration of its elements, the Broadway musical was a well-tuned machine for delivering. Nevertheless, as will be seen, the integrationist model loomed large in the responses of reviewers. Even before the show began the audience would have been confronted with several signs of the evening's 'Scottishness'. The bright red souvenir programme had, on its cover, executed in simplified, quasi-art-deco style, a smiling and dancing highlander, kilt and plaid swirling, with the title of the show spread across the centre of the programme in red tartan lettering. This image would become stylistic shorthand for the show, reproduced on the programmes for its many revivals in the USA and on that of the first London opening in 1949. Like operas and operettas, Broadway shows have overtures which foreshadow the main melodies of the show and, as several of the *Brigadoon* songs incorporate Scottish musical motifs (or, more accurately, motifs which had come conventionally to signify 'Scotland'), the overture would also have oriented the audience to an (albeit imaginary) sense of place. Evasive to the last about his intentions, Fritz Loewe tended to downplay the Scottish elements in his score, claiming that his main inspiration had been Brahms. However, this is contradicted by the analysis of the score by American musicologist Jennifer Lynn Oates:

> The entire score imitates the sound of bagpipes through open-fifth drones, grace notes and rhythms. The Overture… evokes the traditional music of Scotland through its rhythms and the use of the pentatonic and hexatonic scales… Even though the Scottish musical elements do not dominate the score and the same Scottish musical traits are used over and over again (open-fifth drones, grace notes, Scottish reel rhythms, and raised fourth or lower seventh scale degrees), it is sufficient to convey the Scottish guise through the music.
>
> *(Oates undated: 1–9)*

The imaginary sense of Scotland would have been further reinforced when, the overture ended, the main curtain rose to reveal *tartan* running tabs, those inner curtains which open horizontally. Against those closed running tabs would have been played the Introduction which, as mentioned previously, deploys the same four bagpipe-like notes that had figured in 'Macpherson is Rehearsin' and to the same end, signifying 'Scottishness'. Still with the tartan tabs closed, the Prologue, executed by an off-stage chorus and solo tenor, fulfils a crucial information-giving function. One of the great strengths of Popular Art is its directness, its bending over backwards to ensure that the audience is in no doubt about what is going on (apart, of course, from genres like the thriller and horror movie in which audience misdirection is part of the appeal). Three crucial pieces of information are conveyed in the brief Prologue: that the setting is the Scottish highlands; that the two hunters are lost there; and that a strange event is about to unfold. The first two points are reinforced by the lyrics repeating them and the 'strange thing that happened' is given extra emphasis by switching to the solo tenor to point it up, the tenor voice being best suited to ensuring clarity since its lower registers are closest to what the ear finds most congenial. Roland Barthes makes the distinction between the denotative and connotative dimensions of signs, the former being explicit and informational, the latter suggestive and, often, ideological. Clearly the main function of the Prologue is denotative (although the musical mood is connotative), while the main function of the Overture, Introduction and tartan running tabs is connotative. It is only after the Prologue that the tartan tabs open to reveal the first of Oliver Smith's sets: a 'large outcrop of rock', a 'rough wooden bridge' and a backcloth depicting 'a distant, fertile valley'. The libretto also tells us that the time is 5am on a May morning, 1946. Smith's initial set illustrates perfectly the Barthesian distinction between denotation and connotation in the same sign. At the denotative level it delivers precisely what the libretto says, but the jagged shapes of the rocks and bridge and the grey, early morning colours suggest something altogether darker. In Chapter 1, I spoke of the austere, sometimes surrealist sets Smith had designed for other shows such as *Rodeo* and *Oklahoma!*. He draws on quite different artistic traditions for his *Brigadoon* sets: what come to mind are the dark forests of German Romanticism and the skewed shapes of German Expressionism. Consciously – he, it will be remembered, like Lewis and De Mille, recoiled from the sentimentality of the original libretto – or unconsciously, Smith may have heard the sombre heartbeat of *Brigadoon* under its shining skin.

Recently there has been a torrent of DIY books purporting to lay bare the structure of popular narrative, particularly the two-hour classical Hollywood fiction film. The claim of these books, which collectively could be described as 'story structure discourse', is that

5. Romanticism and ruins. A key Oliver Smith set for *Brigadoon*.

all popular narratives have the same basic structure involving a central protagonist who lacks something in his (and it usually is 'his' rather than 'her') life and who fights the obstacles (most usually including a villainous antagonist) which seek to thwart his desire, eventually (most usually) overcoming them to achieve his aims. The nature of the desire may, of course, vary. It may be external, such as tracking down the killer of a friend or relative, or internal, the conquering of a flaw in his own makeup. More ambitious narratives try to give the protagonist both external and internal goals. *Brigadoon* certainly fits the less sophisticated end of the story structure spectrum, with Tommy being driven solely by desire. The protagonist is often given a companion who, by the nature of his personality, will point up the qualities of the protagonist's makeup. We can see this structure – and the lack in the protagonist's life – being articulated in the opening scene of *Brigadoon*. Tommy Albright is about 30 and has 'an attractive but sensitive face' and Jeff Douglas is about 35 and is 'retiring but good-natured, primarily because he does not care'. The dialogue exchange sets up both the lack in Tommy's life and the differing ways each will respond to the 'strange thing' we have already been told is going to happen:

TOMMY	There's something about this forest that gives me the feeling of being in a cathedral.
JEFF	If we were, I'd know where the exit was.
TOMMY	You don't believe in anything, do you?
JEFF	Of course I do.
TOMMY	Really? What?
JEFF	Practically anything I can understand, you know, anything that's real to me. Like things I can touch, taste, hear, see, smell, and – (*he indicates the flask*) swallow.
TOMMY	What about the things you don't understand?
JEFF	I dismiss them.
…	
TOMMY	You seem very satisfied.
JEFF	I am. Aren't you?
TOMMY	No, I'm not… I don't know. But something seems wrong, especially about Jane and me. And that makes everything wrong. Look how I postpone getting married. I just can't get myself to that altar.

Thus is Tommy's 'lack' and romantic desire, and Jeff's oppositional hard-headed cynicism, set up right from the start.

The appearance of the ghostly village is signalled by the offstage chorus singing the title song and the village – painted on the backdrop, but thus far invisible – comes into view through lights behind the backdrop. One critic has written of the magical, talismanic quality of certain names in Broadway musicals, including 'Brigadoon' and 'Bali Hai' from *South Pacific* (1949). Even Kurt Weill constructed his own magical land, 'Youkali', although, characteristically, the song of which it is the title carries within itself the awareness that all such lands are chimeras. This talismanic quality is exploited in the slow title song, which signals the emergence of the village from its hundred-year sleep. The repetition of the word 'Brigadoon' – elongated by the musical form – has an incantatory quality. It is at this point that Tommy and Jeff catch sight of the village and move towards it, Tommy eagerly and Jeff hesitantly, as befits their different temperaments. Jeff's remark, 'Wait till Cook's Tours hears about this', confirms what the earlier dialogue exchange has indicated: Jeff is constructed not only as cynic, to point up Tommy's passionate openheartedness, but also as comic, to contrast with Tommy's seriousness. The character of Jeff will be the source of much of the comedy (some of it bitter), a necessary element in any Broadway show. In many tales of the supernatural there is a threshold which must be crossed to leave the 'real' world and enter the magical realm, from the mirrors of *Alice in Wonderland* and Jean Cocteau's *Orphée* to the portal in *Being John Malkovich*. Here the bridge fulfils this function, the first scene ending as the hunters cross it. As will be seen when we come to discuss the film version, what can be achieved with a simple cut or dissolve in the cinema may often have to be realised in the theatre through the opening and closing of tabs and the raising and lowering of front and backcloths. Such is the case here. After they cross the bridge the closing of the tabs permits the unseen lowering of the front cloth for the next scene which shows 'the low wall of a country road with fields beyond and hills in the distance'. *Brigadoon* subscribes to the traditional view that the machinery of *mise-en-scène* should be invisible to the audience since to see it would 'break the spell'. It has become the practice of more radical theatres – not least the Brechtian – blatantly to foreground the mechanics of scene-changing, sometimes to the extent of using the actors (though rarely the stagehands) to accomplish the change. Like much popular art, however, the Broadway musical tends to be conservative, both formally and, as we shall see, ideologically. The brief second scene has both a practical and a musical function. It is part of the genre of the Broadway musical – which it shares with operetta and, indeed, opera – that, shortly after establishing the basics of the story, there should be a big production number, usually involving most of the cast, an upbeat musical tempo and the glowing spectacle of actors and costumes in colourful movement. In Viennese-style operetta, for example, this would be the early 'village green' scene where the aristocratic principals encounter the happy, forelock-tugging peasants and drink, sing, flirt and, sometimes dance with them. At the same time, the big production number has to be carefully structured in terms of rising tempo and gathering crowds so that it reaches a climax of music, colour and movement. At the mechanical level, the brief second scene on the road permits the unseen removal of the bridge and jagged rocks and their replacement with the scenery and extensive props for the upcoming big production number. Musically the scene provides the space to begin the escalation towards the big number by way of a series of sung vendors' calls, which, incidentally, through the extensive use of grace notes, reasserts the Scottishness of the milieu. Individual members of the cast pass across the stage. 'They wear simple Scottish garb' and 'some of them are carrying baskets, some have pitchers on their shoulders, some have long sticks with ducks and pheasants hanging from them, and others have trays with food and other articles for sale'. They greet each other in silent mime as the vendors' calls – such as 'Come all to the square', 'Come ye to the fair' and 'Come ye from the hills' – sound off stage. As some of the vendors begin to sing their calls on-stage, the front cloth rises to reveal the scene of the first big number, 'Down in McConnachy Square'. The libretto goes into considerable detail about what is, indeed, 'an eighteenth-century community' engaging in the weekly fair which 'was the custom in Scotland then'. Several minor principals are named and described as is the intense movement and colour of the scene. One of the characters is Harry Ritchie 'who is aged about twenty-four. He is a slender, extremely sensitive-looking lad. He carries a book.' Amid all the colour, bustle and excitement of the scene 'Harry goes to a stool... sits and reads'. Harry is, indeed, the malcontent who will endanger the existence of the village by attempting to cross the bridge into the 'real' world. His description is interesting. Although the prime motivation for his wishing to leave is his rejection as a suitor, his description suggests that very rejection may have been symptomatic of his Otherness. Harry is constructed as an artist/intellectual, a figure of profound suspicion in popular art and – it might be added in relation to the 'McCarthyism' unfolding in post-war American society – in the demonology of the Cold War.

In Preston Sturges' acerbic comedy *Sullivan's Travels* (1941), the rich film director Sullivan, having announced that he intends to live among the poor to research a socially-conscious film, is subjected to a scathing diatribe from his butler about the condition of the poor and their attitude to rich do-gooders who seek to study them. By way of explanation and comfort to the crestfallen Sullivan, his valet looks at the departing figure of the butler and, shaking his head sadly, observes: 'Always reading books, sir.' This suspicion of people who read books has a long history in Anglo-American popular culture. Intellectuals and artists have often been represented as crazed or effeminate as in, for example, the first *film noir* cycle of the 1940s and 1950s (e.g. *Laura* [1944], *Phantom Lady* [1944], *Crack-Up* [1946] and *The Big Sleep* [1946]). A remarkable number of villains were associated with producing, selling, collecting or writing about art or with intellectual activity more generally. This extended to other genres as well, for example the musical, in which 'artists' as opposed to 'artistes' were often figures of fun, as in *The Barkleys of Broadway* (1949) and *The Band Wagon* (1953), particularly if they were of a modernist orientation. However, the popular cinema's most vitriolic hatred was reserved for 'political intellectuals', as in *The Fountainhead* (1949), *My Son John* (1952) and *Viva Zapata!* (1952). If this seems to put an untoward weight on a figure who is not the most major character in *Brigadoon*, it indicates that there are massive hidden icebergs of ideology lurking underneath the seemingly most throwaway characterisations in Broadway musicals.

The brief second scene also allows the escalation of the music of 'McConnachy Square' and, importantly, provides a mechanism to segue spoken dialogue into song. Robert Lewis addresses this question:

> I remember that Agnes De Mille... tried, wherever possible, to blend her movements from walking to dancing and so eliminate the 'seams'. So too I would ask the singing actors to intensify their speaking... as they got right up to their singing cue. Also, where possible, I had them half talk the opening words of the song. In this way you can completely obliterate any break in the dramatic line as you go from the dialogue scene into the musical portion. Then, at the end of the number, I always found a way to attach the beginning of the speaking part with a significance that grabbed the audience's attention and allowed for no letdown from the number.
>
> *(Lewis 1980: 171)*

In line with the macro-integration of music, story and dance which increasingly preoccupied Broadway in the 1940s, Lewis is here practicing micro-integration. Significantly, the vendors' cries, half-spoken, half-sung, are all individual voices, but the overall effect is of depth and variety, achieved by alternating bass, soprano, contralto, baritone and tenor voices. It is only when the front cloth rises, the lights come on full and virtually the entire company bustle around McConnachy Square that there is collective singing of what is, in effect, the refrain to the verse sung by the vendors, this time rendered in an altogether more brisk tempo:

Come ye from the hills.
Come ye from the mills.
Come ye in the glen,
Come ye bairn, come ye men.
Come ye from the loom,
Come from pail and broom.
Hear ye everywhere
Don't ye ken
There's a fair
Down in McConnachy Square.

In between its initial rendering and its show-stopping reprise, there are spaces for individual verses and the orchestration becomes more complex with vendors' cries, individual verses and main refrain intermingling and rushing towards the climax. The Broadway musical, because it is popular, is often thought of as a simple form. If the stories and their exposition are relatively one-dimensional, the music (or, more correctly, the orchestration) is often quite complex. The orchestration of 'Down in McConnachy Square' shows some of the features which would come to their most complex articulation in 'The Rumble' sequence in *West Side Story* (1961). However, the relative sophistication of the orchestration is somewhat at odds with the Kailyardesque vocabulary of the lyrics.

Part of the organisational complexity of a Broadway show, and of popular narratives more generally, is that particular scenes may be made to have more than one function. In addition to delivering the requisite early big production number, the McConnachy Square scene brings to the audience's attention – by having her sing one of the choruses – Meg Brockie who, with Jeff, will emerge as the major source of comedy in the show. The nature of the comedy is hinted at when she is surrounded by the four men she has been flirting with. The song ended, the scene incorporates further exposition by introducing the two main female characters, the sisters Fiona and Jean, by explaining that Jean is to be married to Charlie that very day, and by retaining the malcontent Harry in the scene long enough to make clear – by a series of looks and glances – that he is the suitor Jean has rejected in favour of Charlie. Several critics have pointed to Lerner's eight marriages and sought to relate them to the ever-hopeful romanticism of his work and, the reverse of that coin, its implicit misogyny. Certainly both these qualities are present in *Brigadoon* but they are as much a characteristic of the unquestioned patriarchal culture of the time as of Lerner's psyche. Certainly, some of the ostensibly jocular exchanges about the necessity of wives to hold their tongues in the McConnachy Square scene might raise eyebrows today and, I would hazard a guess, might be excised from modern (particularly American) productions. The grossness of the patriarchy of Broadway shows of this time – as with other areas of popular art – is sometimes breathtaking. For instance, *Carousel* manages to present male violence against women as 'really' a sign of love. At the same time we should be alert to those (albeit secondary) counter-patriarchal impulses, for example the strong matriarchal figures in, say, *Oklahoma!* and *The Sound of Music* (1965), who sustain and encourage younger women, often through songs such as 'You'll Never Walk Alone' and 'Climb Every Mountain'.

The only guide to costuming in the libretto is the brief description of the first appearance of the 'natives' as being in 'simple Scottish garb'. Unsurprisingly, given the hegemony of Tartanry, the production personnel interpreted this as kilts and other tartan accoutrements. The costumes were designed by David Ffolkes who, though the greater part of his costume- and set-designing career was to be in the American theatre, was in fact an Englishman who had, during the Second World War, served in a Scottish regiment, the Royal Scots Greys. It is not widely known that tartan – particularly as a set of distinctive patterns assigned to named clans – is shot through with falsity and invention, part of that (primarily) nineteenth-century phenomenon associated with the manufacture of national identities which Eric Hobsbawm and Terence Ranger have called 'the invention of tradition' in their edited collection of that title. There is no particular reason why Ffolkes, as a Briton, should have been any more aware of tartan's dubious history than his American colleagues, for the British generally, and even more grievously, the Scots themselves, have internalised the Scottish Discursive Unconscious. With regard to the invention of tartan, the process – and its chief architect, in imagination if not action – are succinctly rendered in Murray Grigor's caustically witty film *Scotch Myths* (1982). Sir Walter Scott, flanked by a servant with an armful of diverse tartan patterns, is considering which one will best suit

King George IV, whose 1822 visit to Edinburgh Scott was to choreograph:

SERVANT   What about this one here. This is a scarlet red.

SCOTT   Mm, what check?

SERVANT   Well, it's known as Number 137. It's a fraudulent check.

SCOTT   Call it 'Stewart'.

SERVANT   'Stewart'. Just plain 'Stewart'?

SCOTT   No, call it '*Red* Stewart'.

SERVANT   Aye, that's more appropriate. 'Red Stewart'.

SCOTT   '*Royal* Stewart'.

SERVANT   'Royal Stewart' you have.

SCOTT   '*Ancient* Royal Stewart'.

SERVANT   Oh, I like that. 'Ancient Royal Stewart' it is.

SCOTT   'Ancient, Royal, *Dress* Stewart'

SERVANT   As you wish. 'Ancient Royal Dress Stewart'.

SCOTT   'Ancient, Royal, *Hunting*, Dress Stewart'.

6. Sir Walter Scott (John Bett) and servant (Chic Murray)
invent tartan, in *Scotch Myths*.

SERVANT Oh, there's no doubt about it, Sir Walter. You're a man of
     words. 'Ancient Royal Hunting Dress Stewart' I name it!

SCOTT Then bring furrit the tartan and we'll tartan the
     kingdom!

The vogue for tartan swept through the Scots aristocracy and those foreign grandees who imagined themselves to have some claim to Scots ancestry and, over the course of the nineteenth century, it percolated downward through the various layers of Scots society, greatly aided by the imprimatur of Queen Victoria and her German consort, to the extent that people bearing certain names now live in the delusion that they are 'entitled' to wear a certain arrangement of checks and colours, a belief ardently fostered by commercial interests. Throughout the nineteenth century, this grotesque act of mythmaking became sedimented in a number of expensively produced volumes of prints purporting to show the tartans of the various clans. The best known of these are probably the McIan prints, which may be glimpsed gracing the walls of many Scottish hotels, restaurants and 'collectible' shops. Historically inaccurate but ideologically fulfilling, these prints are the most likely sources of David Ffolkes' costumes. The more general question of the relationship of *Brigadoon* to Scottish history did not greatly preoccupy its makers. The issue, however, was to be more sharply posed by the London production of 1949.

In such a patriarchal form as the Broadway musical, collective singing and dancing usually divides along gender lines with women and men singing and dancing sentiments 'appropriate' to their gender. With regard to Agnes De Mille's choreography – to judge from its survivals in the film versions of *Oklahoma!* and *Carousel* – although men and women do, of course, dance with each other, the overall impression is of phalanxes of men and women divided along gender lines and performing movements which rarely stray far from classical ballet and are defined by cast-iron conceptions of gender identity. One such recurrent trope is the group of young women who sing and/ or dance about marriage. Fiona's song 'Waitin' For My Dearie' falls into this category. The dialogue segues into the song with an exchange between Fiona and Meg which is remarkable for its near-explicit sexuality with Fiona opining that 'getting married is the only way you can do it that's respectable!'. Fiona's song contains the lines:

I hold a dream and there's no compromisin'
I know there's one certain laddie for me.
One day he'll come walkin' o'er the horizon;
But should he not then an old maid I'll be.

Just as Tommy and Jeff are constructed as opposites, Jeff cynical and gregarious as far as women are concerned, and Tommy passionate and searching, so too are Fiona and Meg constructed in terms of the same binary. Fiona's song is not only conventional with regard to gender, it also exemplifies another key trope of the Broadway musical – the 'I Want...' song which may be sung by a man or a woman. Just a few years earlier the male lead of *Annie Get Your Gun* had his own 'I Want...' song – 'The Girl That I Marry'. This being the post-*Oklahoma!*, integrated musical period, Fiona's song also extends the exposition and, the world of the Broadway musical being highly structured, the man who will end her yearning does indeed 'come o'er the horizon' as Tommy and Jeff enter. Every Broadway musical (and every romantic comedy) has the moment of 'the long look' when the lovers first meet and cannot take their eyes off each other. The Rodgers and Hammerstein musical *South Pacific* would actually incorporate this moment into a song, 'Some Enchanted Evening' with its line about seeing a stranger across a crowded room. The libretto does not make much of this moment, but it is usually *played* with great intensity. The scene also develops the relationship between Meg and Jeff, with her making all the running and Jeff being, as usual, sarcastic. Charlie enters and kisses Fiona. For a brief moment Tommy is allowed to believe that Fiona is the bride-to-be, until it is revealed that Charlie is to marry her sister Jean. More will be made of this misunderstanding in the film version.

Throughout the scene there have been ambiguous asides by the locals about the status of Brigadoon but Charlie nearly lets the cat out of the bag when, calling for drinks all round on the occasion of his marriage, he proposes a toast to Mr Forsythe (whom we will learn is the schoolmaster who engineered the miracle) 'for postponin' the miracle for me', causing some embarrassed lies to Tommy and Jeff. When Tommy and Fiona find an excuse to exit together, Charlie launches into his 'gender-appropriate' song 'I'll Go Home With Bonnie Jean', which is all about having to eschew philandering when he gets married. Analogously to Fiona's song with the female chorus,

Charlie's song is delivered with the male chorus. Again, the song has a near-explicit sexuality:

Hello to married men I've known
I'll soon have a wife and leave your's alone...

The libretto indicates at this point that there should be a 'Bonnie Jean Ballet' opened by Maggie who has previously been said to fancy the lovelorn Harry. Having danced flirtatiously with Charlie, she transfers her attention to Harry and, the dance completed, they exit, looking daggers at Charlie. Apart from the removal of a few movable items such as vending booths, all of the foregoing singing, dancing and exposition has taken place on the McConnachy Square set which will be the site of more expository dialogue in which Tommy once more confesses his unwillingness to marry his fiancée and Fiona indicates her attraction to him. When she says that she has to gather heather, this segues into the duet that was to become the most famous song from *Brigadoon*, reprised on radio and on concert platforms thereafter – 'The Heather on the Hill'. Part of the refrain runs:

The mist of May is in the gloamin'
And all the clouds are holdin' still
So take my hand and let's go roamin'
Through the heather on the hill.

As is evident from the dialogue quoted throughout this chapter, the 'Scottishness' of *Brigadoon* is sustained in the language as well as the music, décor and costumes. In the last chapter it was suggested that a key 'subconscious' element in the shaping of the show was the vaudeville persona of Harry Lauder. That influence seeps to the surface in the vocabulary of 'The Heather on the Hill', the generative influence being Lauder's song 'Roamin' in the Gloamin'. However, the music for 'The Heather on the Hill' contains none of the 'Scottish' elements of other parts of the score. It is very much a Tin Pan Alley ballad, which may explain its success. However, Tin Pan Alley ballad or not, it remains an integrated element which advances the relationship between Tommy and Fiona, almost making explicit their growing love for each other. Indeed, one part of the dialogue which intersperses among the sung lyrics, Tommy's line 'It almost

sounded like I was making love to you, didn't it?', has the function
of raising the question of love without too early a declaration and of
foreshadowing Tommy's next solo song 'Almost Like Being in Love'.
At the end of 'The Heather on the Hill' the audience is in no doubt
about the pair's feelings for each other. The libretto reads 'at the end
of the song, Tommy and Fiona stand looking at each other' signalling
the place where Lerner had wished to incorporate 'the long look'. It
will be recalled that, as played, this look often occurs when Tommy
and Fiona first meet. The scene closes with a foreboding storm with
several villagers, Harry and Jean among them, passing to and fro. It
is clear from the looks Harry directs at Jean, which the libretto has
clearly indicated since they first appeared on stage together, that a
'pay-off' is being built up to. That said, before the tabs close, the
final image is upbeat. Against a reprise of the choral 'Come ye from
the hills...' refrain, the recurrent references in the dialogue to the
making of clothes for the wedding receive their pay-off when some
of the men left on the stage unfold lengths of tartan and hold them
aloft, reminding us that a Broadway show involves visual spectacle
as well as singing and dancing.

Shaping such a show – as with many other genres of popular art –
is, at a formal level, very much about balancing tones so that passion
and drama are interspersed with lighter moments. This interweaving
also creates crucial spaces for scene-changing in preparation for the
next big set and for allowing principals who may have been on stage
for a long period, and performed taxing songs and/or dances, to rest
momentarily before plunging into further punishing routines. Such
is the multiple function of the next scene which takes place in 'The
Brockie Bothy', Meg's dwelling, to which she has taken Jeff to mend
his trousers. However, since the whole depth of the stage is used in
the bothy scene, the show is obliged to close the running tabs and
make use of 'Change of Scene Music' to allow the set to be put in
place. As has been noted, Meg and Jeff are the main sources of
comedy, he through his cynical wisecracking, she on account of her
ardent pursuit of any male in sight. However, Meg's scarcely
contained sexual aggressiveness posed something of an ideological
problem for *Brigadoon*. Although the Tartanry narrative constructs
Scotland as a faery realm in which the natives are unsophisticated
and close to nature, it has difficulty in incorporating a key element
of analogous noble savage myths such as those relating to, for

example, the South Seas – innocent and unrestrained sexuality. The difficulty may have come about partly from historical awareness of Scotland's post-Reformation Calvinism with its fierce repression of any kind of pleasure – a repression which has produced at least two literary masterpieces, Robert Louis Stevenson's *Dr Jekyll and Mr Hyde* and James Hogg's *The Private Memoirs and Confessions of a Justified Sinner* – but more particularly from the interweaving of Tartanry with Kailyard. Kailyard is symbiotic with Calvinism not in some vague general sense, but specifically with the 'Auld Lichts' tendency, that narrowest and most repressive strain associated with those who seceded from the Church of Scotland in 1733 to uphold the Solemn League and Covenant. This is arid soil indeed out of which to grow a sexually omnivorous woman. What *Brigadoon* does therefore, in a skilful ideological manoeuvre, is to locate Meg within a different Other, but one which is synonymous with unbridled sexuality. Meg is made part-gypsy. Because the audience too will live within the narrative of the gypsy as sexualised Other, this feature of Meg offers sufficient 'explanation' for her predatory sexuality.

Brigadoon operates at many levels. Drawing on deep-seated historical ideologies, it nevertheless keys into contemporary events as well. With the Cold War unfolding in 1947 – Churchill, in 1946, had delivered his epochal Fulton, Missouri speech in which he coined (or gave more public currency to) the phrase 'Iron Curtain' – the audience would have picked up on the following exchange:

MEG   What happened to the lassie you were engaged to?

JEFF   She fell in love with a Russian…

MEG   Russia is in Europe, isn't it?

JEFF   Yes, more and more…

The bothy scene is structured to underline Meg's tireless pursuit of men and to set up her first song, 'The Love of My Life', in which she works through a list of named men each of whom had been 'the real love of my life'. Replete with barely masked sexual innuendoes, the song would pose problems for the film version. Its barefacedness is evident in lines such as:

I never went back for what I heard was true;

That a poet only writes about the things he cannot do.

and also:

> We skirmished for hours that night in the glen,
> An' I found that the sword was more mighty than the pen.

The role of Meg calls for both acting and singing and the libretto calls for it to be assigned to a contralto. The galloping rhythm of the above lines indicates that the song is very up-tempo, indeed polka-like. There is a particular kind of singer, generic to the Broadway musical, known as a 'belter', the archetype being Ethel Merman who, with her raucous contralto, had belted out 'There's No Business Like Show Business' in *Annie Get Your Gun* the previous year. Merman and her style – invariably show-stopping – may well have influenced the inclusion of this kind of song in *Brigadoon*. Comic songs may be more difficult to deliver than romantic songs since they often call for more acting than the latter. The last chapter referred to Cheryl Crawford as not just a number-cruncher but as having a real sense of theatre. This is reflected in her description of the work she did with the actor playing Meg in 1947:

> For every moment of her big number I gave her exact and detailed business. Her song… described her attempts to attract four different men, all of whom abandoned her. All alone on the stage [the actor] didn't know what to do with her hands. I gave her a piece of heather to play with for greeting and flirting and showed her how to imitate the different men as she sang about them. These bits of business relaxed her and the song came to life. When the last man had had his pleasure and disappeared, she tossed the heather over her shoulder in disgust. On opening night her performance was so well received that we decided that she should have a number in Act Two.
>
> *(Crawford 1977: 165–166)*

Apart from showing the continuing artistic involvement of Cheryl Crawford, this quotation reminds us of the detailed micro-work on performance and *mise-en-scène* which goes into rehearsals so that the performance will look seamless and 'natural', but also that a Broadway show is invariably flexible enough to respond to what the audience is telling it from one performance to another. In the same section of her memoirs Crawford reveals the electrifying fact that one of the figures she engaged to carry out this kind of detailed work with the actors was none other than her old colleague Lee Strasberg. Oh, to have been a fly on the wall at those rehearsals! It is both amusing and sobering to learn that the *mise-en-scène* of *Brigadoon* – an artefact which, especially for Scots intellectuals, has elicited nothing but derision and contempt – should have been partially fashioned by possibly *the* foremost theoretician of actorial performance in the American theatre. Regrettably, however, no record seems to be extant of the nature of the work Strasberg did with the cast. Meg's song, and the scene as a whole, ends as Jeff appears to go to sleep. Meg, reprising her earlier account of how her mother had wooed her father, sits in a rocking chair and waits for him to wake, an unspoken, but unmistakable, signal that, like her mother before her, she intends to have sex with her catch.

Since the next scene, the interior of Fiona and Jean's family home, also uses the whole depth of the stage, the bothy scene too has to end with drawn tabs and 'Change of Scene Music'. The new scene opens with a choric song and dance involving Jean and several of the women, 'Jeannie's Packing Up', during which the women pass Jean's clothes along their line for packing in a trunk. Much innuendo revolves around their decision to exclude a red flannel nightie from the clothes she will need. If the main plot is about the deepening love of Tommy and Fiona, the main subplot concerns Harry's growing despair at Jean's impending wedding. Like the romantic main plot, the subplot must be kept on the boil and, indeed, carefully built in intensity until its culmination at the wedding. This scene, therefore, has Harry deliver a finished garment (his father is a tailor) to Jean's father, which is the occasion of his most bitter statement of his predicament – 'I hate everythin' and everybody in this cursed village' – and the darkest foreboding about its outcome. Harry gone, the scene even finds space for a song when Charlie, come to sign the family bible, serenades the off-stage Jean with 'Come to Me, Bend to Me', after which Jean and the women perform a ballet anticipating, as the libretto tells us, 'the joys of marriage and the sorrow of leaving her father's house'. Clearly economic use is being made of this scene and this set by having several plot strands advanced within it. Tommy and Fiona return with the heather from the hill and, before she goes upstairs, Tommy kisses her. When Jeff also enters, his question about how Tommy is feeling allows Tommy to segue into another of the most popular songs from *Brigadoon* – 'Almost Like Being in Love'.

There were, in the 1940s, several show songs which refreshed the romantic love ballad by taking one step backward from it and thereby rendering it more oblique and interesting. Once again, *Oklahoma!* seems to have been the blueprint for this development with 'People Will Say We're in Love'. That song is a series of injunctions from each lover to the other – 'Don't throw bouquets at me... Don't laugh... Don't sigh...', for if you do all those things, 'people will say we're in love'. Rodgers and Hammerstein seem to have patented this strategy, for it reappears in *Carousel* in 'If I Loved You'. This kind of oblique love song, which has no overt declaration of love (and no 'moon' rhyming with 'June') is reprised in 'Almost Like Being in Love' in which Tommy and the returned Fiona play out a love duet without once saying 'I love you'. It is at this point that Tommy picks up the family bible and discovers that the entry for Charlie and Jean's wedding is 24 May 1746. He asks Fiona for an explanation and she says she has to speak to the dominie, Mr Murdoch. Absorbing as the relationship between *Brigadoon* and Scottish history may be to Scots intellectuals, it was clearly of tangential concern to the makers of the show. This date, 24 May 1746, probably arrived at by Lerner counting two centuries back from the time of writing, is less than six weeks after one of the most bloodily resonant events in Scottish history, the Battle of Culloden. That day, on a moor not far from Inverness, was ended the last attempt by the Stuart dynasty to reclaim by force the British crown from which the Catholic members of that family had been dispossessed by the 'Glorious Revolution' of 1688. Six weeks after that date – the ostensible time of *Brigadoon* – the Highlands would have been in turmoil as the redcoats of the victor of Culloden, the Duke of Cumberland, hunted down (and often slaughtered) the remnants of the vanquished Jacobite forces. For those aware of it, Culloden and its bloody aftermath sounds in distant counterpoint to the generally upbeat music and spectacle of *Brigadoon*, adding the question of historical veracity to the Scots intelligentsia's High Art-oriented disdain for *Brigadoon*, a situation which was to recur, with rather more point, in relation to *Braveheart* in 1995.

Although *Brigadoon* makes dramatically economic use of every scene by nursing along diverse plot strands, it is part of the sumptuousness of the Broadway musical that there be a sufficient number of scene-changes to alleviate audience boredom and display the set designer's art. It is not at all unusual in the theatre for the audience to applaud the set before any actors appear in it. Once again, there is 'Change of Scene Music' as the tabs close and open again on a new set, the outside of Mr Murdoch's house, to which Fiona has brought Tommy – with Jeff firing off cynical wisecracks such as 'Should I wear my three-cornered hat?'. Murdoch explains that he and Mr Forsythe, 'the Minister of the Kirk', concocted a plan whereby Brigadoon avoided the turmoils of the world by falling asleep and coming out of that sleep for only one day every 100 years. Forsythe had made a bargain with God that in return he would offer the sacrifice of himself being excluded from Brigadoon's future. Two points are worth raising about this aspect of the show. As Tom Nairn has pointed out, the key figures in the Kailyard landscape are middle class professional men, most usually ministers and schoolteachers, but later television versions such as *Dr Finlay's Casebook* and *Sutherland's Law* brought in doctors and lawyers as well. Here, it is the two earlier professions who engineer the miracle. Also, the precise reason for the miracle bears closer attention. As Murdoch says:

> Two hundred years ago the highlands of Scotland were plagued with witches; wicked sorceresses who were takin' the Scots folk away from the teachin's of God and puttin' the Devil in their souls. They were, indeed, horrible destructive women…

Quite apart from the misogyny of this, it implicitly refers to another text which has been important in imaginings of Scotland – Shakespeare's *Macbeth* – the text which, more than any other, casts Scotland as a 'here-be-dragons' terrain, prey to the darkest supernatural. However, *Brigadoon* cannot exploit the full implications of its reference to *Macbeth*, for to do so would evoke, in Arthur Melville Clark's words:

> a 'Caledonia stern and wild', a chilly and thinly-populated land of mountains and shaggy woods rather than ploughed fields… of barren moors and battlefields and grim fortresses rather than towns, villages and farms… with thunder, rain and hail as accompaniments…
>
> *(Melville Clark 1981: 32)*

This was the Scotland that Orson Welles was to conjure up in his 1948 screen version of *Macbeth* (McArthur 2001).

There is a technique of (mainly) literary criticism, much favoured by French Marxist critics, whereby they probe the silences of texts, forcing them to utter what they would rather remained silent and repressed. Much in the way that we have already probed the silence behind the date in the family bible, so too might we ask what kind of Scotland did Brigadoon wake up to, after its first century of sleep, in 1846. As it happened, Scotland would have been reeling from another important event in its history, the Disruption, wherein one third of the ministers of the Church of Scotland broke with the established church, primarily over the issue of the freedom of congregations (as opposed to rich patrons) to appoint ministers. It would also have been a Scotland in painful transition to an industrialising modernity, again incompatible with the bucolic idyll of *Brigadoon*. In 1846 there was also a failure of the potato crop (as in Ireland), which added to the already existing pressure on highland tenant farmers to vacate their arable land to make way for (from the great landlords' point of view) the economically more profitable sheep – a process which has entered Scottish demonology as 'the Highland Clearances' with the Scottish aristocracy, particularly the Duke of Sutherland, cast as the main villains. On the subject of *Brigadoon*'s silences, there is no sign, in the text as we have it, that figures of the class and geographical location of the Brigadooners would have been subject to the overlordship of the kind of powerful magnates into which the clan chiefs had mutated post-Culloden. This question of 'real' history will return with a vengeance in our discussion of *Braveheart*. It would be utterly pointless to accuse *Brigadoon* and *Braveheart* of falsifying history as though they had set out to deliver historically accurate accounts of the Scottish past. At the same time, the issue is important and cannot simply be tossed aside – as many are wont to do – with the observation 'What do you expect from Broadway (or Hollywood)?'. The question has to be formulated more sophisticatedly, along the lines of 'What is there in the Broadway or Hollywood production set-ups that systematically *requires* them to falsify and/or repress "real" history?'. The answer lies, of course, in the pleasures Broadway shows and Hollywood movies deliver and the aesthetic forms and ideological manoeuvres necessary to ensure their cultural transmission.

Going back to the scene in which Tommy learns the secret of Brigadoon and, crucially, that an incomer may remain in the village as it passes once more into its century of sleep if he loves someone in the village, the scene, and the tabs, close with the announcement that the wedding is about to begin, but not before Murdoch articulates the yearning that the concept of 'Brigadoon' speaks to. In response to Tommy's question as to what the hundred-year sleep is like, Murdoch speaks of hearing 'strange voices' which are 'filled with a fearful longin'.' He reckons they are the cries from the outside world and that 'there mus' be lots of folks out there who'd like a Brigadoon'. The arriving scene is referred to in the libretto as 'Outside the Kirk' and is dominated by a ruin 'of what was perhaps a large church' rendered more dramatic by Oliver Smith's expressionist set. *Brigadoon* is romantic in the popular sense of that term. But it is also Romantic in the more precise sense that one of the tributaries feeding into it was German Romanticism. One of the elements of the 'picturesque' so highly regarded by the Romantics was the frequent inclusion of a ruined church or abbey in pictures and prints, which reflected their interest in history and their dark passion for *memento mori*. This dramatic scene is the setting for the second 'big production number' – 'The Entrance of the Clans' – which tended to come towards the end of the first act of any Broadway show. As the libretto describes it:

> When the RUNNING TABS open, MURDOCH is standing LC, a few paces from the kirk steps. All the TOWNSFOLK are proudly dressed according to their Clan for a special occasion and a member of each announces the name of his clan at the appropriate music cue.

The Scottish Discursive Unconscious is made up of diverse images and narratives right down to particular words and phrases. One such phrase is 'the gathering of the clans' which most people will have heard and will vaguely associate with Scotland. Another such phrase is 'lone piper'. Why 'lone' and not 'a' or 'one' or 'a single' piper? The answer is that the phrase 'lone piper' is encrusted with a larger narrative the dominant allusions of which are barrenness, loss and elegy. On a similar note, Compton Mackenzie has spoken of young girls suffering from 'a lone sheiling complex'. The phrase 'gathering of the clans' has sufficient general currency for it to build into the *mise-en-scène* and provide a ready-made source of music and spectacle which, given the gender ideologies of the Broadway musical, is heavily masculinised. The alleged hardness and warlike spirit of the

Scots is a central part of the Scottish Discursive Unconscious, hanging like an albatross round the necks of émigré Scots, the more mature trying to live it down, the less mature trying to live up to it. In *Braveheart* this masculinism will take on a darker, proto-fascist hue. So it is, then, that the 'clansmen' enter, chests and bagpipes inflated, and become the guests for the wedding of Charlie and Jean. Murdoch explains that, in the absence of a Minister, 'it is perfectly proper, accordin' to the laws of Scotland, for two people to be wed by sincere mutual consent'. This was indeed legally acceptable in Scotland until 1927. There is then a brief wedding dance before the major dance, the 'Sword Dance and Reel', which was to elicit much admiration in reviews. The Sword Dance is performed initially by Harry who is then joined by the other young men, the point of the dance being to move with increasing speed among the four quadrants of the crossed swords on the ground without the feet touching the blades. Although Agnes De Mille had overall charge of the choreography, she brought in a specialist in Scottish dance, James Jamieson, to advise on the specifically Scottish dances. The Sword Dance is exciting in itself but, given its location in *Brigadoon* and with Harry in particular dancing frenziedly over naked swords, it racks up the dramatic tension until, of course, the violence which has been simmering under the surface of *Brigadoon* erupts. As the Sword Dance segues into the Reel and everyone joins in, Harry begins to dance with Jean but, unable to contain himself, starts to kiss her violently. When she runs to Charlie, Harry finally grasps the hopelessness of his situation. The first act ends with Harry's despairing cry – 'I'm leavin' Brigadoon. 'Tis the end of all of us. The miracle's over'.

The high dramatic note on which Act One ends is immediately picked up in Act Two. The sombreness of the scene, 'A forest near the border of Brigadoon', is reflected in the description in the libretto – 'the backcloth depicts large gnarled trees'. This simply makes explicit the expressionist tendency of Oliver Smith's sets throughout the show. It is also at this point that Loewe's score – previously very much grounded in late nineteenth-century Romantic music – becomes more modernist, at times even Stravinskian, as it launches into 'The Chase', in which the young men of Brigadoon, Tommy among them, try desperately to stop Harry crossing the bridge and sending the village into oblivion. It is also one of the key masculinist moments in *Brigadoon*, with an upbeat, percussive male chorus accompanying the chase. The libretto does not spell this out, but as played this scene is often homoeroticised by having the pursuers stripped to the waist. The Sword Dance and The Chase provide the opportunity for the actor playing Harry to demonstrate his athleticism as he jumps from trees and tussles with his pursuers. The original Harry in 1947 was the Metropolitan Ballet dancer James Mitchell whose good looks and physique and intensely athletic dancing were often commented on in reviews. Although no film record of the original 1947 production seems to exist, Mitchell's qualities as a dancer can be appreciated by looking at, among other things, the film version of *Oklahoma!* in which he dances the role of Curley in De Mille's famous dream ballet, which, unlike her choreography for *Brigadoon*, survived onto the screen. Harry will die accidentally by hitting his head on a stone, thus ensuring that Brigadoon will not vanish forever. Broadway musicals of the time seem to have been reluctant to stage the deliberate killing of characters who, for plot reasons, have to be disposed of. This may be related to the general lightness of tone of the form, but may also have been a reaction against the carnage of the Second World War. Jud in *Oklahoma!* and Billy in *Carousel* die accidentally, each falling on his own knife. The fact that Hammerstein should be so 'careless' as to repeat this motif in contiguous shows confirms – despite historians' insistence on the growth of integration – the extent to which song, dance and spectacle rather than plot are the primary focus of attention. The chase and the death of Harry is the point at which *Brigadoon* comes closest to grand opera. Following the discovery of his body, the music becomes funereal and what in other scenes would have been spoken dialogue here becomes *recitative*.

The narrative arrangement of the next few scenes is interesting as a technical exercise in how a Broadway show can manipulate diverse emotional tones, passing from tragedy to romance to broad comedy and back again to tragedy. Fiona and Tommy have become so overwrought and anxious about each other in the chase sequence that they are at their most emotionally naked when they are reunited. This scene, directly following that of Harry's death (which the pursuers conceal from the rest of the villagers) is where they speak of their love for each other most explicitly and Tommy segues into one of the least memorable of the show's songs, 'There But For You Go I', which is, indeed, often dropped for this reason. Their declaration of love is given added poignancy as the time nears for Brigadoon's day to end. The next scene, 'The Glen', opens with the wedding still going on – the villagers still in the dark about Harry's death – and narrows down to Meg's second song 'My Mother's Weddin' Day', about the fact that Meg had been present at her mother's wedding, a feature of the show which was to alarm the film censors when the screen version was proposed. Like Meg's first-act song, 'The Love of My Life', this too is delivered at a galloping tempo:

> MacGregor, MacKenna, MacGowan, MacGraw,
> MacVittie, MacNeil and MacRae;
> Ay. All the folk in the village were there
> At my mother's weddin' day

The linguistic structure slots into another trope of the Broadway musical – the patter song, the *raison d'être* of which is to showcase the singer's capacity to race through an enormous number of words at breakneck speed. This particular song may have been suggested by the number that made Danny Kaye a Broadway star, 'Tchaikowsky' from *Lady in the Dark* (1941) in which he galloped through the names of innumerable classical composers in seconds. It will be recalled that Meg's second song was not originally in the score but was added because of the success of her first song. This illustrates that, despite the largely justified claims for *Brigadoon* as a post-*Oklahoma!* integrated musical, it still displayed some features of earlier musicals in which interpolation, often of popular hits of the day by other composers and lyricists, was the norm. It was by this latter route that George Gershwin, for example, first made his mark on Broadway. To repeat a point made recurrently in this book, popular art (perhaps *all* art except the minimally modernist) loves dramatic reversals of tone. Meg's song rouses the audience – and the cast – to a high pitch of energy and good humour. It segues into a resumption of the wedding dance, but the festivities are broken off abruptly by the sound of a lament being played on the bagpipes – needless to say, by a 'lone' piper. The bagpipe lament is yet another part of the bricolage of the Scottish Discursive Unconscious, something which the world recognises as 'essentially' Scottish. In a sense, Harry's death is too rich dramatically not to be 'milked' for as much emotion as it will bear – a tendency to which popular art often succumbs. His body, draped in tartan, is carried on-stage by his grieving father, and Maggie, who has been signalled in Act One as being attracted to Harry, performs a funeral dance the elements of which are spelled out in the libretto. Much of the dramatic action thus far in Act Two has excluded Tommy who has mainly been an onlooker, but it seems to firm up his resolve to stay in Brigadoon with Fiona and he announces this to Jeff as Harry's body is carried off-stage. Jeff, revealing that it is he who has killed Harry, albeit accidentally, reminds Tommy of the dreamlike (or, in his own case, nightmarish) experience they have had to the extent that Tommy becomes confused and his resolve to stay falters. This, of course, occurs as Brigadoon's day is coming to an end. Tommy and Fiona sing a duet, 'From This Day On' after which Brigadoon recedes into the mist with Fiona's repeated call 'I love you' dying into silence.

Strictly speaking, *Brigadoon* should have ended at that point, but with Tommy remaining in the village. However, this would have made the conventionally-shorter Act Two unacceptably short. There was much adverse comment at the time about the unsatisfactory nature of *Brigadoon*'s Act Two. What Lerner did to get round the shortness which would have resulted from ending on the first return to sleep was to anticipate the 'second ending' which would become popular in the horror movie decades later with the monster, apparently dead, reaching out of the depths to clutch the ankle of (usually) the heroine. *Brigadoon*'s version of this is to return Tommy to New York to a scene described as 'A bar in New York City. Four months later' and to his 'fiancée' Jane. In this scene, Tommy is lethargic, preoccupied, interested in nothing anyone says to him, clearly still entranced by Brigadoon and Fiona. Ingeniously, Tommy's memories are given external form by certain phrases spoken by figures in the bar, triggering reprises, by off-stage voices, mostly of the songs he and Fiona have sung together, Fiona even becoming visible by means of a scrim or gauze screen through which she can be seen from time to time, ghostlike. For example, Jane's line 'After all, darling, I did think the minute you'd get in town you'd call me – or come to me', triggers a reprise of Fiona singing 'Come to Me, Bend to Me' and similar phrases provoke other songs. All of this has the effect of making Tommy break with Jane and, with Jeff, hurry back to Scotland. The final scene is a reprise of the opening scene of the show, the forest where they had become lost. When they find no trace of the bridge or of the village, Tommy is ready to concede that it has all been a dream. As they are about to leave, they hear the reprise of the title song as the bridge and village once more come out of the mist. Murdoch appears and beckons Tommy across the bridge, assuring him that 'when you love someone deeply, anythin' is possible – even miracles'. Trance-like, Tommy crosses the bridge, leaving a bewildered Jeff as the final curtain falls. Inexplicably, but perhaps reflecting the uncertainty about the show's ending, Tommy and Fiona are not reunited on stage.

Brigadoon would become – with *Finian's Rainbow* – the most celebrated show of the 1947 Broadway season, would run for 581 performances and would transfer to an even more extensive run in London in 1949. Looking at the London programme, however, one is struck by two significant differences from the Broadway show. Instead of being set in 1946, the action is now set in 1935 and the credits contain an additional member of the company – Scottish Technical Adviser. The two are connected since the latter, actor/ singer Ian Wallace, pointed out that to set the date of the miracle which put Brigadoon into suspended animation as 1749 would be to locate it within the post-Culloden proscription of the wearing of tartan. Wallace would also be helpful in authenticating the cast's Scots accents. Following its spectacular success on Broadway and in London, *Brigadoon* proceeded to acclaimed tours and revivals throughout Europe, the Americas and the rest of the world. It is among the most popular shows to be mounted by amateur groups, averaging 40 revivals annually. An important element in all this, which we have not yet addressed, is the critical discourse surrounding *Brigadoon* and how this widened out and, in certain quarters, darkened to the point – certainly by the late 1970s – when the very word 'Brigadoon' would send Scots intellectuals into paroxysms of rage. We shall address this presently but, by the 1970s, the original stage show had, in popular consciousness, merged with, indeed, was largely replaced by, the film version of 1954. It is to the latter that we now turn.

3

Brigadoon and Metro-Goldwyn-Mayer

When MGM was making *King Solomon's Mines* (1950) [t]he moviemakers arrived in the Congo and... were appalled to find the natives wearing tennis shoes and Hawaiian shirts. Worst of all, their hair was slicked down and did not look right... Finally MGM solved the problem by shipping two hundred Afro wigs from Culver City...

Peter Hay

During the Second World War there appeared, in the pages of *Life* magazine, in lavish double-page colour, a photograph captioned 'MGM's Boss Mayer and His Top Talent'. In it, MGM President Louis B Mayer sits surrounded by most of the top stars of the studio, some of them, like Captain James Stewart and Private First Class Desi Arnaz, in military uniform. Shot on a characteristically grandiose MGM set complete with marble pillars and a life-size statue of an Oscar, the photograph speaks sumptuousness, incarnating the MGM slogan 'More stars than there are in the heavens'. Mayer, in the centre of the front row, is flanked on one side by Katharine Hepburn and on the other by Greer Garson. Spencer Tracy sits immediately behind him. Less prominent in the photograph are two (then) young actors who would go on to play Tommy and Jeff in MGM's adaptation of *Brigadoon* – Gene Kelly and Van Johnson.

Researching a Broadway musical and its screen adaptation are two very different activities. Roughly speaking, it is rather like comparing the product of a cottage industry with that of a multinational corporation. Although probably less true today, this was certainly the case in 1953/4 when MGM put into production the 'property' it had acquired several years before. The break-up of the studio system post-1960 makes the organisation of stage and film musicals nowadays rather similar, but prior to that the differences were enormous. Characteristically, in the organisation of a stage musical, the individual impresario is the key figure, the one who organises the finance, seeks out the libretto and composer, appoints the production team and – doubtless in consultation with them – selects the principal actors, singers and dancers and schedules an appropriate theatre. Cameron Mackintosh would be perhaps the best-known such figure on the British scene today. *Mutatis mutandis* Cheryl Crawford fulfilled that role in the easing of *Brigadoon* onto Broadway. Within such an arrangement, all the major creative personnel are freelance, engaged for the single production with the director, choreographer, costume and set designer being responsible for their own research. During the heyday of the Hollywood studios, all of this would be carried on in-house, the individual studio having vast tracts of studio space, vast armies of carpenters, plasterers, painters, electricians through cameramen, editors, designers, musicians, all the way up to writers, directors and producers. This was particularly true of MGM, always the most glamorous and lavish of studios. This means that screen musicals are invariably better documented than stage musicals, with the key papers – scripts, inter-office-communications (hereafter I-O-Cs), schedules, market research and promotional campaigns – all belonging to the same organisation and therefore, in general, being better preserved than the papers of individuals connected with stage musicals. Such is the case with *Brigadoon*.

I described the shaping of the Broadway version primarily in terms of the input of six figures, Lerner and Loewe, Crawford and Lewis, and De Mille and Smith. I will describe the film version principally in terms of producer Arthur Freed, director Vincente Minnelli and choreographer/dancer/actor Gene Kelly, although, of course, the adaptation was of the Lerner/Loewe work and Lerner wrote the screenplay. We must never lose sight of the fact, however, that all their talents were assembled within the crucible of MGM and drew on the resources of that vast organisation. Arthur Freed joined MGM as a songwriter and plugger from Broadway and got his first production credit on *Babes in Arms* (1939). Thereafter, the output of what would come to be the Arthur Freed Unit at MGM reads like a roll-call of the greatest screen musicals: *Strike Up the Band, Little Nellie Kelly* (1940); *Lady Be Good, Babes on Broadway* (1941); *Panama Hattie, For Me and My Gal** (1942); *Cabin in the Sky+, Best Foot Forward, Du Barry Was a Lady*, Girl Crazy* (1943); *Meet Me in St Louis+* (1944); *The Clock+, Yolanda and the Thief+* (1945); *The Harvey Girls, Ziegfeld Follies*+, Till the Clouds Roll By* (1946); *Good News* (1947); *Summer Holiday, The Pirate*+, Easter Parade, Words and Music** (1948); *Take Me Out to the Ball Game*, The Barkleys of Broadway, Any Number Can Play, On the Town** (1949); *Annie Get Your Gun, Pagan Love Song* (1950); *Royal Wedding, Show Boat, An American in Paris*+* (1951); *The Belle of New York, Singin' in the Rain** (1952); *The Band Wagon+* (1953); *Brigadoon*+ (1954); It's Always Fair Weather*, Kismet+* (1955); *Invitation to the Dance** (1956); *Silk Stockings* (1957); *Gigi+* (1958); *Bells Are Ringing+*. To indicate the cohesiveness of the Freed Unit, no fewer than 11 of these, marked thus +, were made with Vincente Minnelli as director, and 12, marked thus *, with Gene Kelly, sometimes as actor, sometimes choreographer and sometimes co-director. The credits of *Brigadoon* are replete with the names of figures long part of, or associated with, the Freed Unit, all of whom had worked previously with Minnelli and Kelly: Associate Producer Roger Edens, Art Directors Cedric Gibbons (the long-time head of art direction at MGM) and Preston Ames; Set Decorators Edwin B Willis and Keogh Gleason, Musical Director Johnny Green, Orchestrator Conrad Salinger and Costume Designer Irene Sharaff.

The role of the director in the theatre and the cinema are equally crucial, but there is a substantial difference in the way they have been discussed in the history and criticism of the two fields, the film director having received much more critical attention than the theatre director. Very broadly speaking, it is the writer in the theatre who has been the main focus of critical interest. These different emphases have come about for complex cultural reasons, but two are worth mentioning. In the first few decades of cinema, as it emerged primarily as a scientific preoccupation, a technical toy and a source of popular entertainment, many of the figures responsible for artistic innovation were directors, for example DW Griffith, and many of those arguing for the cinema's artistic autonomy, like Erich von Stroheim, or socio-political relevance, such as SM Eisenstein, were also directors. Somewhat later, in the 1950s, one of the most important movements in the history of film criticism – the emergence of *auteurism* first in France then in the USA and Britain – focused on the film director, particularly in the popular Hollywood cinema, as the major source of critical interest. It was as a result of this latter movement that Vincente Minnelli became critically visible. Greatly respected as Robert Lewis is in the history of theatre, he is nowhere near as well documented as Minnelli, who has several books and innumerable journal articles devoted to him and his work. It is these publications which help facilitate our understanding of what he brought to *Brigadoon*, what he found most interesting about it and how he left a visible 'signature' on it. A central principle of the auteur method is to scrutinise the entire output of a filmmaker to lay bare the recurrent thematic and stylistic features of the films. Thomas Elsaesser has written of the characters in Minnelli's films as engaged in a struggle

> for total fulfilment, for total gratification of their aesthetic needs, their desire for beauty and harmony, their demand for an identity of their lives with the reality of their dreams...
>
> (Elsaesser 1981: 15)

The extent to which this description fits Tommy hardly needs to be spelt out, but the auteur method considers all of a director's films in its analysis, so the description is equally true of Minnelli's melodramas, several of which, like *The Bad and the Beautiful (1952)* and *Lust for Life* (1956) – his biography of Vincent van Gogh – are explicitly about tortured artists who are quite literally searching for 'an identity of their lives with the reality of their dreams'. Minnelli's recurrent obsession may be *one* of the reasons – the powerful presence of Gene Kelly as choreographer is another – why the screen version of *Brigadoon* brings dance much more to the foreground.

Gene Kelly is also a well-documented figure. He had four separate Hollywood careers, as actor, dancer, choreographer and director, very often fulfilling all four roles on the same picture, as in *On the Town*. According to his biographer Alvin Yudkoff, both the moment of

Brigadoon and the project itself were unhappy for Kelly. He had left the USA for Europe in 1951, partly for economic reasons to take advantage of the American tax laws, and partly for political reasons. His known liberalism had brought him into conflict with more than one anti-communist committee and his then wife, Betsy Blair, more leftist than Kelly, had been effectively blacklisted. He was also, according to Yudkoff, deeply resentful that his contribution to the Oscar-showered Freed/Minnelli picture *An American in Paris* had not been recognised by a 'Best Actor' award or one shared with Minnelli as 'Best Director'. Yudkoff, describing Kelly's return from Europe to participate in *Brigadoon*, writes:

> His return to Hollywood contrasted starkly with his first arrival fourteen years earlier. The competition of television had ground down MGM's annual output of films to a new low. With two European flops and *Invitation to the Dance* [which Kelly wrote, directed, choreographed and starred in] still bogged down in expensive post-production, auguring little or no eventual profit, Gene was not exactly king of the hill, as he found out at his first meeting with Dore Schary [Head of Production at MGM] on the subject of his next musical, *Brigadoon*. Vincente Minnelli would direct, Schary explained... Gene didn't believe a word of what he was hearing. He was being shunted aside as director and as a participant in the crucial production decisions on *Brigadoon*. While in Europe he had broken away for a location survey in Scotland and had worked out a plan for shooting exterior locations in the highlands there, interiors at the Boreham Wood Studios near London and, finally, the songs and dances in Culver City. He had spoken to the legendary English [sic] ballerina Moira Shearer about the lead female role opposite himself and had planned to engage the Sadler's Wells Ballet Company for the ensemble numbers. Schary cut him short... No location shooting; painted backdrops will be fine, thank you. Forget Shearer and Sadler's Wells. Cyd Charisse, under contract, would do nicely. And to beat the competition of television, *Brigadoon* would be shot in CinemaScope.
>
> *(Yudkoff 1999: 229)*

This passage needs to be 'unpacked' at several points. In the late 1940s, the money men in New York had effectively lost confidence in Louis B Mayer and his costly, highly bureaucratised operation at Culver City and had instructed him to 'find another Thalberg', Thalberg being the legendary inter-war Head of Production at MGM who had steered the company towards its sumptuous identity and healthy balance sheet. Mayer lighted on Dore Schary, an odd choice politically for the arch-conservative Republican Mayer since Schary was a New Deal liberal Democrat who, as Head of Production at RKO, had specialised in 'social problem' films such as *Crossfire* (1947) which dealt with anti-Semitism. Despite Schary's attempts to reorient MGM towards less costly genres, his early years at MGM coincided with the 'golden years' of the MGM musical, testimony to what a juggernaut a Hollywood studio could be in any attempt to change direction. Kelly had, indeed, gone to Scotland with Freed to scout locations for *Brigadoon* – Freed has been widely quoted as saying that 'Scotland did not look Scottish enough' – and the story of Moira Shearer being approached to play Fiona has intrigued critics for years. If she were to be cast because she was *Scottish* (and not English as Yudkoff says) this might mean that, as in the London stage version, some measure of authenticity was in the minds of the MGM personnel. On the other hand, if what attracted them was Shearer's work on two films by Michael Powell and Emeric Pressburger, *The Red Shoes* (1948) and *The Tales of Hoffman* (1951), then the attraction would have been Shearer's capacity to function in a deliriously non-naturalistic form. As it happens, the story of MGM's interest in Shearer seems to be a myth since she herself denies that any such discussions took place. Arthur Freed had acquired the screen rights in the late 1940s as a 'property' within which to showcase Kathryn Grayson, an MGM singing star then under contract, but her contract had expired by the time *Brigadoon* went into production and the casting of Cyd Charisse, primarily a dancer, as Fiona further tipped the balance of the project towards dancing. It was indeed Schary's decision to shoot on the MGM back lot and in CinemaScope. He had, after all, been hired to bring MGM's financial extravagance under control. CinemaScope was seen at the time as the cinema's answer to television. It had been introduced by Darryl Zanuck, Twentieth Century Fox's Head of Production, in 1953 with *The Robe*, a biblical epic which had been very successful at the box office. There is a further passage in Yudkoff's biography of Kelly which is rather controversial:

> When Gene started [on *Brigadoon*], there was an immediate tension between him and Minnelli... Later, explaining the debacle, Gene

explained: 'Vincente and I were never in synch. I remember him telling me that he hadn't liked the Broadway show at all, and I loved it'. Gene envisioned *Brigadoon* almost as a Scottish western, an outdoor picture radiant with vistas of heather on which he and the company would dance. He was aware, nervously so, that the stage play had been hailed for the brilliant choreography of Agnes De Mille, linking classical ballet to traditional Scottish dancing in a way that moved the story along – an approach entirely consistent with Kelly principles. But he had no intention of collaborating with her; at this point it would do his fading career no good merely to serve as a conduit for De Mille, ushering her well-received dance concepts into the film version. Just the thought of being elbow-to-elbow with a strong-minded woman choreographer (whom he personally abhorred for her conservative politics and her homophobic prejudices) set him firmly on the path of sweeping aside De Mille's work...

(Yudkoff 1999: 230)

As we saw in Chapter 1, De Mille's work certainly displayed a hard and fast conception of gender with her dancers often behaving as stereotypical men and women, the former excessively macho, the latter girlish but, aside from a few references to the high incidence of homosexuals among male dancers, she can hardly be said to have been homophobic. Also, although she came from a strongly Republican family – her uncle was the film director Cecil B De Mille – there is scant evidence of her allegedly conservative politics. Indeed, she crossed swords with the notoriously rightwing, anti-communist gossip columnist Hedda Hopper on Ed Murrow's television programme *Small World* in 1959 and was a consistent activist for the unionisation of dancers and choreographers. However, the above extracts from Yudkoff's book do suggest that the major overall creative decisions on *Brigadoon* were in hands other than Kelly's.

It was suggested at the beginning of this chapter that – on account of their different institutional status – film musicals are better documented than stage musicals. For information about the setting-up of the Broadway and London stage versions of *Brigadoon* we have had to rely largely on the memoirs of figures such as Crawford and Lewis and the recollections of surviving personnel such as Ian Wallace. With regard to the film version, however, quite apart from having the film itself, there are two separate collections of papers.

The Arthur Freed Unit papers are lodged, as part of the MGM collection, at the University of Southern California and Minnelli's papers at the Margaret Herrick Library of the Academy of Motion Picture Arts and Sciences, both in Los Angeles. From the former we learn that Lerner and Loewe received $180,000 in adaptation rights and that Lerner received a further $35,000 for the screenplay. As was the norm at the time, the script was sent to MGM's legal department which suggested some changes to avoid offending the Duke of Fife (over the use of the name of his estate) and the American automobile industry (over a reference to a foreign car), and to that curious institution the Production Code Administration since, between 1934 and 1966, no film could be shown in American cinemas without a PCA seal of approval. Following a series of Hollywood sex scandals in the 1920s, a Catholic Jesuit priest, Father Daniel Lord, drafted a code of propriety for the movies which called upon them to stop glorifying gangsters, adulterers and prostitutes. Gregory Black, historian of the PCA, writes:

> Lord's code, which soon became the Bible of film production, banned nudity, excessive violence, white slavery, illegal drugs, miscegenation, lustful kissing, suggestive postures, and profanity from the screen... [H]is code also held that films should promote the institutions of marriage and home, defend the fairness of government and present religious institutions with reverence.
>
> *(Black 1994: 1)*

Will Hays, at the time President of the film trade body, the Motion Picture Producers and Distributors of America, adopted Lord's code but over the next four years there was dissatisfaction among religious groups with its implementation and the Catholic Church inaugurated the Legion of Decency campaign with the specific aim of having a tougher code formally adopted. In response Hays created the PCA with a lay-Catholic anti-Semite, Joseph I Breen, as its director. There is among the Freed papers a copy of a letter from Breen to Schary clearing the script of *Brigadoon* except for the song 'The Love of My Life' and the chorus of 'The Chase' since 'the former is an unacceptably light treatment of illicit sex' and the latter contains the expletive 'By God!'. Knowing that Meg's second song 'My Mother's Weddin' Day' had no hope at all of being passed by the

PCA the producers did not even include it in the script. They also dropped 'The Love of My Life' but had some small compensation in learning that Breen had relented on 'By God!'. However, some months later Breen had become concerned once more about the script, specifically Meg's attempted seduction of Jeff. These exchanges occurred in the summer and winter of 1953 before *Brigadoon* was shot, but as late as May 1954, with the film well 'in the can' Schary was still apprehensive, urging Freed to do something about 'some little dialogue about divorce – probably just enough to put the picture into the "B" category of the Legion of Decency – something which can hurt this particular picture'. What Schary was referring to was the four-part classification against which the Legion of Decency measured every film before awarding their seal of approval:

A1 Unobjectionable for general patronage
A2 Unobjectionable for adults
B   Objectionable in part
C   Condemned

Shorn of all its 'objectionable' elements, *Brigadoon* would go on to win the plaudits of diverse religious and pro-family groups and be presented with a Blue Ribbon Award, sponsored by the National Screen Council, 'for the best release of the month suitable for the whole family'. The Film Estimates Board of National Organisations rated the film 'F' as being suitable for all the family and Freed, Minnelli and Lerner all received Christopher Awards, given to those showbiz people 'whose work reflects positive values and shows how a person can use his God-given talent for the benefit of all'. Clearly in the 1950s the 'moral majority' policed the film industry with a formidable armoury of sticks and carrots. Certainly, at this time, the film industry had a dismal record of caving in to strong-arming by political and religious groups.

MGM's adapting *Brigadoon* sent a buzz through the North American sector of the Scots diaspora, and indeed further afield. Included in the Freed papers are many letters, mostly from Scots-American performers or their agents and well-wishers, soliciting parts. There is even a letter from a Glasgow woman who had played Fiona in the South African run and had been offered the role in Australia. Such letters are interesting in their own right but, by noting to whom they are addressed or assigned in the MGM set-up, the historian can deduce something about the division of labour on *Brigadoon*. The financial papers indicate when personnel came on the payroll, what their rate was and how long they served. We learn, for instance, that Minnelli came aboard from 21 August 1953 and remained on the payroll until 15 June 1954. We can deduce from the dates and sources of other I-O-Cs that he and Lerner were in New York in September 1953 auditioning some of the minor principals from outside the MGM stable while Roger Edens, the Associate Producer, was in Culver City handling unsolicited bids for parts and dealing with more general and minor matters, for instance replying to the Palos Verdes Pipe Band, thrice winners of the California State Pipe Band Championship and suppliers of pipers to what appears to have been a version of *Brigadoon* on ice. Letters to Freed from the New York talent agency organising Lerner and Minnelli's auditions speak of Minnelli being impressed by the 'gaunt appearance and brooding quality' of Hugh Laing, a dancer with the New York City Ballet, who would be cast as a very effective Harry in the film.

Two particular factors emerge from all the Freed papers. There was intense interest in the project among Scots-American performers and seemingly some genuine commitment on MGM's part to deal – as they saw it – authentically with the Scots dimension of *Brigadoon*. Among the extensive papers is a box marked 'Research Materials' which contains two copies of Lerner's libretto and a number of postcards and tourist brochures relating to Scotland including a photograph of a bridge with, on the rear, the words 'Bridge near Robert Burns' birthplace – Scotland. Re *Brigadoon*'. The visual material would certainly have helped the in-house design people who would have designed the film quite independently of the designs for the stage show. However, as we shall see, Minnelli was carrying out his own research on the visual look of the film.

The I-O-Cs from Schary to Freed indicate that, in general, he was well pleased with the way the project was developing. His praise for the 'simple and illusory quality' of the set was modest given that it was the largest ever built on the MGM back lot. 'Illusory' indeed: there were stories of local birds crashing into the set thinking it was real. However, there was one issue on which Schary remained nervous. In December 1953, he wrote to Freed with a copy to Minnelli:

Dear Arthur

I've seen some of the early work on *Brigadoon* and for style and general effect we should all be pleased, but I am becoming quite alarmed over the use of the dialect. I think much of it will be incomprehensible to an American audience, and while it can be argued that dubbing will take care of some of it, it would be absurd for us to continue playing the entire picture with so much burr in it. Please discuss this with Vincente...

It would seem that, for Schary, the Dialect Coach was doing his job too well. Just as Lewis in London had hired Ian Wallace as Scottish Technical Adviser, so too had Freed mobilised a Los Angeles-based Scot who styled himself Commander KD Ian Murray, RN. We know nothing about Murray's input to the accents in the film, apart from its worrying Schary, but we do know something about the significant role Murray played in the marketing of *Brigadoon* in the USA. Extant photographs reveal what is often referred to as a 'professional Scotsman', portly, bearded and in full highland dress with an impressive array of campaign decoration miniatures on his jacket. He will reappear in the next chapter.

About a year previously, this time in Edinburgh, another professional Scotsman was getting into the *Brigadoon* act. Minnelli, working so regularly for MGM, maintained an office in Culver City. Minnelli's papers contain an I-O-C from his secretary to Freed to the effect that Minnelli had been conducting personal research on Scotland in the course of which he had written to the Scottish Tourist Board in Edinburgh looking for pictures of the country. His letter had been passed to the Assistant Secretary (Administration) to the board, one Iain F Anderson, FRSGS, FSA, who it seems had seen the touring version of *Brigadoon* in Edinburgh, was an expert on eighteenth-century Scotland and, having sent on some visual material, offered himself as technical adviser. Attached to the I-O-C are copies of Anderson's letters, six in all, amounting to 19 densely-typed pages of historical and other advice regarding the making of the film. The voluminous letters were not due entirely to Anderson's being verbose, though he was certainly that, but also to the indications in his letters that Minnelli had been bombarding him with questions. Anderson offered advice about historical background and social *mores*, the design of highland housing, the form of highland fairy tales, what might have been on sale in McConnachy Square, details of highland weaponry and female and male attire, right down to the minutiae of sporran design – at one point he boasts that his own sporran is 180 years old. Anderson is meticulous in describing the visual material he is sending, including photographs of Muckerash Castle, the Falls of Glencoe, the grounds of Brodick Castle, the Hermitage of Braid, the Linn o'Dee, the village of Luss, a thatched cottage and a woman spinning. Anderson also sent photographs of the costumes for the Australian production of *Brigadoon*, which had been made by an Edinburgh kiltmaker, and a number of weighty books, the heavy postal charges on which Anderson laments. Crucial among these was *MacIan's Highlanders* which, oddly, Anderson describes as an accurate representation of highland costume. Anderson seems to have been representative of a type of Scot, mercifully less common nowadays, with an inordinate pride in what he imagined to be Scottish history but which was, in fact, an armature of linked ideologies about the Scottish past interspersed with some real historical knowledge of a Gradgrindian kind. Invariably decked out in 'highland dress' – despite the preponderance of potbellies and spurkle shanks among the type – such professional Scotsmen were objects of derision, particularly among younger Scots. In addition to being entranced with the 'romance' of the Scottish past, Anderson was, it seems, something of a dramatist *manqué*. One of his letters bemoans the lack of 'any strong traditional element or rhythm' in *Brigadoon* and recommends that it be re-scored to include tunes such as 'Loch Lomond', 'Annie Laurie', 'Robin Gray' and 'Afton Water' – a fondness for 'traditional' Scots songs (and a deadly propensity to perform them on every occasion) is a mark of the professional Scot. Warming to his theme, Anderson suggests that there is a key character missing from the script – a fiddler. This character 'could be introduced as the joyous fiddler serenading the bride-to-be and later on lead the orchestra in the duet "Almost Like Being in Love"'. Anderson proceeds to rewrite whole scenes to include his creation:

Act II, Scene 3 – The Glen
This scene would open as one of bright gaiety with THE FIDDLER playing a Scottish Country Dance Tune. With a group of eight dancers executing the dance. As the dance is proceeding, the

distant wailing of the pipes playing a lament drifts into the scene of the gay music and the dance. The spectators are first noticed picking up this awesome message foretelling death. They race to watch the dance and peer into the distance. The dancers continue for a little dancing on gaily to the fiddler's music. Then the fiddler hears the distant wailing. He falters in the speed of his playing, stops, goes on... The whole actors freeze in a position of a realised horror of this wailing message. 'Whose death?' is in every mind. The piper is still unseen, and as the effect of the sorrowful lament increases with his approach, the sad cortege comes into view. (The foregoing is an adaptation of an actual experience of the writer's when the distant playing of a lament changed a happy company to one of sadness.) The intensity of the arrival of the body could be increased by the 'keening' of the women present. A wailing note of extreme sorrow which in past centuries was not uncommon...

The 'lone piper' syndrome, referred to in the last chapter is here writ large, calling to mind the words of that inveterate romanticiser of Scotland, HV Morton – 'Grief locks the English heart, but it opens the Scottish. The Celt has a genius for the glorification of sorrow' (Morton 1929: 54). It would seem that – whatever benefit they may have derived from the material he sent – Minnelli and his production team were able to resist Anderson's rewriting of *Brigadoon*. The correspondence concluded with Minnelli expressing the hope that he and Anderson might meet in person 'when we commence preparations for *Brigadoon* in the early Spring'. At this point Anderson vanishes from the documentation surrounding the film.

The 'whims of executives' had already asserted themselves in Schary's insistence that the project be shot on the back lot and in CinemaScope (in fact it was shot in two formats to accommodate those theatres not technically equipped to run CinemaScope) and some of the compromises, such as the demands of the PCA and the less than wholehearted participation of Kelly, have already been referred to. Minnelli was deeply immersed in the history of art, as his 17-minute ballet, based on the French Impressionists and Post-Impressionists, in *An American in Paris*, and his film biography of Van Gogh, *Lust for Life*, testify to. Not surprisingly, his vision of Scotland in *Brigadoon* was partly conceived in art historical terms. Drawing on whatever materials Anderson sent him, supplemented by what MGM had assembled, he came to the conclusion, it seems, that available film stocks used individually would provide too bright an effect. The Scotland of Minnelli's imagination was of a more sombre hue. As he has said:

> I studied photographs of Scotland – misty monotones, yellows and greens, and based the film on those subdued colours...
>
> *(Casper 1977: 96)*

He seems to have had in mind for the interiors Dutch painting and for the exteriors English Romantic painting. He tried several experiments with cinematographer Joseph Ruttenberg and decided that the dark Scotland of his imagination would best be realised by using a Technicolor negative and printing the positive in Anscocolor, a cheaper alternative which MGM under the cost-conscious Schary was increasingly opting for. Anscocolor had the effect of dulling down the piercing tones of Technicolor although *Brigadoon* – to the eyes of audiences used to the more naturalistic Eastmancolor common nowadays and allied to the film's discernibly studio-based landscapes – appears wildly non-naturalistic, an important factor in the detestation it was to elicit from Scots intellectuals. The mist-shrouded landscape that is the first image after the credits is as dark as anything in Constable or, for that matter, Caspar David Friedrich, truly the Scotland of Romanticism. Indeed, it is pushed to such a level of unreality that, rather than the art historical tradition of academic Romantic painting, a more appropriate point of reference might be the postcard representations of Scotland by the artist Ernest Longstaffe for the London postcard publisher S Hildesheimer and Company at about the turn of the century. Many of these were printed in Bavaria and – rather analogously to the Minnelli/Ruttenberg colour experiments – the very distinctive German colour printing process of the period lent an added unreality to the landscapes.

The credit sequence of *Brigadoon* is very characteristic MGM. Against the snarling lion of the well-known MGM logo, we hear the characteristic four bagpipe-like notes and added grace-note of Loewe's Overture which is played out against the credits. They consist of the artistes' and production personnel's names on a series of white calling cards lying on a ruffled piece of Royal Stewart tartan gathered by a 'Celtic' badge, the music, the tartan and the badge, of course, signifying 'Scottishness' and orienting the audience to what is to come. This form of credits – calling cards on a background of fabric – was used extensively by MGM at this time and itself signified the high-gloss production values of the company. There is no doubt that Minnelli shared the general Hollywood commitment to the 'agreed' shape of classical film narrative. Von Ellstein, the European film director in *The Bad and the Beautiful* (widely supposed to be based on Alfred Hitchcock) is thought to reflect Minnelli's view when, in an argument with his producer, he tells him that a picture consisting solely of dramatic high points 'is like a necklace without a string; it falls apart'. That said, Minnelli's considerable reputation among film critics and historians unquestionably rests primarily on his superb visual flair and, in particular, the energy, dynamism and colourfulness of his *mise-en-scène*, all deployed in realising that utopian other world which, for Minnelli, is the very antithesis of quotidian dullness. Indeed, the driven producer in *The Bad and the Beautiful* is shown to lapse into a state of neurosis when not producing art, again a view widely ascribed to Minnelli himself. Minnelli's reputation for visual flair had been achieved within the pre-widescreen standard screen aspect of 1.33:1. It is no secret that he disliked the CinemaScope aspect ratio of 2.35:1, sharing the view of the German director Fritz Lang who – appearing as himself in Jean-Luc Godard's *Le Mépris* (1963) – opined that CinemaScope was good for photographing snakes and funerals.

The key question is the extent to which Minnelli's celebrated colour and dynamism survive the cumbersome CinemaScope frame in *Brigadoon*. Following the credits and the Overture, there is a brief sequence in which Tommy and Jeff are located in the Scottish landscape. Minnelli gets around the constant tendency to stasis in the CinemaScope frame by a combination of languid crane shots and pans across the landscape with a long, slow lap dissolve while, as in the stage version, the essential information is given by the chorus. Whereas the stage version immediately picks up the two men's first conversation, the film embarks on a sequence which has no parallel in the stage version – it dramatises Brigadoon's coming awake with a highly mobile camera picking up the village landscape as a magical golden light begins to suffuse it. Windows open, villagers awake and stretch and animals lurch to their feet. The sequence has been described as:

very reminiscent of Genesis' account of creation's dawning, and
very appropriately since this is the story of the rebirth of the village
and Tommy...

(Casper 1977: 141)

7. Contemproary advertisements for the film of
Brigadoon stressed the novelty of CinemasScope.

The main point to be noticed is Minnelli's confidence in the handling
of the CinemaScope frame, its fluidity very reminiscent of those
marvellously mobile (often opening) sequences common in
Hollywood in the late 1930s and early 1940s, as in *Dead End* (1937)
and *The Killers* (1946). However, other things are worthy of note.
An image of an old lady waking up in a rocking chair as the golden
light streams in the window renders concretely Minnelli's basing his
interiors on Dutch painting and, in the image of the built-in bed
with doors, we may have one of the moments when Anderson's
research was incorporated into the film's design. Further departing

from the stage version, Minnelli segues his wholly cinematic reawakening sequence into the first big production number, 'Down in McConnachy Square'. It is noteworthy that, despite the blaze of colour and movement which is the focus of this sequence, it finds space, in the meeting of Charlie and Harry, to foreshadow the central conflict. The stage version mentions primarily the vending of vegetables and flowers although, as will be recalled, one scene closes with the villagers unrolling and holding aloft lengths of tartan cloth. Minnelli augments this by foregrounding the dying and selling of cloth thereby extending and dynamising the scene's colour range. Referring back to Minnelli's experience as window dresser and stage designer, James Naremore has written about Minnelli's remarkable 'feel' for clothes and fabrics in motion, achieved most sensuously in the washerwomen sequence in his *Yolanda and the Thief*. It is only after these early 'cinematic' departures that Minnelli returns to the Broadway version through a dissolve from the Brigadooners concluding their 'McConnachy Square' song to a map being studied by the lost Tommy and Jeff, who have not yet spotted Brigadoon. It is at this point that Minnelli presents the exposition which differentiates the cynical, worldly Jeff from the romantic, yearning Tommy. As they are about to leave the spot, Tommy – to a brief reprise of the title song – spots the village and they head for it. Given Minnelli's acute sense of the resonance of colour, it is worth pointing out that Jeff is dressed in very cool blues and greys. Tommy's main garment is a dark green shirt, but a bright red tee shirt can be seen underneath it and his socks too are bright red. In other words, the only 'hot' colours are associated with Tommy, a foreshadowing of the passion to come.

In the stage version, it will be recalled, this scene is followed by the 'Down in McConnachy Square' number, which is that version's way of marking the reawakening of Brigadoon. Minnelli has already done this cinematically and segued it into the 'McConnachy Square' number, the effect being that many of the song and dance numbers in the film are brought forward. Fiona's song 'Waitin' For My Dearie', in the stage version, takes place in McConnachy Square: it makes sense in the theatre to pack as much action as possible into one set. In the film, after Tommy and Jeff make for Brigadoon, there is a scene by and inside Fiona and Jean's cottage. There is a brief bit of business in which Charlie comes by and is sent packing lest he see Jean on her wedding day. Once inside the cottage, where the village women are packing Jean's trousseau, Fiona sings 'Waitin' For My Dearie', Charisse's voice being dubbed by a professional singer since she was primarily a dancer. Solely a sung number on the stage, and in keeping with the stronger presence of dance in the film, it becomes here a dance involving Fiona and the women, Minnelli patently more comfortable composing the CinemaScope frame with up to a dozen people in it rather than with simply Tommy and Jeff as in the earlier scene. As will be seen, Gene Kelly – as both choreographer and dancer – is intensely eclectic in terms of the range of dance styles he is prepared to include in a single number. The dance styles of 'Waitin' For My Dearie' include quasi-ballet movements, a minuet (to which certain rhythms in the song lend themselves) and a mime in which one of the women dresses as a man and pretends to woo Fiona. Again, Minnelli has colour-coded this sequence. While the other women wear darker, multi-coloured dresses, Fiona is luminous in a primrose dress, but her dormant passion – the theme of her song – is hinted at in the flashes of tangerine in her underskirt. The song and the dance close with Fiona looking wistfully out of the window. We will be talking extensively about Kelly's choreographing of the dances, but Minnelli also choreographs the actors throughout, arranging them so that both information-giving and subtexts are made clear. For instance, when an elder is spelling out the boundaries of Brigadoon which must not be crossed on pain of the village's disappearance forever, the frame is extensively populated by villagers, but a space is left right at the centre of the frame into which Harry – the threat to the village's survival – appears, delivering to Fiona an account of his torment which is even more sombre than that in the stage libretto:

> I've got nothing, nothing but to be trapped in this peasant village all my life. Look at it! The boundaries of a town? Not to me. 'Tis more the dimensions of my jail.

The film makes more of the entry to Brigadoon of the two Americans than does the stage show, with them asking directions from three separate villagers all of whom run away in alarm or refuse to give information. It is at this point that the film engineers the first meeting of Tommy and Fiona. Again, it exemplifies Minnelli's confident choreographing of actors within the CinemaScope frame.

Tommy and Jeff are in the mid-foreground when Fiona enters in the right rear of the frame. As she comes into the foreground she enters the space between Jeff and Tommy which has opened by the latter moving slightly to the right so that, throughout virtually the remainder of the scene, Fiona faces Tommy and has her back to Jeff, thus permitting the 'long look' between them. Tommy learns that her name is Fiona Campbell – unaccountably, there are several name changes from stage to screen – and she gives directions to McConnachy Square. The stage libretto mentions an inn, but Iain Anderson's detailed briefing for Minnelli on eighteenth-century Scotland speaks of this as being unlikely. The film plays up the fear and amazement of the villagers. But it is Charlie who smoothes things over with his invitation to the Americans to drink his health on his wedding day. Hearing that the bride's name is 'Campbell', Tommy assumes it is Fiona, the film making more of this confusion than the stage show. In the stage show there is Charlie's song, 'I'll Go Home With Bonnie Jean' and, separately, 'The Bonnie Jean Ballet' with Tommy and Jeff simply as onlookers to both. The ballet is dropped from the film – doubtless because it had De Mille written all over it – and, instead, Kelly reworked 'I'll Go Home...' so that it becomes a way of integrating Tommy and Jeff into the village both as singers and dancers. Kelly was, of course, an expert dancer and Van Johnson had himself been a 'hoofer' on Broadway – he and Kelly had appeared together in *Pal Joey* there – before becoming MGM's 'young lead' *par excellence* in the 1940s. The role of Jeff in the film was originally slotted for Donald O'Connor – a much more athletic dancer than Johnson – because of the success of his partnership with Kelly in *Singin' in the Rain*, but by the time *Brigadoon* went into production his contract had lapsed.

We have spoken of the eclecticism of Kelly's choreography and dancing. Although he had been offered a position in the Ballet Russe, in some respects he was too proletarian and humorous a dancer to have been a convincing leading man in the classical ballet. This is partly a matter of physique. From the moment he arrived in Hollywood he had been compared with Fred Astaire and it was generally agreed that Kelly was much more athletic, physical and – in terms of body language – blue collar than Astaire. On the only occasion Astaire's legs had been seen outside elegantly tailored slacks – in kilts for the 'One And Only Highland Fling' number in

8. The eclecticism of Kelly's choreography: Tommy (Gene
Kelly) and Jeff (Van Johnson) quote from *The Spirit of '76*. The villager
third from the right, in particular, might have stepped out of a Scottish
comic postcard.

The Barkleys of Broadway – they were revealed as gazelle-like. Kelly's
legs, on the other hand – as revealed in the dream sequence of *The
Pirate* – were akin to those of a pit pony. Astaire is usually
remembered in white tie and tails, Kelly in baseball cap, slacks
and tee shirt. The choreography of 'I'll Go Home With Bonnie
Jean' involves some simple marching movements by Charlie and
the villagers between verses of the song and a vaudevillian tap cum
soft-shoe duet by Kelly and Johnson which is much more 'down-
market' than the analogous dance by De Mille. The eclecticism of
the Kelly version even extends to a brief pastiche of the patriotic
painting *The Spirit of '76* with Kelly and Johnson limping as they
play imaginary fifes. Whether the credit should go to Kelly,
Minnelli or both, the *mise-en-scène* of the dance elements of 'I'll
Go Home With Bonnie Jean' is an object lesson in how to move
figures around unostentatiously so that they are in the right
positions to be incorporated into the collective dance which, to

accommodate the CinemaScope frame, is arranged as a horizontal line of about seven arm-linked villagers with Tommy and Jeff at the centre of the line (see plate 7). As was noted in the last chapter, some of the lyrics of this song approach sexual frankness, so it might be wondered why the PCA did not object to their remaining in the film. Demented and repressive the PCA might have been but, like many crazy ideological systems, it was internally coherent. A key element was that the institution of marriage be honoured so, since Harry's song is about a man giving up his dissolute ways to settle down to marriage, the lyrics remained intact. Similarly, part of Meg's dialogue – both her 'belter' songs having been excised as unacceptable to the PCA – was altered to make the object of her pursuit of Jeff marriage rather than seduction.

Fiona hastens to the square in the hope of seeing Tommy again and, the brief misunderstanding about her marital status resolved, the way is clear for their first big number together – 'The Heather on the Hill'. In both stage show and film this is a courtship moment, the point at which, even if they do not explicitly say so, they signify conventionally to the audience that they are falling in love. On stage this was by way of a sung duet but in the film, although it begins as a song by Tommy, it quickly becomes one of the big dance numbers of the film and also one of the least eclectic choreographically. From start to finish it is stylistically unified as a popularised version of classical ballet. Charisse is never *au pointe* but makes several movements reminiscent of the classical repertoire, including *attitude effacé* in which she leans on Kelly and raises her leg backwards to shoulder height (see plate 7). Kelly functions as an orthodox classical ballet male partner who – even if his movements are less refined than in classical ballet – supports and, on several occasions, lifts Charisse. Conceptually, the choreography suggests a patriarchal wooing with Kelly quite literally chasing Charisse across the hill and she feigning resistance and then succumbing. However, this initial dance can only, with propriety, go so far. It has to be seen in relation to the reprise of 'The Heather on the Hill' near the end of the film, which is altogether more passionate and sexualised. The chase elements of this dance are underlined by the rapidity of the motion Minnelli introduces to the camera movement. In every Minnelli picture there is always what can be called a 'Minnellian moment' when the frame detonates in an explosion of colour (or, in black and white movies, contrasts), movement and, according to genre, passion or violence. Minnelli's rapid movement of the cumbersome CinemaScope camera reminds us that, if the 'Minnellian moment' has not yet arrived, the straitjacket of CinemaScope is not going to inhibit it for long. In the stage version, the love duet of 'The Heather on the Hill' ends quietly with Tommy and Fiona looking at each other. Minnelli uses the freedom the cinema confers by ending on a grander note with the camera pulling back rapidly into long shot to reveal the highland panorama with Tommy and Fiona, just like the audience, turning to admire its 'picturesqueness'. This is a very appropriate strategy on Minnelli's part since he understands, intuitively if not consciously, that the 'magic' of *Brigadoon* is very much bound up with the grandeur of the Scottish terrain, albeit reconstructed on the MGM back lot. However, the intended seriousness and grandeur of this scene was undercut for Scottish audiences – to the point of eliciting laughter – by the fact that the 'heather' being gathered was manifestly sumac from North California. Having acquired shaggy highland cattle for the film, it might be thought that the producers would have imported some heather.

The endings of songs and dances in musicals are always interesting moments, for they often present the technical problem of how to engineer a change of tone from the (often) emotional or comic 'high' back to the quotidian or even to something more sombre. At the end of the song duet of the stage version, a darker note is introduced by having the 'Rain Scene', which sparks a kind of foreboding by including a further encounter between Harry and Jean. The film achieves

9. Quasi-classical ballet: Tommy (Gene Kelly) and Fiona (Cyd Charisse) dance 'The Heather on the Hill'.

a more sombre mood without recourse to this scene when Tommy attempts to cross the bridge to pick some 'heather' and is stopped by Fiona's alarmed cry. Her terror provides the occasion for Tommy to rehearse the strange events of the day and to set up the two subsequent scenes in which Tommy will discover the eighteenth-century dates of Fiona's and Jean's birthdays and be informed by the dominie, Mr Lundie – another unaccountable name change – about the true nature of Brigadoon. However, before these scenes, the tone again changes when, chasing the runaway Fiona, Tommy tumbles down a bank and lands at the feet of Jeff fleeing Meg's amorous advances. Prompted by Jeff, Tommy launches into 'Almost Like Being In Love' which, in the stage version, was again a love duet sung by Tommy and Fiona but here – again confirming the stronger presence of dance – becoming a song and dance for Tommy. Reflecting yet again the eclecticism of Kelly's dancing and choreography, this is mainly a soft-shoe shuffle with a bit of athletic leaping. The present writer had a colleague to whom Kelly's singing and dancing was anathema, the reason being that 'he always looks so damned pleased with himself'. If that charge can be made against Kelly, then the choreography of 'Almost Like Being In Love' supplies the smoking gun. Stephen Harvey is merciless in traducing what he describes as Kelly's 'throbbing falsetto' and his 'patented irresistible grin'. The charge that Kelly's work on *Brigadoon* was repetitive of his own previous work would recur significantly in audience responses to the film.

Jean's and Charlie's wedding is entered in their family bible as 24 May 1754. It will be recalled that the libretto for the Broadway opening had it as 24 May 1746, quite unaware of the resonance this would have for Scottish audiences, as Ian Wallace was to point out in the context of the London production. The year 1754 would certainly have been deep into that post-Culloden period in which, among other prohibitions, the wearing of the tartan was proscribed. Hollywoodean imperialism has, in the last analysis, scant regard for historical accuracy and no regard at all for the feelings of peripheral peoples. After Tommy's discovery of the entries in the bible, Fiona takes him to the croft of Mr Lundie. Minnelli gives added resonance to this scene by entering it by way of a blaze of yellow flowers then raising the frame to pick up Lundie gardening. Curiously for a rural setting, this is the only agricultural work we see in *Brigadoon*, so it raises the moral stature of Lundie. Within European culture, post the Industrial Revolution, pastoral and agricultural work has been endowed with a spiritual quality, often in binary opposition to the 'evil' city. This is a binarism which European immigrants took with them to the Americas and which became even more intense and polarised there. The pastoral/agricultural half of this binarism has been explored by Henry Nash Smith in his resonantly titled *Virgin Land: The American West as Symbol and Myth* and is discernible in many Hollywood films, particularly those pre-Second World War films dealing with the 'opening' of the West such as *The Covered Wagon* (1924), *Wells Fargo* (1937) and *The Westerner* (1939). It is most poignantly rehearsed in the films of John Ford who, appropriately, would signal the *post*-Second World War souring of the vision in *The Man Who Shot Liberty Valance* (1962) and *Cheyenne Autumn* (1964). Minnelli, by having Lundie till the earth, locates him in a moral narrative the audience would unanimously share. The other side of the binarism, the city as hell, will be expressed with great force later in the film. It will be recalled that one of the key shaping discourses of *Brigadoon* was Kailyardism within which

10. The moral status of pastoralism:
the garden of Mr Lundie (Barry Jones).

the major moral reference points were the dominie and the minister. Forsythe, the minister, having been evacuated from the story before the action of *Brigadoon* begins, Lundie must fulfil the theological role. It is no accident that, in a film blazing with colour, Lundie should be seen consistently in black.

Kelly has spoken in interviews of his conception of shooting outdoors in Scotland so that *Brigadoon* might have been like 'the way John Ford would shoot a Western', further evidence that he was disenchanted with the project as realised. However, despite the argument on behalf of the 'real' which will be made in relation to a certain scene in *Braveheart*, there is no intrinsic reason why shooting outdoors should be more artistically valuable that shooting on a built set. Indeed, a strong argument could be made that the long sequence which includes the wedding, Harry's interruption of it, his consequent hunting and death, and Tommy and Fiona's dance reprise of 'The Heather on the Hill' achieves its force precisely because of the unreality of the set and the control over all the aspects of *mise-en-scène* which studio-shooting facilitated for Minnelli. Also, the Longstaffean luridness of the lighting contributes significantly to the delirium Minnelli achieves in this sequence, making it a 'Minnellian moment' on a par with, say, Lana Turner's unhinged car dash in *The Bad and the Beautiful* or the 'Mack the Black' nightmare ballet in *The Pirate*. In terms also of the overall theme of the film, the unreality of the studio is entirely more appropriate than the stubborn authenticity of actual landscapes would have been. Certainly, the way Minnelli films 'the gathering of the clans' for the wedding has no sense of spatial restriction. Its expansiveness is achieved partly through camera movement, partly by skilful choice of camera position (for example, shooting through the broken windows of the ruined church). The power of the *mise-en-scène* is added to by setting the sequence at dusk, rendered in shades never seen on land or sea through control of the studio lighting, and having the 'clansmen' bearing lighted torches. The origin for this – the same reference point for an analogous scene in *Braveheart* – may have been a late-nineteenth-century issue of the *Illustrated London News* depicting the arrival of Queen Victoria at Balmoral Castle.

The Brigadooners assembled and the bagpipes stilled, Lundie announces simply that 'there's goin' to be a wedding' whereupon the cynical Jeff, still carrying his rifle, strides off into the forest, leaving

Tommy to be joined by Fiona who has changed from primrose into a dress of Minnellian red with a plaid of green Campbell tartan, reprising the colours Tommy is wearing. The choreography provides a ritual perhaps evocative of pre-Christian times when Charlie carries his bride, in white, across a bed of sumac, again standing in for heather, and she loosens her hair. Interestingly, *Braveheart* invents a similar quasi-pagan ceremony for Wallace and his bride. There follows a brief dance, involving Charlie, Lundie and Jean, which is one of the few in the film to incorporate Scottish dance movements, specifically from the Highland Fling. Beginning slowly, it increases in tempo until many more, particularly young men and women, are drawn in. It is at this point that Harry appears and, thrusting aside the other dancers, seizes Jean and kisses her violently, being seized in turn by Charlie on whom he pulls a dirk. Measured against the stage version, the film may have lost dramatic force by dropping the Sword Dance in which symbolically violent activity Harry was the main actor. Calmed by a menacing ring of villagers, Harry speaks a poignant line: 'All I've done is to want you too much' after which he utters the line with which Act One of the stage version ended: 'I'm leavin' Brigadoon. 'Tis the end of all of us. The miracle's over'. There is, of course, no interval in the film which moves directly to the chase, opening with the male chorus chanting 'Harry Beaton' (another name-change, it being Ritchie in the original). The change does, however, make the chant deeper and more resonant. We have spoken of Loewe's score at this point shedding its dominant, nineteenth-century Romantic sound and becoming more modernist and percussive. The film retains the stage show's use of opera-like *recitative* in this scene and the general upping of tempo and emotional register is more than matched by Minnelli's *mise-en-scène* which is very reminiscent of the boar hunt in his film *Home From the Hill* (1960). It becomes a *mélange* of flashing torches, naked torsos and violent encounters between Harry and his pursuers, all coming to a climax when Jeff, following the flight of a grouse, fires into a tree, killing Harry. As in the stage version, Tommy takes an active part in the pursuit, but is not present when Harry is shot. Jeff's later revelation that he has killed Harry will be an important element in destabilising Tommy's initial decision to stay in Brigadoon. Harry's body being removed, and the elders deciding not to reveal his death till the morrow, the sequence continues with Fiona desperately seeking Tommy, fearful that he may have strayed beyond the bounds of Brigadoon. They meet in the clearing beside the ruined church, where the wedding dance took place. On stage, this had been the occasion for a slow love song by Tommy, 'There But For You Go I', which was, in fact, recorded for the film – Kelly's rendering of it can be found on the CD of the music from *Brigadoon*. In the event, it was dropped from the released version. Kelly has spoken of there being a general problem of the songs from *Brigadoon* being rather slow, but we can speculate that Minnelli very likely (and Kelly possibly) found the song too low-key emotionally after the frenzy (both musically and in terms of *mise-en-scène*) of the chase. In the film, therefore, the song is replaced by a danced reprise of 'The Heather on the Hill'. If the first version is a courtship dance, the reprise is a consummation dance. Kelly is ardent and Charisse – in her flame-red dress – clinging and yielding. The dance ends with them on the ground in a long, passionate embrace. It is at this point that Tommy confesses he cannot leave her and, as dusk begins to descend on Brigadoon, he rushes to find Jeff to inform him of his decision to stay, only to be told bitterly about Jeff's killing of Harry. Jeff's speech is much tougher in the film than on the stage and is greatly enhanced by Johnson's surprisingly (given his previously genial career profile) bitter playing. Commiserated with by Tommy for having killed Harry, Jeff rounds violently on him:

> What am I supposed to feel in a hoodoo joint like this! Dream stuff, boy, all made up of broomsticks and wishing wells. It's either that or a boot camp for lunatics. I don't know what goes on here, but it's got nothing to do with me and nothing to do with you... And you want to give up your family, your friends, your whole life, for *this*!

His resolve shaken, Tommy bids a sad farewell to Fiona, her cries of 'I love you' receding as the mist swirls in to encompass Brigadoon once more. There then occurs one of the most resonant cultural transitions in the American (or any other) cinema. As Tommy passes across the bridge and leaves the frame, the image of the mist gives way, through a swift dissolve, to a vertiginous overhead view of a sky-scraper city. It could be any city, but it is New York. What is being signified here is 'cityness', the City of Dreadful Night. On the soundtrack is a blaring, cacophonic brass sound, evoking demented

11. Tommy (Gene Kelly), back in New York with his fiancée
(Elaine Stewart), cannot forget Fiona and Brigadoon.

modernity. This gives way to a New York bar which, on the
stereophonic soundtrack, sounds like the Tower of Babel with the
patrons all talking at once and with great rapidity. The contrast with
the silence and repose of Brigadoon is startling. Jeff, already pretty
drunk, is there as a subdued Tommy enters dressed, like most of the
other men in the bar, in a white suit. It is not to put too great a
symbolic meaning on this element to suggest that all the colour has
been washed out of their lives. As in the stage version, he explains to
Jeff that the single word in a conversation can send his thoughts back
to Fiona and Brigadoon. He is joined by his 'sophisticated' fiancée
Jane, whom moviegoers of the time would have recognised as the siren
who comforted Kirk Douglas' darkest hours in *The Bad and the
Beautiful*, Elaine Stewart. Jane, like the other denizens of the bar, never
stops talking and it is throughout her long monologues that, cued by
a word here and there, Tommy drifts into daydreams about Brigadoon.

On stage this was done through a scrim, with Fiona and Brigadoon being visible. Here it is done solely on the soundtrack, with Jane's prattle periodically being engulfed by the songs Tommy has heard or sung in Brigadoon. As in the show, the scene ends with Tommy breaking off his engagement with Jane and dragging Jeff back to Scotland to the place where they had stumbled on Brigadoon but which is now desolate, provoking Tommy's poignant line: 'Why do people have to lose things to find out what they really mean?' As they are about to depart, the talismanic title song is heard and Brigadoon once more emerges from the mist. The stage version ended with Tommy beckoned across the bridge by the dominie, leaving Jeff scratching his head in the 'real' world. In the film, Tommy crosses the bridge, rushes to McConnachy Square where Fiona's cottage door opens, revealing her in a blaze of light. As the lovers move slowly towards each other she opens her arms to enclose him.

At about the time *Brigadoon* was being shot in Culver City, another film was being shot, largely in Scotland. This film was the Ealing comedy *The Maggie* and it bears a curious similarity to *Brigadoon* (McArthur, 2003). It too is about an American who comes to Scotland and is entranced by the land and the people. At a key moment, when he has shed most of his associations with his American life, he attends a *ceilidh* during which he is led into a dance by an ethereally beautiful woman, in some sense representing 'the spirit of Scotland', who approaches him with the same wide-armed gesture with which Fiona engulfs Tommy at the end of *Brigadoon*. This 'coincidence' testifies to the extent to which both films – despite being the products of different cultures – are locked within the Scottish Discursive Unconscious within which Scotland is heavily feminised, for which the most appropriate image would be a beautiful woman with her arms wide open. It is perhaps not without significance that both films were made at the moment of the USA's highest level of investment in foreign economies, including that of Scotland.

To indicate the difference in scale between mounting a Broadway show and making a Hollywood movie, the stage version cost $167,000 – by a strange coincidence just $35,000 above the cost of the footage excised from the film; the film cost $2.3 million. Such an investment had to marketed with care, the starting point of our next chapter.

4

Marketing, Using and Abusing *Brigadoon*

Asked about his obsession with biblical themes, Cecil B. De Mille
replied 'Why let two thousand years of publicity go to waste'.

Peter Hay

Hollywood's impulse to give the audience what it wants translated
into serious and organised market research, the core of which
was the double sneak preview followed by the sampling of the
audience by way of a questionnaire. Usually the studios would
preview their upcoming releases unannounced in suburban theatres
in Los Angeles or the surrounding conurbation. Thus it was that, at
the Encino and Picwood Theaters on 4 and 15 June 1954, *Brigadoon*
was first seen by ordinary cinemagoers, between 220 and 230 on
each occasion, all of whom afterwards filled in the standard MGM
questionnaire which consisted of seven questions:

1. How would you rate the picture:

OUTSTANDING   EXCELLENT   VERY GOOD   GOOD   FAIR

2. How would you rate the performance of the following?

EXCELLENT   GOOD   FAIR

Gene Kelly as Tommy Albright

Van Johnson as Jeff Douglas

Cyd Charisse as Fiona Campbell

Elaine Stewart as Jane Ashton

Barry Jones as Mr Lundie

Hugh Laing as Harry Beaton

Virginia Bosler as Jean Campbell

3. Which scenes did you like most?

4. Which scenes, if any, did you dislike?

5. Would you recommend this picture to your friends?

6. Any added comment?

7. We don't need to know your name, but we would like to know the following facts about you:

(A) Male (B) Please check your age group

  Female   Between 12 and 17

        Between 18 and 30

        Between 31 and 45

        Over 45

The data gathered at the previews would have been encouraging for the studio, since the great bulk of responses to the first question were in the OUTSTANDING/EXCELLENT bracket and to the second in the EXCELLENT/GOOD category. The responses to the first two questions were first collated on a gender-neutral basis but, thereafter, with all the questions, on a gendered basis, which reflects Hollywood's tendency to think of particular genres (for example, gangster movies, westerns, films noirs and war movies) as primarily 'male' and others (for example, melodramas and musicals) as 'female', even though all of these genres (though not necessarily *all* the films constituting them) will have some element of heterosexual romance. This gendering extended to naming certain films 'women's pictures', 'weepies' and 'tear-jerkers'.

Histories of Hollywood are littered with examples of particular films – having elicited negative reactions at preview – being extensively re-cut and, in certain instances, re-shot, to take account of comments made in audience questionnaires. However, when – as in the case of *Brigadoon* – responses were generally favourable, it is often difficult to ascertain what use has been made of this kind of market research other than to confirm that what has been offered is generally acceptable. Regrettably, there is no evidence as to what action, if any, the producers of *Brigadoon* took on the basis of its questionnaires nor, indeed, what their general attitude was to the mechanism of the sneak preview. Assuming, however, that the attitude was the same across the industry, a memo from the Head of Production at another major studio, Daryll Zanuck of Twentieth Century Fox, may shed some light. This is a memo written in 1948 to Charles Skouras, President of Fox West Coast Theaters (presumably before the Supreme Court decision of that year which, interpreting anti-trust legislation, ruled that production had to be divorced from distribution and exhibition):

> My Dear Charlie
>
> The purpose of a first sneak preview on a picture is to *try out* the entertainment values, particularly the comedy values. We do not have first sneak previews on dramas, because I feel that I am sufficiently qualified to edit a drama in the projection room; and the only time I preview a drama is *after* I have cut it down to footage and it is ready for release… On comedies, however, a sneak preview is practically essential. And, for this reason, we leave in many things that we would ordinarily take out. We go to the preview expecting the picture to drag and not to screen anything resembling a finished product…
>
> *(Behlmer 93: 155)*

The 'dislikes' and 'added comments' of the responders do reveal certain tendencies. Strongest among these was the large number of complaints about the sound being too loud, which may have been due to *Brigadoon*'s being the first MGM musical to have used stereophonic sound. There was also an enormous number of complaints about the dropping of 'The Sword Dance' and, to a lesser degree, the song 'Come To Me, Bend To Me'. Clearly many patrons had seen the stage show and were making comparisons with it, often to the detriment of the film. However, this did not preclude a generally favourable response to the latter. Perhaps most interestingly, there were recurrent criticisms of Kelly's choreography, dancing and singing. This overall criticism of Kelly is to some extent reflected in the performance ratings, generally upbeat though they were. In the first report, 152 rated Kelly excellent, while 178 rated Charisse and

174 Johnson excellent. Even Barry Jones, with 136 votes in this category, although in a minor role, came close to equalling Kelly's score. The analogous figures for the report on the second preview were Kelly 136, Johnson151, Charisse 160 and Jones 119. However, it is in the specific comments that the overall tendency of the audience to be losing patience with Kelly shows most clearly:

> Kelly's dances getting to look all alike (female)
>
> I'm tired of him doing the same dances in every picture (male)
>
> Enough of Kelly's hat dances by now (male)
>
> Gene Kelly should not sing (male)
>
> Kelly is on his way out (male)

As these comments indicate, Kelly's attraction was waning rather more among males than females. It would be a gross over-simplification to suggest that comments such as these in themselves brought an end to Kelly's dancing career at MGM. The general economic situation in the company, the waning of the dance-based musical in the light of changing musical tastes – rock and roll was on the rise and Kelly's last traditional musical for MGM, *It's Always Fair Weather* was released at the same time as the Elvis Presley vehicle, *Love Me Tender* – and the economic difficulties of Kelly's all-ballet film, *Invitation to the Dance* – its failure is said to have hastened Dore Schary's departure from MGM – were probably all more important in diminishing Kelly's standing, but the questionnaire responses certainly would not have helped.

Overall, however, the sneak preview responses must have convinced MGM that they had an eminently marketable product, so the well-funded MGM promotional machine swung into action. The measures included selling the picture on the back of its music by holding special screenings for DJs and making up a special 'platter' for them, and having the music played on the Muzak system which was piped into areas such as department stores, offices and factories. Extensive use was made of the actual props and costumes from the film by setting up displays in department stores. One fashion house designed several dresses on the theme of *Brigadoon* and advertised them in *Vogue*. Tie-ins were arranged with MacGregor Sportswear and Lux Toilet Soap, the latter using an advertisement Cyd Charisse had recently done for that product. Contact was made with 'Scotch

Societies' and MGM donated a special *Brigadoon* trophy which was presented at the 22nd Annual Gathering of the Southern California Scotch Societies, and Elaine Stewart – who played Tommy's New York fiancée – cut the ribbon to open the new Highlander Motor Hotel in Hollywood. One of the recurrent complaints in the questionnaire responses was that Elaine Stewart received excessively high billing given her limited on-screen presence. The reason for this seems to have been the well-known Hollywood practice of using younger contract players in minor roles and attempting to promote their careers by 'over-billing'. Resistance to this practice – as evidenced by questionnaire responses – indicates that audiences are somewhat less passive than 'Mass Culture' theorists paint them.

The last chapter referred to the appointment as Technical Adviser on the film of 'Commander' KD Ian Murray RN, revealed in photographs to have been something of a professional Scotsman in his full highland dress. More sinisterly, we had discussed – in the context of *Brigadoon* – the disposition to fantasy of Lerner and Loewe. There is some evidence that 'Commander Murray' may have been prone to fantasy himself. Without directly accusing him of being a conman, his name is strangely absent from the Navy List over the period – the mid 1930s to the mid 1950s – when one would expect to have found it. The Navy List is the Admiralty's regular publication, which gives the names (and certain other details) of serving, reserve and retired officers of the Royal Navy and related arms. Whether or not Murray's naval credentials were genuine (the Navy List is a notoriously difficult document to negotiate), he was mobilised by MGM as a Scottish icon and accompanied *Brigadoon* to cities such as Boston, Philadelphia, Baltimore, Richmond, Norfolk, Atlanta, Memphis, New Orleans, Dallas and Chicago. Murray can be seen smiling from the pages of the trade press of the time which informs us that 'he will wear kilts on the tour and discuss Scottish legends, customs, etc.'. MGM set in train a second promotional tour for the film, this time to cities such as Detroit, Cleveland, Pittsburgh, Buffalo, Toronto and New York for which they engaged two 'Scots lassies', air hostesses working for Scandinavian Air Services who 'will appear in their native dress of tartan and kilts and distribute to all they meet real Scots ties and sprigs of heather'. It was during this second tour that there occurred what was surely the most bizarre phenomenon of *Brigadoon*'s promotion. MGM prevailed upon the inhabitants of Saratoga Village, Maryland to change the name of their village to 'Brigadoon' with the two 'Scots lassies' and MGM officials in attendance at the formal ceremony. One of the air hostesses read an extract from Burns' 'The Cotter's Saturday Night' standing on a platform above a sign which read 'This is Brigadoon, the happiest village in the U.S.A.' At this point the promotion of *Brigadoon* becomes almost surrealist, the MGM lion, Leo, even doing the Highland Fling in the pages of *Variety*. Certain aspects of the British promotion would retain this surrealist quality.

12. Saratoga Village, Maryland is renamed 'Brigadoon' during the marketing of the film.

As well as supplying local cinema managers with posters and stills to promote the particular films they are running, film companies – most expansively the Hollywood majors such as MGM – supplied campaign books for each film. The British campaign book for *Brigadoon*, whose UK release began on 27 June 1955, as well as containing technical information about the nature and dimensions of publicity material such as posters, stills and pennants, also had an extensive section entitled 'Showmanship' – an extremely important concept among film distributors and exhibitors (there was an American trade journal called the *Showmen's Trade Review*). This section consisted of promotional advice ranging from the low-key to the Barnum-like. For example, following the American strategy, it recommended that

13. Leo, the MGM symbol, dons kilts
to trumpet the virtues of *Brigadoon*.

emphasis should be put on selling the film through its music, therefore cinema managers should contact local music stores well in advance of the film's playdate to ensure that adequate supplies of records and sheet music would be in stock. The reference to sheet music suggests that the promotional mindset was lagging somewhat behind the changing pattern of domestic entertainment with singing the latest hits round the family piano rapidly giving way to television watching. It also recommended that managers arrange window displays in local music shops, send copies of orchestrations of the film's music to local bandleaders (the *quid pro quo* being that the bandleaders announce where the film is playing when they introduce the numbers), and send free cinema tickets to the same bandleaders and music shops. However, it is in the merchandising tie-ins that the surrealist dimension reappears. A special tie-in was arranged with the *Draper's Record* involving prizes for window displays and the involvement of several

British firms selling goods specially related to *Brigadoon*: tartan shirts for men and, for women, not only tartan slacks, skirts, blouses and berets, but tartan lingerie as well. One wonders if, long secreted in some deep drawer, there still exist examples of the *Brigadoon* bra, slip and panties. This heightened note is continued in the suggested promotional stunts which included inviting local centenarians to the opening – the reasoning being that they would have been around when Brigadoon last came out of its sleep in 1855; covering the cinema foyer with tartan wallpaper (available from MGM at ten shillings a roll); dressing the 'usherettes' in highland dress; inviting local 'kilted gentry' to the opening; and having local florists send sprigs of white heather tied with tartan ribbon to 'women journalists, heads of women's clubs, female heads of large departmental stores, publicans' wives, etc'. Bizarre as some of the suggested stunts are, there is, underlying the MGM campaign book, a hard-headed comprehensiveness which seeks to exploit every opportunity to promote not just the film itself, but the MGM stable of actors. For instance, as well as stills from the film there are on offer special studio portraits of the leading stars tailored to fit into the windows of local businesses; for example, Cyd Charisse with two puppies for insertion into local pet shop windows; Van Johnson with an electric shaver for electrical goods windows; and Elaine Stewart in a fur coat for the windows of up-market department stores. The campaign book even includes a suggested layout for an advertisement to be inserted in local papers, which spelled out the title of the film and incorporated diverse local businesses. Its headline 'Och aye! These are the thriftiest bargains for many a day!' slots into another trope of the Scottish Discursive Unconscious, the legendary stinginess of the Scots. The film historian Kenneth Cameron has suggested – on the analogy of the phrase 'harmless fun' which is usually thrown at anyone protesting about demeaning jokes – that we need a concept of 'harmful fun' to describe statements such as the above, insulting to groups which have subordinate status in dominant discourses and therefore, usually, in the 'real' world. The libretto and screenplay are surprisingly free of references to Scottish stinginess, although it lurks in Jeff's disavowal of 'Scottish frugality' and Fiona's father's stated intention that the wedding supper should be 'hospitable, not philanthropic'.

Clearly, then, MGM had very much more resources to put into the promotion of the film than did the producers of the stage show.

How then did reviewers respond to both? Given the cultural differences between the USA and the UK, the conception of the function, practice and critical vocabulary of theatre reviewers in both societies is remarkably similar. In short, they are consumer guides. To be sure, the reviewers of the more serious newspapers and journals will suggest that a particular work may or may not achieve the status of 'art' and the tabloid press concentrates more on 'entertainment', although the division is not entirely hard and fast – but the injunction is usually the same, see or do not see this show. As was mentioned in Chapter 1, the enthusiastic response of the New York reviewers to the Broadway opening of *Brigadoon* was almost unanimous. The single dissenting voice was George Jean Nathan (in Lerner's view for personal reasons) and even he described the show as 'one of the most thoroughly engaging entertainments in a long time'. In the citation which accompanied their awarding *Brigadoon* the title of 'Best Musical of 1947', the New York Drama Critics Circle set out their reasons:

> Because of [its] altogether original and inventive blending of words, music and dance; because its taste, discretion and thoughtful beauty mark a high note in any season; and because it finds the lyric theatre at its best.

Two statements from the New York reviews set the framework within which the reviewers' responses would be cast:

> The sweetest, cleanest, liveliest and loveliest musical to hit the boards since *Oklahoma!*
>
> *(Danton Walker)*

and:

> A thoroughly engaging evening... Robert Lewis has fused the show's various elements with authority and spirit.
>
> *(Louis Kronenberger)*

These statements join with the reference, in the citation, to the *blending* of elements to reveal that, as has been mentioned in Chapter 1, what the New York reviewers used as a measuring rod of a show's success at that time was the extent to which its diverse elements such as narrative, song and dance no longer operated as autonomous entities, but were *blended*, and that the Ur-Musical which would become the touchstone for all shows was *Oklahoma!*, the show which, in 1943, had delivered the 'book' musical in which all the elements contributed to the narrative. Thus, Russell Rhodes described *Brigadoon* as bringing

> A thrill in direction, acting, singing, design and colour not sparked since *Oklahoma!*

and the anonymous reviewer of the *New York Times* saw it as

> a plastic work of art which carries dialogue into dancing and dancing into music with none of the practical compromises of the Broadway stage.

Oklahoma! (and the 1940s Broadway musical more generally) would become a major point of reference in the London reviews as well. However, the 'integrationist' impulse of the New York reviewers was cut across by what had become a standard element in their reviewing practice deriving from the non-integrated, revue-style musical entertainments of the past – the singling out of particular artistes for praise. Clearly this was an important aspect of the consumer-guide nature of reviewing, providing ready-made quotations which might be extracted from reviews and used in the show's advertising thereafter. Examples of these include:

> Agnes De Mille has staged ballets that are simple, dramatic, colourful and exciting
>
> > *(Richard Watts, Jnr)*

> Perfectly staged by Bob Lewis
>
> > *(Brooks Atkinson)*

> The scenery by Oliver Smith is imaginative and delightful
>
> > *(Robert Garland)*

We have referred recurrently to the Scottish Discursive Unconscious, that deep-seated, historical *bricolage* of images, sounds and stories that immediately comes into the heads of people throughout the world at the word 'Scotland'. As we saw, the discourses of Tartanry and Kailyard are dominant within the Scottish Discursive Unconscious, the latter in particular suffused with sentimentality. One of the pernicious effects of the SDU – probably experienced by every Scot who has set foot outside Scotland – is that the way he or she speaks will be noted as 'charming' and, here it becomes positively grating, will probably be jocularly imitated. The appearance of a show like *Brigadoon* provokes reviewers to just this kind of baleful practice. Thus, throughout the New York reviews, the cast are referred to as 'lads' and 'lassies' who dance 'mang the heather' and are invariably 'bonnie'. Often this noxious syndrome is saved for the reviewer's peroration, as in:

> Ay, laddie, 'tis a bonnie, brave show, a daisy
>
> *(Russell Rhodes)*

> The talk of the town… Scotch and so-da-lightful
>
> *(Walter Winchell)*

This discourse would also emerge, hydra-like, in the London reviews. Partly to demonstrate the continuity of the tropes of reviewing, it is useful to consider the London reviews of 1949 alongside those of *Brigadoon*'s revival in 1988. Although we could tease out differences between the New York and London reviews (of which more presently) it is the similarities which assert themselves most strongly, as in the common commitment to the integrated musical:

> The piece strives for, and in great measure achieves, unity of impression. Dances, songs and dialogue – in that order of importance – are worked into the single light-hearted, beguilingly sentimental statement of a fantastic idea… The director keeps a controlling hand on all the details, carefully relating them to each other and to the general idea
>
> *(The Times)*

and, from the same review, as though to insist on the integrated nature of the work and unwillingness to foreground any particular aspect:

> The songs, though plentiful, are comparatively short, and demands that they shall be repeated go austerely unheeded.

This last quotation illustrates how far the Broadway musical had come from simple revue. In the latter the songs – often imported *ad hoc* as Tin Pan Alley hits of the day – might be repeated with several encores according to audience demands. *The Times'* use of the term 'austerely' suggests that the integrated Broadway musical was now pursuing a more elevated conception of art and that the London audiences were somewhat behind the times, responding to *Brigadoon* as an old-fashioned revue. As in the New York reviews, *Oklahoma!* became a reference point for the excellence of the show:

> It has many of *Oklahoma*'s charms – the same youthful dash and freshness, the same kind of seemingly effortless and spontaneous ballet-style dancing
>
> *(Cecil Wilson, Daily Mail)*

Although – as these remarks indicate – reference to *Oklahoma!* need not be couched solely in terms of integration. It is the same *Daily Mail* review which conjoins reference to *Oklahoma!* with the kind of twee mock-Scotchery of the New York reviews when it described the show as 'Och-aye-lahoma!'. The 1949 London reviews have their fair sprinkling of 'lads' and 'lassies' but it is in the 1988 reviews that this discourse becomes unpleasantly omnipresent, perhaps reflecting the increasing 'tabloidisation' of some reviewing practices by this time:

> Leslie Mackie is delightfully effervescent as a wee Scots lassie despairin' of ever finding 'the right lad' (the style of Lerner's dialogue is woefully catching)
>
> *(Francis King, Sunday Telegraph)*

and:

> [T]ake the high road or the low road to the Victoria Palace. You'll have an awful bonny time
>
> *(Hilary Williams, What's On)*

One tabloidesque review invoked another trope of the SDU, this time relating to the alleged virility of Scots men:

> One of the greatest mysteries in life has finally been solved by the new production of Lerner and Loewe's first big musical hit.

> Despite rumours to the contrary, Scotsmen do wear something
> under their kilts
>
> *(Maureen Paton,* Daily Express*)*

One of the notable things about the 1988 London reviews was that
they no longer felt the need to praise *Brigadoon* as an integrated musical
since that was now the standard form. Paradoxically too, despite the
frivolous and empty tabloidesque reviews cited above, the 1988
production elicited some of the most insightful and knowledgeable
notices, more so even than the New York reviews of 1947:

> It belongs not to the Broadway realism of Rodgers, Hammerstein
> and Hart, but to the fantastical Edwardian theatre of Barrie and
> musical comedies like *The Arcadians* which promised metro-
> politan audiences the idyll of a loving Utopia beyond the
> pressures of town and time
>
> *(Michael Ratcliffe,* Observer*)*

and:

> Though his entire career was based in America, the Austrian Loewe
> wrote music which was redolent of Lehár, Kálmán, Oscar Straus
> and Leo Fall which he would have seen during his adolescence in
> Vienna and Berlin... [His score] could so easily have accompanied
> a story about gypsies in Transylvania
>
> *(Charles Osborne,* Daily Telegraph*)*

There is one aspect of the London reviews that is wholly lacking
in those of New York. It will be recalled that Robert Lewis, sensitive
to what the Scots might think of *Brigadoon*, had engaged Ian Wallace
as Scottish Technical Adviser, a task Wallace had set about with gusto.
One finds in certain of the London reviews the implication that
Scots are liable to be rather prickly about stage representations of
themselves or their country. This is evident in the following:

> I can well imagine that Caledonian sticklers for historical accuracy
> will be amused or indignant at liberties which have been taken
> with accent and dress. Yet the show itself is of a quality to make
> the sternest Scot abandon criticism in enjoyment
>
> *(WA Darlington,* Daily Telegraph*)*

There are several stock characters who stalk the SDU. Its Tartanry dimension supplies the virile, warlike Scot and the Scot who is close to nature, often with 'second sight', while its Kailyard dimension furnishes the thrifty, often religious, Scot and his structural opposite, the drunken Scot. The thrifty Scot often segues into the stern, unbending Calvinist to whom pleasure of any kind is anathema. This is the stereotype evoked above.

Given the occasional sensitivity London reviewers displayed with regard to *Brigadoon*'s representation of Scotland and the Scots, it might be thought that the reviews in the Scottish press would have been foaming at the mouth. That this was not so – or was so only in a highly qualified way – was due to a complex set of circumstances. In 1955 there were upwards of 50 national and local newspapers in Scotland. To have consulted all of them would have been a mammoth task which – given that critical discourse at any one time tends to oscillate round a few recurrent ideas – would probably not have yielded more than the limited trawl deployed. This consisted of looking at the newspapers in and around the four major Scottish cities – Aberdeen, Dundee, Edinburgh and Glasgow. Of the three Aberdeen papers, the *Evening Express* had a low-key, descriptive item on its entertainment page and the most substantial response to the film was in the *Weekly Journal*. What is surprising about this review is that, first of all, it is not given any more space than the other films opening in Aberdeen that week and, secondly, that it is almost entirely descriptive. Beginning:

> It's here. *Brigadoon* – the American's eye view of the Scottish Highlands, complete with mists, tartans, clansmen and grouse shooting...

it then goes on to mention that the film mobilises many of the artistes from *An American in Paris*, that Gene Kelly and Arthur Freed had visited Scotland and that the painted MGM backdrop was the longest ever made before giving a brief summary of the plot. There is absolutely no dissent from the film's view of Scotland and the Scots, no sign that there might even be an issue in this regard. Why is this? Janet Staiger, in her magisterial book *Interpreting Films: Studies in the Historical Reception of American Cinema*, deploys the term 'reading formation' in her account of the responses of American reviewers to certain films at particular historical moments. Central to this concept is the idea that only certain questions will be raised within particular reading formations, other questions being repressed. One of the most obvious examples of repression would be the discourse of feminism among reviewers in the 1950s, both male and female. An explicitly feminist discourse would appear in American film reviewing only in the late 1960s and early 1970s and was of course related to (second-wave) feminism's agitation in the wider social context. Needless to say, feminism was absent from Scottish film reviewing in the 1950s but, in the context of *Brigadoon*, a more marked absence was the question of the film's representation of Scotland and the Scots or, more accurately, the broaching of this question in a highly circumscribed form, the terms of which will be examined directly. To have raised this question would have, at the very least, *implied* a nationalist politics at a time when unionism reigned supreme in Scotland – on the left partly for internationalist reasons, partly on account of political opportunism, and on the right for conservative reasons – with Scottish Nationalists being regarded as pitiable eccentrics. It would be another two decades – particularly after the failed referendum of 1979 – before the interrogation of culture from a left-nationalist perspective would become part of the reading formation of Scottish film critics and reviewers. The Dundee reviews were virtually identical to those of Aberdeen, with the *Courier* and *Advertiser* carrying no reviews whatever – the existence in Scotland of newspapers which eschewed film reviews may have been due to a residual Calvinism within which entertainment in general, and cinema in particular, was viewed with suspicion – and the *People's Journal* providing a brief descriptive review.

The most extensive coverage of *Brigadoon* was in the Glasgow press. In 1955, Glasgow, far and away the most populous city in Scotland with one fifth of the population, sustained a daily broadsheet, the *Glasgow Herald*, two daily tabloids, the *Daily Record* and the *Bulletin* – actually the latter was tabloid in format but quasi-broadsheet in tone – three evening papers, the *Evening Times*, the *Evening Citizen* and the *Evening News*, and a Sunday tabloid, the *Sunday Mail*. In addition there was a Glasgow edition of the Dundee-based *Sunday Post*. All of these offered substantial arts/entertainment coverage. Looking over the Glasgow reviews of *Brigadoon*, one gets the impression of an incestuous gaggle of entertainment journalists tumbling out of the press show and laughing together at the film's howlers in its representation of Scotland. The title of Mamie Crichton's piece in the *Evening News* – 'But this can't be Scotland' – seems to promise a cultural critique, but what is delivered is a low-level 'it's not like that' complaint:

> [C]urious accents and the laughable sight of Hollywood studio sets of the Scottish Highlands, complete with heather a yard long, English sheep dogs, foreign breeds of sheep, tartan and pipers galore and a couple of Americans 'huntin' grouse among trees with the wrong kind of guns and without dogs and beaters...

This is echoed by Robins Millar in the *Evening Citizen* which had, in the previous week, serialised the story of *Brigadoon* in five extensively illustrated parts:

> [The] sets are too obviously painted, but since the whole affair is unreal, that may pass, along with some other things that strike the Scots native as odd. I accepted that one wee clachan was able to muster four masterly pipe bands. Half-heartedly I wished that Van Johnson had not gone grouse shooting by torchlight...

As well as indicating their incestuousness, this preoccupation may say something about the social composition of the Glasgow reviewers. Even the film reviewer of the broadsheet *Glasgow Herald* – like that of *The Times* discreetly anonymous as 'our film critic' – sounds off on this:

> [The two Americans] discover the fantasy village while on what they call a grouse hunt – a pursuit on which they appear to have embarked some hours before dawn with repeater shot guns.

In fact, despite their carping, almost all the Glasgow reviewers were very well disposed to the film, seeing it as excellent entertainment and strongly recommending it to their readers. The *Evening Times* ('Hollywood makes a grand job of *Brigadoon*') and the *Bulletin* ('It Charms and Disarms') were particularly indulgent and the *Sunday Post*'s headline – 'It's the Queerest Village in the Highlands' – was unconsciously perceptive given the strong leanings to homosexuality, including Minnelli himself, within the Freed Unit (Tinkcom 1996). Again, one is profoundly disappointed by the absences in the reading formation of the time, particularly any glimmerings of the cultural – and ultimately political – implications of *Brigadoon*'s construction of Scotland and the Scots. The review in the Edinburgh broadsheet the *Scotsman* also had some good things to say about the film but, on the surface at least, it closely resembles the carping of the Glasgow reviewers:

> Purple backcloths and excesses of tartan are tolerable on the stage but, seen through the giant eye of CinemaScope, they are ridiculous. Even more galling are the 'phoney' Scots accents, the Doric being reduced to 'dearie', 'laddie' and 'canna'. The bagpipe 'music' emanates, almost certainly, from a theatre organ. The director seems to have gone out of his way to make the film as unauthentic as possible. He came to Scotland looking for a filming location and went away disappointed. Scotland was not 'Scotch enough'. Evidently Scottish actors are similarly handicapped. There is not one in the cast.

In common with several up-market newspapers of the time, the film reviewer of the *Scotsman* was anonymous. However, we know him to have been Forsyth Hardy, friend and biographer of John Grierson and, like him, a powerful advocate of documentary cinema, and of realist cinema more generally, throughout his life. Given the aesthetic position Hardy lived within, it is perhaps understandable that he should attack *Brigadoon* (though ultimately endorse it for its entertainment value) in the terms he did. One of the contradictions of the Scottish reviewers' response is that Hardy's piece in the *Scotsman* – by its own and by general consent the most socially and intellectually elite newspaper on the Scottish scene – occupies exactly the same critical terrain as Donald Bruce's review in the most hydrophobically tabloid Scottish paper, the *Daily Record*. As would be expected, however, the tone and layout of the latter are several octaves higher than that of the *Scotsman*. Bruce's piece is headed:

> Its got colour... It's got CinemaScope... It's got Kelly
> BUT IT'S PHONEY BALONEY.

Listing the film's ostensible attractions, Bruce continues:

All mighty impressive except for one thing: somewhere, somehow, someone should have told them just a little about Scotland and how the place looks and how the natives talk. MGM spent a couple of years and millions of dollars on transferring this musical show to CinemaScope. They might have spent a few thousand of it on coming over here to photograph Scotland as it really is and taking back a bloke who could have guided them on how to speak Scots. Gene Kelly and Arthur Freed spent some time in Scotland before the picture was made, so there is less excuse than ever for the gigantic, built-up, painted backdrop... which is supposed to represent Highland mountains and glens... This is an elementary blunder the French or the Italians, those impressive sticklers for film reality, would never have made...

Despite its tabloid tone, Bruce's review is at one with Hardy's, even to the point of evoking the two film moments which, along with British documentary of the 1930s, Hardy consistently canvassed as the high water marks of fictive cinema, pre-war French poetic realism and post-war Italian neo-realism. This – reductive and badly-expressed as it is in so many of the Scottish reviews – is an unspoken, perhaps even barely conscious, part of the reading formation of the time. Faced with this kind of aesthetic, *Brigadoon* never really had a chance, except to be damned with faint praise as a charming piece of escapist entertainment. Quite apart from the absence – in the reading formation of Scots film reviewers generally – of the means to make a historically grounded cultural/ideological critique of *Brigadoon*, such as the concept of the Scottish Discursive Unconscious seeks to facilitate, the influence of realist aesthetics blinded them to the capacity of highly stylised forms of cinema to deliver their own kind of truth, as in the auteurist perception that Minnelli's being drawn to projects which explored the tension between life and art gives some clue to his own deepest pre-occupations which, precisely because they were deeply held, expressed themselves in the passionate and dynamic *mise-en-scène* of his films. The Scottish reviewers' low-level carping about quotidian accuracy would be replayed 40 years later with regard to *Braveheart*. None of the foregoing should be read as a blanket attack on cinematic realism, particular expressions of which – British documentary of the 1930s, Italian neo-realism and its Third-World disciples, the films of Ken Loach and Mike Leigh – constitute the most honourable traditions of cinema. However, there is every difference between the practice of, say, Roberto Rossellini, who found all the imaginative images he needed within the already-existing world, and those who, like the Scots reviewers of *Brigadoon*, fetishise quotidian 'reality' at the expense of every other aesthetic consideration. The nuances within such a distinction will be important in the consideration of certain aspects of *Braveheart*.

What none of the Scots reviews ever did was to take *Brigadoon* out of the confines of cinema and use it as a reference point for Scottish culture in general. Yet this is precisely what became of *Brigadoon* in the recent past. By 1992, the *Scotsman* had a strip cartoon set in a place called 'Brigadoom'; in 1993 the *Herald* (formerly the *Glasgow Herald*) ran an article on Scots law entitled 'Romantic Tales of Scots Law "as real as Brigadoon"'; and in the same year the *Scotsman* had a piece on the Scottish Tory Conference entitled 'Beware the Brigadoon factor'. In 1994, a newspaper's weekly feature entitled 'The Alternative Encyclopaedia of Scotland' had an entry 'B is for Brigadoon'; a columnist in 1997 referred to BBC Scotland as 'the Brigadoon Broadcasting Corporation'; and in 2000 *Scotland on Sunday* reported on a special St Andrew's Day celebration at the notorious Millennium Dome under the rubric 'Welcome to Big Mac day at the Briga-dome'. In the same year, the *Guardian*, reporting on Madonna's wedding in the Scottish Highlands, headed the piece 'Brigadoon is alive with the sound of money'. Finally, there is Simon Callow's cry in *Four Weddings and a Funeral*, referred to in the Introduction, on seeing the Scottish baronial interior: 'Christ! It's bloody Brigadoon!' How did *Brigadoon* come to enjoy such discursive centrality? Greatly to oversimplify, one strand of the explanation could be described as the insights of theorists being taken up by critics and in turn spinning outward to the literate population principally by way of journalists. To be more specific, an important shift occurred in the 1970s in Marxist theory wherein the relationship between economics and politics on the one hand and culture on the other became more attenuated, with the consequence of ceding much more autonomy (and therefore more political importance) to the latter. Several key Marxist thinkers were central to this shift, but subsequent accounts have tended to privilege the name of Antonio Gramsci, particularly in relation to his concept of *hegemony*, which he deployed to explain how ruling blocs retain control mainly by consent rather than coercion. Within such an explanation, culture becomes a key site in the struggle for hegemony. Such a re-emphasising of culture (it had, of course been a preoccupation of many Marxists beforehand) naturally provoked Marxist-inclined critics to examine their particular cultural sites with renewed interest, not least Scottish critics in the wake of the failed devolution referendum of 1979. Greatly influenced by the writings of Tom Nairn on Scottish culture, 'the local intelligentsia', to quote Angus Calder, 'fell like hyenas on Nairn's Great Tartan Monster' (Calder 1994: 230). Important examples of this feeding frenzy were the *Scotch Myths* exhibition by Murray and Barbara Grigor in 1981, the *Scotch Reels* retrospective and publication at the Edinburgh International Film Festival in 1982, subsequent writings over the next several years in the journal *Cencrastus*, increasingly numerous books and the Glasgow Tramway Theatre's production, *Jock Tamson's Bairns*, in 1990 which, again to quote Calder, 'revealed a very earnest attempt... to deconstruct tartanry, the Burns cult and Scottish machismo'. This work, by critics and artists – within which *Brigadoon* was an important reference point – fed outwards to the wider population to the point where the ideas became common currency and hence usable in journalistic headlines such as those quoted above. To apply the terms of this analysis, the anti-Tartanry/Kailyard position became, in the 1980s and the 1990s and at least as far as the Scottish intelligentsia is concerned, *hegemonic*. Every hegemony is, by the nature of the definition, fragile and contested and the anti-Tartanry/Kailyard position is no exception, having been attacked in its turn (see McCrone 1992 and Craig 1996) principally for seeking to replace one essentialist national identity with another at a moment when (national) identity needed to be theorised as open, complex and hybrid, an identity constantly being remade rather than fixed. *Scotch Reels* makes a brief reference to *Brigadoon* as follows:

> The cinematic apotheosis of this tradition [Scotland as tartanised dream] is both articulated and deconstructed in... *Brigadoon*. At one level it takes the Romantic representation of Scotland as a given, but at another level – that of the working through of the personal obsession of its director, Vincente Minnelli, with the question of illusion and reality – this representation is revealed as the dream *par excellence*, as a fiction created to escape from the urban horrors

of the twentieth century. No British feature film [about Scotland]
has the progressive force of *Brigadoon* in this regard.

(McArthur 1982: 47)

It is a matter of some regret that *Scotch Reels'* fierce polemic against
the romantic construction of Scotland is what became hegemonic
among Scots intellectuals at the expense of the more subtle argument
of the second part of the quotation, which – to be pursued – requires
detailed attention to *Brigadoon's mise-en-scène*. The often crudely
realist aesthetics of Scottish, and British, film culture puts films like
Brigadoon at a distinct disadvantage. It is instructive to compare the
Scottish reviews with concurrent reviews of the film in France.
Although the French response was not uniformly favourable – the
first line of *Positif's* review read 'To put it plainly, *Brigadoon* is a
disappointment' – none of the reviews got hung up on the
'inauthenticity' of the film and the most favourable review, by Jean
Domarchi in *Cahiers du Cinéma*, was ecstatic, being headed 'Minnelli
the Magnificent'. Some extracts from this review will demonstrate
the gulf between the critical vocabularies of the British (including
the Scots) reviewers and the French:

I tend to believe that *Brigadoon* is a film of genius (if not
perfection. [Minnelli] has found the exact point of balance where
cinema and painting, far from clashing, combine and accumulate
their efforts to enthral the viewer. It is possible that here Minnelli
was thinking of Brueghel, there of Patiner, Vermeer or certain
seventeenth century Mannerists. However, what would elsewhere
have become retrospective and fake becomes here a great work of
art... The dancing camera remains fixed for a splendid still shot
then moves on, then stops again... The game is played out between
the camera and the décor's colours. Minnelli has incomparable
knowledge of cinematographic language. He knows perfectly how
to alternate still shots with camera movements... The chase of the
unfortunate Harry... is one of cinema's greatest achievements
through Minnelli's perfect synchronisation of camera movement,
song and colour. Truly, it is less a case of Harry trying to escape
his pursuers than *a battle of light and shadow*... Which director
could have better rendered the harsh fleeting light of the torches
playing on the ferns and the scarlet flash of Cyd Charisse's dress
against the Scottish landscape's dusky green? ... I had considered

Minnelli the last of the 'Mannerists', in the sense historians give to that term, slightly cloying perfection and not devoid of eclecticism. I recant that view: Minnelli is indeed a *great European artist* to whom both old and modern painting will owe an extended life and cinema two or three essential films.

One need not wholly endorse Domarchi's review – its hyperbolic tone, its application of the prevailing discourse of High Art to popular cinema, its exclusive preoccupation with the figure of the director, its formalism – to appreciate that it supplies what Anglo-American (particularly Scottish) reviews of *Brigadoon* manifestly lack: detailed attention to the film's *mise-en-scène*, a necessary precondition for articulating the idea (which Domarchi does not proceed to) that *Brigadoon*, through the force of its *mise-en-scène,* demonstrates the artificial construction of Scotland in discourse. Domarchi's review being almost entirely formalist, its principal limitation is to leave *Brigadoon* within the realm of 'art' and ignore its connection with politics and history. To make that connection, the concept of the Scottish Discursive Unconscious needs to be mobilised.

Why, then, is Domarchi's review (and French responses more generally) so markedly different from English-language reviews of *Brigadoon*? The answer is complex, but a useful starting point is the different perceptions of the USA held by France and Britain. To the former, America has been seen as a revolutionary progenitor, to the latter, an errant younger sibling with the temerity to separate itself from the mother country (which is not to say there are not powerful anti-American currents in French life as elsewhere in the world, the more so as particular American administrations bully the rest of the world). More directly, the two leading art movements in twentieth-century French life, Surrealism and Existentialism, were both warmly disposed to popular art, including cinema, while the British intelligentsia (relatively untouched by both) traditionally saw American popular art as a sink of tasteless vulgarity. In general, certainly at the time of *Brigadoon*'s release, British culture would have endorsed Oscar Wilde's view that the United States of America was the only society to have passed from barbarism to decadence without the intervening stage of civilisation. The French cinematic intelligentsia's broad endorsement of *Brigadoon* – principally on account of its formal properties and their venerating of its director

– did not occur in Scottish film culture, although it was to emerge in British film culture primarily in the pages of the journal *Movie* and in student film journals influenced by it and by French criticism, such as *Brighton Film Review*. The brief indication in this direction in the passage cited from *Scotch Reels* fell on dead ground, so to speak, the Scots intelligentsia being much more preoccupied with the first part of that passage in which *Brigadoon* is described as the apotheosis of the tradition *Scotch Reels* polemicised against. It is this preoccupation which underpins the diverse hostile references to *Brigadoon* in the newspaper headlines cited above. It can be said, therefore, that *Brigadoon* – unlike *Casablanca* – had a profoundly negative intertextual life at the hands of the Scots intelligentsia. It is probably also true to say that *Brigadoon*, as apotheosis of the romantic tradition rather than *Brigadoon* as formally rich text deconstructing that tradition, preoccupied that fragment of the Scots intelligentsia professionally concerned with teaching about film and television and/or about Scottish culture.

In an earlier conception of this book, it was envisaged that a substantial section would be given over to responses to *Brigadoon* from a number of Scots among whom this fragment was well represented. Space precludes the inclusion of such a section in the present volume, but the submissions made by these Scots throws light on several unsuspected dimensions of *Brigadoon*. Margaret Hubbard, a teacher of Media Studies, describes the intriguing experience of directing *Brigadoon* for an amateur operatic society in Australia in 1973:

> I was invited to direct it because I 'would understand its nuances' and I 'could make a production which was authentic'... From nowhere many expats arrived to join the chorus or work back stage, and then became extremely vitriolic if I tried to suggest Scotland was not, and never had been, as it appeared in *Brigadoon*. My accent was wrong. Why did I not speak with the soft highland lilt? Why was my name not Mac...? Scotland's *Brigadoon* image is very necessary to those who have left... The hostility to my exploding the *Brigadoon* myth matched only the hostility to my leaving to come home. How could I prefer the wet, cold weather and the poverty to the Lucky Country? A magical land it was no more. *Brigadoon*, then, is vital to the psychological stability of millions of ex-Scots and their descendants who do not live here...

I returned last year to visit [Australia]. *Brigadoon* is alive and well
– once again I didn't fit the Scots lassie they wanted me to be...
As long as we allow ourselves to be created in the image of those
who choose not to live here, we will continue to be seen as
backward, quaint and comic.

Margaret Hubbard raises the important points of the time-warped,
not to say imaginary, view so many diasporic peoples have of their
'homelands' and the *Brigadoon* image having been shaped furth of
Scotland (though internalised by the Scots themselves). Her final
sentence, about the grievous *political* effects such images may have
on modern Scotland – an important part of *Scotch Reels'* polemic –
sounds a note reprised in several of the contributions. Thus,
filmmaker Murray Grigor:

What makes *Brigadoon*'s fantasy of a past that never existed
important is its potential to fuel the *themeparkisation* of Scotland
today. In a country which allows standing stones to be bulldozed
away and awards tourist grants to historical blasphemies, the fakelore
of *Brigadoon* begins to dominate the folklore of our real yesterdays

and novelist Carl MacDougall:

The extent to which the *Brigadoon* perceptions have distilled down
to us who live here is obvious, when there is a serious lobby to
turn *Flower of Scotland* into a national anthem. Is *Brigadoon* more
or less than *Flower of Scotland*? The sentiments are, to my mind,
even more distasteful; romantic nonsense, which is clearly
nonsense, is one thing, dying for a wee bit hill and glen [part of
the lyrics of *Flower of Scotland*] is another.

MacDougall's, like the other contributions, was written in 1993.
Regrettably, the lobby on behalf of *Flower of Scotland* was successful
and its inane lyrics and clichéd music can be heard issuing from the
mouths of Scottish soccer and rugby players as they line up before
international matches. The effect of 'the *Brigadoon* discourse' on
Scottish artists can be quite inhibiting. Thus, dramatist Donald
Campbell:

[*Brigadoon*'s] success has promoted a perception of Scotland which,
although grotesquely erroneous, is curiously persistent, creating a

very real obstruction to the understanding of genuine Scottish culture throughout the world. I have lost count of the number of times that people from other countries have told me – intending it as a compliment – that my work 'isn't really Scottish'. What they mean, of course, is that my drama has nothing in common with *Brigadoon*. This makes me feel like the grandson of Cochise who, on applying for work as an extra on a film about his grandfather, was turned down on the grounds that he didn't look like an Apache.

This echoes the statement attributed to Arthur Freed that 'Scotland didn't look Scotch enough' or MGM's shipping afro wigs to Africa for *King Solomon's Mines*.

Critic and academic John Caughie, stumbling dazed from his first experience of *Brigadoon* at the *Scotch Reels* event in Edinburgh in 1982, was heard to say 'Now I know what it feels like to be a woman'. Being both Scottish and female creates a double bind, alluded to by academic Myra MacDonald in her contribution:

> Watching *Brigadoon* again, I was reminded of the metaphor that the cultural critic Judith Williamson applies to the condition of femininity. Women, she writes, function as a kind of 'zoo... a dumping ground for all the values society wants off its back but must be perceived to cherish'. *Brigadoon*, too, would make an ideal zoo. Alluring to the fascinated gaze of the outsider, denying aspiration to those inside, its enchantment lasts only as long as it exists outside history, where culture and materiality cannot touch it... Scottishness, like femininity, still ranks high in the cultural exchange-rate mechanism: as long, that is, as others can impose their own value on it. The minor Brigadoonians raise all the interesting questions. Harry Beaton, understandably anxious to escape from this burlesque paradise, and the 'lass' who propositions Jeff at least have enough spirit to challenge Brigadoon's mystique and articulate their own desires. One ends up dead: the other, we suspect, has the makings of one of those evil witches Brigadoon cocoons itself against. Wrestling with the bars of the cage is not, after all, a pastime that zoos encourage.

It was, however, another female respondent, academic Adrienne Scullion, who – though accepting *Brigadoon*'s ideological perniciousness – nevertheless suggested a possible way of slipping through the bars of the cage:

Brigadoon offers a frighteningly familiar version of Scotland. The film highlights many of the recurring discourses of Scottish culture. The *faux* romance of the Highland landscape, peopled by fey young maids and a generous sprinkling of benign father figures; the courtly values of the Kailyard, with dominie, minister and two contrasting versions of the lad o' pairts [a poor but clever boy] in Charlie and Harry; and, perhaps most challengingly, the anti-Kailyard moment *par excellence* of the hunting down of Beaton, possibly the most sympathetic character in the narrative. However, most exhilarating is the element of irony that the film may activate in contemporary audiences. The gaudily-painted backdrops and the corseted and tartan-clad Highland villagers present some Hollywood precursor of Vivienne Westwood-meets -1745 and allows the viewer to negotiate a set of distinctive and unexpected pleasures of misrecognition.

Adrienne Scullion is here recommending reading *Brigadoon* against the grain, specifically with an irony that comes more easily to her postmodern generation of critics. We will return to a somewhat different conception of reading against the grain at the end of this chapter.

Several of the respondents took the present writer to task for dwelling on a phenomenon which, as they saw it, had no importance in contemporary Scotland. This book has been a running argument against that view, but perhaps the perception that *Brigadoon* – as the apotheosis of a wider phenomenon – may have done considerable political damage to modern Scotland is best expressed by Donald Dewar, the late First Minister of post-devolution Scotland:

[T]he *Brigadoon* image has done Scotland no favours. It has encouraged a whimsical, romantic vision of a land full of peat smoke and Harry Lauder which is awful to behold. The one consolation I can offer is that the image has not got through to everyone. Speaking at a recent Labour Party Conference, I coupled a particularly outrageous piece of Scottish National Party propaganda with *Brigadoon*. On leaving the platform I was approached by a well-known London political journalist who asked, with genuine concern, if Brigadoon was a battle in Scottish history. In a sense it is – a battle to throw off an unwanted image which never had its roots in reality.

It is relatively easy to measure the hostile response of the Scots intelligentsia to *Brigadoon*. It is there in the books and articles of film critics, in the letters of the respondents cited above, and in the headlines and other intertextual references in (mainly) Scottish journalism. But what of those other Scots (and non-Scots) for whom *Brigadoon*, far from offering the kind of problematic constructions described herein, offers a charming and frivolous entertainment, or even connects with their sense of Scottishness? Aside from noting that *Brigadoon* is among the most popular revivals, both inside and outside Scotland, among amateur drama and opera groups, how might 'ordinary' responses to *Brigadoon* be gauged, what is its intertextual life outside the Scots intelligentsia? A possible answer might be found on the worldwide web where a search for the word 'Brigadoon' throws up nearly 50,000 results. These include the official Frederick Loewe Website, which offers biographical inform-ation and details about his musicals. It has an interesting sub-site, the Brigadoon Forum Archive, which seems to consist mainly of cries of help from American high school students who have been cast in one of the show's roles and reassuring advice from those who have done the gig. The following is a characteristic exchange:

> I hope to be working soon on a community version of *Brigadoon*. I get the Scottish accent, but sometimes slip into a quasi-Irish-British sort of thing. Does anyone out there have any information for on-line dialect help?
>
> Unfortunately, dialect is the kind of thing you really need to HEAR to polish up on... Just rent a movie that takes place in Scotland like *Rob Roy*. The Scottish accent is not particularly difficult and as long you try, most audiences won't be nitpicking. Good luck! Huch-Hi!

This is reminiscent of a production mounted in a Midwest high school where the cast prepared their accents by listening to Scotty in *Star Trek*. Several of the sites are of local theatre companies advertising their productions and commercial enterprises selling cast albums, DVDs of the movie and 'Scottish clan badge shirts'. The name 'Brigadoon' recurs in two curious contexts, the breeding of dogs and the breeding of flowers. Thus, there is a Brigadoon Kennel in Massachusetts, a Brigadoon Bearded Collie website and separate sites devoted to thoroughbred dogs called Banchory Mist o'Brigadoon and Percival Burns o'Brigadoon. It seems the recurrent name in these compilations refers to an original dog, Brigadoon, 'sire of 20 champions'. Several sites advertise for sale a hybrid tea rose called Brigadoon and several promote objects and artworks relating to *Brigadoon*. One site appears to be some kind of virtual community with a figure called 'Fiona, Protector Goddess of Brigadoon' and yet another offers an electronic novel entitled *Searching for Brigadoon*, which begins 'Come and join us as we walk into the heart of the mist that is Scotland...' Far and away, however, most Brigadoon websites use the name to advertise idyllic holiday retreats (including golf courses) and retirement accommodation. Such sites figure in Scotland, Australia and Canada, but are overwhelmingly in the USA. There are Brigadoons in California, Michigan, Connecticut, Tennessee and Washington State. The Tennessee site invites the reader to 'discover the magic of Brigadoon Resort... a special place in time'. As has been suggested earlier, the popular appropriation of the name and concept of 'Brigadoon', far from the hostility evinced by the Scots intelligentsia, locates it with those other talismanic 'places' Shangri-La and Bali-Hai, in the sure knowledge that the very word will conjure up a repertoire of associations amounting to an escape from the modern world.

The situation of *Brigadoon* in the twenty-first century is paradoxical. Constantly revived (mainly by amateur, but sometimes by professional, groups) it continues to be enjoyed by popular audiences, its songs part of the repertoire of the 'middlebrow' concert platform, while at the same time being reviled by the Scots intelligentsia. Hopefully, the foregoing account of *Brigadoon* on both stage and screen may introduce some measure of nuance into what has been a too easy dismissal of the piece, proceeding from debatable aesthetic assumptions. That said, this book is not an out and out attempt to rehabilitate *Brigadoon* on all fronts. It still amounts to a problematic embodiment of the Scottish Discursive Unconscious and, as such, requires constant interrogation. An earlier part of the book spoke about the silences of *Brigadoon* and speculated, among other things, about the kind of Scottish world the Brigadooners might have encountered on first waking from their hundred-year sleep in 1847. Ethan Morrden has pondered fruitfully what a reconceptualised *Brigadoon* might look like:

I'd like to see a rethinking... in which the fascism latent in
Brigadoon's confining social and religious structures is emphasised.
More should be made of Jeff's nihilism, of the New York fiancée's
pestering conventions. *He* [Tommy] could be played as Jerry Lewis,
she [Jane] as Martha Stewart. The bar scene could be reset in a
television studio, where she is far too busy revealing needlepoint
and eulogising the soufflé to listen to Tommy. And consider the
Brigadoon afterstory: Tommy has vanished, Jeff was the last person
to see him alive, and his alibi will be some babble about a ghost
village. Will some bold director, one day, give us a de-fantasised
Brigadoon, with a very short final pantomime of detectives grilling
Jeff in an interrogation room?

(Morrden 1999: 175)

The crucial omission from Morrden's engaging list of possible
revisions is, of course, a *Brigadoon* which deconstructs the Scottish
Discursive Unconscious within which it was itself conceived.

Will some bold director one day...?

5

Scotland and the
Braveheart Effect

Happy the nation whose annals are vacant
Thomas Carlyle

Brigadoon could be described as having a long, slow intertextual life, providing for some people a reassuring reference point – cashable as the name of a retirement home or species of flower – of an imaginary Scotland of highland beauty, peace and romance, and evoking for others, particularly the Scots intelligentsia, a ready shorthand for the kind of sentimental *kitsch* they see as having defined Scottish life. Vehement as the latter's references to *Brigadoon* often are, they could not be said to have affected Scottish society as a whole. It is quite the reverse with *Braveheart*. From the moment of its announcement as a possible project to its delirious European premiere in Stirling and beyond, it has convulsed Scottish society, seen by some as manna from heaven and by others as an unmitigated curse.

The reasons for *Brigadoon*'s relative invisibility and *Braveheart*'s omnipresence are not hard to fathom. Their respective 'moments' were very different. *Brigadoon* entered a 1950s Scotland on the face of it securely enveloped in a cosy Unionism, with the few existing nationalist militants being perceived as kilted loonies, the more extreme of whom blew up post boxes because they carried the designation 'Elizabeth II' rather than, as the nationalists averred it should have been, 'Elizabeth I', the crowns of England and Scotland having been united in 1604 with the accession of James I of England and VI of Scotland. It will be noted that even this 'extreme' protest was formulated within the parameters of Unionism and monarchy. Also, by the 1950s, whatever traditions of *cultural* nationalism had been activated during the inter-war period had largely subsided from general visibility.

The 'moment' of *Braveheart* was altogether different. After the failed devolution referendum of 1979, there was intense activity on the cultural nationalist front in literature, music, theatre and film and in the critical discourses surrounding these practices, leading to the most minute scrutiny of any artefact purporting to – or being thought to – speak for Scotland. In addition, *the* crucial difference between *Brigadoon* and *Braveheart* was that the latter was ostensibly about not just Scottish history, but perhaps the most venerated icon within it – William Wallace, the twelfth-century warrior who had resisted, and was ultimately executed by, the English. Graeme Morton, in his *William Wallace: Man and Myth*, has outlined how Wallace came to be the focus of so many diverse imaginings of Scottish history and identity:

> He was not noble by birth, more bourgeois than anything else. He was not part of the Scottish 'state', and his knighthood and his Guardianship of Scotland, for a year after the Battle of Stirling Bridge, was seen as a reward for a man promoted through the ranks by his own efforts, rather than pulled up by patronage and birth. Religiously a Protestant, with a Protestant version of Blind Harry's patriotic verse to confirm it in 1570, he was a suitable role model for post-Reformation Scotland and certainly so in the eighteenth and nineteenth centuries. He was no highlander, although there are highland claims to his memory and his rustic simplicity, honesty, strength and prowess on the battlefield was easily linked to the noble savage, so portrayed in the late eighteenth century view of the Scottish highlands. Nor was he a Jacobite, although this did not stop his deeds of valour appearing in Jacobite songs. However, it did ensure his commemoration would focus Scottish nationhood (freedom) on parliament and governance, not on monarchical restoration...

(Morton 2001: 15–16)

The very meagreness of historical evidence provided the *tabula rasa* on which diverse groups could write their versions of Wallace, opening the way for contradictory claims to his ownership. A film about his life in 1995? A project more calculated to create a 'ferrets in a sack' situation in contemporary Scotland could not be imagined.

To speak of *Braveheart* being made in Scotland is only partly true. It is a mark of Scotland's provincialism that its press becomes starry-eyed at the prospect of any Hollywood celebrity visiting the country. This was writ large when it was announced that Mel Gibson was to direct and star in *Braveheart* and that it was to be shot in Scotland. Although a number of scenes were shot there, the project transferred rapidly to the Republic of Ireland because of tax incentives there and because of the offer of 1,600 Irish Army reservists to swell the crowd scenes (although an alternative story circulates to the effect that the move to Ireland was prompted by lack of access to National Trust land in Scotland). That this came about was due to the diametrically opposed political cultures of the UK and the Republic at the time; in the former a hard-nosed Thatcherite Conservative culture incarnated in the philistine Scottish Secretary (the provincial Governor of Scotland), Michael Forsyth, and in the latter a left-leaning, arts-friendly administration personified by the literate and sophisticated Irish Minister of Culture, Michael D Higgins. The 'stealing' of *Braveheart* by the Irish was to have an electrifying effect on the Scottish political establishment's previously niggardly attitude to funding the arts and, indeed, on the personality and behaviour of Michael Forsyth (of which more presently).

Braveheart was immensely popular with audiences, becoming the tenth-highest-grossing film of 1995. It seems to have been especially popular with Scottish audiences, producing 28 per cent of its British box-office takings in Scotland against the usual average of eight per cent. With a few notable exceptions, reviewers also welcomed it. However, concern was expressed about its xenophobia with regard to the English, a quality much appreciated by teenage Scottish audiences who, it is said, cheered every time Wallace killed an Englishman. Clearly there is a vast difference between responses to acts of violence in works of imagination and to similar acts in the lived world. Nevertheless, several commentators began to look more closely at the film's xenophobia. The influential reviewer of the

London *Evening Standard*, Alexander Walker – himself an Ulster Protestant strongly committed to the continuing political Union of England, Scotland and Northern Ireland – had been prominent in traducing a series of Irish films, among them *The Crying Game* (1992) and *In the Name of the Father* (1993) for their alleged sympathy for the IRA and concomitant anti-Englishness. He extended this argument to *Braveheart*. However, the article which caused Scottish Nationalists to foam at the mouth was by Alan Massie, a distinguished Scots novelist and frequent defender of the Union. What particularly incensed them was Massie's comparing Wallace with General Radko Mladic, the Bosnian Serb commander subsequently indicted by the International War Crimes Tribunal in The Hague for atrocities, mainly against Bosnian Moslems. It became clear at this point that discussion of *Braveheart* would not long remain within the parameters of aesthetics.

The Political Appropriation of *Braveheart*

Possibly unwisely, given the film's xenophobia, the Scottish National Party enthusiastically embraced *Braveheart*. The SNP's then leader, Alex Salmond, spoke highly of the film in several public situations, the party adopted images from it (against, it is rumoured, the wishes of Mel Gibson) in its campaign literature and Salmond, at the party's annual conference, structured his final speech to delegates substantially round the film. Beginning with a reference to *Braveheart*, Salmond's peroration concluded as follows:

> I believe that this party has the ability to change this country, to change Scotland – and that we alone can. That is our task. It is more important than you or me or any person in this hall or any person in the whole of Scotland. To achieve it will require passion and commitment combined with pragmatism and iron self-discipline. So that we can say with Wallace – head and heart – the one word which encapsulates all our hopes – *Freedom, Freedom, Freedom*.

> *(Salmond 1995: 18)*

Quite apart from its explicit invocation of Wallace, the rhetorical shape of Salmond's speech closely follows that of the filmic Wallace's address to his army before the Battle of Stirling Bridge. In the short term at

14. Political appropriation: the card issued
by the Scottish National Party.

least, the SNP's appropriation of *Braveheart* seemed to pay off since, one month after the opening of the film, the party achieved its highest poll ratings for seven years. On the other hand, some Scots intellectuals could be heard muttering that they could not bring themselves to vote for a party which would associate itself with a film of such unmitigated aesthetic vulgarity and ideological unpleasantness.

But Alex Salmond and the SNP were not the only political appropriators of *Braveheart*. Michael Forsyth, up to that point decidedly cool about the ideological dimension of being Scottish, was at the time (until the general election of 1997 eradicated the entire phalanx of Tory members of parliament in Scotland) the sitting member for Stirling, a town particularly associated with Wallace and the site of the imposing national monument to him. Forsyth held the seat by a very slender majority over the SNP challenger. At the film's European premiere there, and to great popular derision, Forsyth arrived attired in highland dress and, more seriously in its longer-term effects, began to reverse government policy with regard to the funding of filmmaking in Scotland. Following a specially-commissioned report by a firm of management consultants, Forsyth created a new public body which incorporated all the previously existing organisations concerned with film culture and film commerce in Scotland. The new body, Scottish Screen, received considerably enhanced funding, but the price was that the emphasis was to shift from film as culture to film as commerce.

Braveheart has also been appropriated by more sinister political forces. There are in Scotland diverse Celtic nationalist groups, often with resoundingly operatic names (in Scots Gaelic, of course) such as *Sìol Nan Gaidheal* (Seed of the Gael). Their politics, which sometimes include dashes of ecologism and animal liberationism, range from republicanism through to crypto-fascism and there is much quasi-theological disputation about the legitimacy of one group over another. However, as David Limond has made clear (Limond 1994) they are united in several beliefs which read like a gloss on the Scottish Discursive Unconscious: that Scotland is a Celtic country which ought to be free of English rule; that Scots of today have lost touch with what the Celticists allege is a particularly Scottish tradition of resistance to oppression; that the 'true nature' of Scotland, materially and culturally, lies in the Highlands; and that Scotland has been betrayed by its academics in general, and its historians in particular, who are seen as spineless apologists for the political *status quo* in the UK. *Braveheart* was clearly manna from heaven for such groups. One such, the Wallace Clan Trust, has a special relationship with *Braveheart*. It seems the trust was set up in 1986 by one Seoras Wallace and its central aim is to bring back clanship to Scotland and 'secure the traditional Wallace lands' for use once more by the Clan Wallace, thereby, to quote one journalist, 'honouring its ancestors and creating a tourist attraction' (McConnell 1995). It seems that Seoras Wallace, animated by his twin passions for Scottish history and martial arts, also founded the Scottish Clan Battle Society in 1986 in which he and his fellow 'clansmen' re-enact – in the garb and bearing the weapons of 'the Scottish warrior' – the great battles of Scottish history. His interest led to the Society/Clan being engaged to choreograph and participate in the battle scenes in films such as *Highlander* (1985) and *Chasing the Deer* (1994), which, in turn, led to their involvement in *Braveheart*. It was during the making of this film that they became close to Mel Gibson (apparently sharing certain ideological predispositions) and at certain moments, as at the Stirling premiere, acted as a kind of Praetorian Guard to the actor. They are also funded by several Scottish local authorities to furnish adventure training for unemployed youngsters. Seoras Wallace sees real significance in the fact that the Clan have worked on both *Braveheart* and *Chasing the Deer*, which recounts the Jacobite Uprising of 1745 culminating in the Battle of Culloden (1746). In Seoras Wallace's words:

[F]or [sic] the Wallace Clan point of view we have told the story of the first fight for independence to the last battle on Scottish soil. So in a sense our vocation has been fulfilled.

(quoted in McConnell 1995)

Both William Wallace and the Battle of Culloden are foci for lachrymose elegiacism in Scotland (McArthur 1994). That the Wallace Clan should foreground them illustrates the extent to which their project is suffused with the Scottish Discursive Unconscious. *Braveheart* continues to have political resonance in Scotland as when, in the run-up to the 1997 general election, the Scottish edition of the London-based *Sun* came out in favour of Labour rather than the SNP with its front page reading 'Bravehearts must wait... it's time for brave heads'. Grotesquely, during the same election campaign, the Scottish Tories ran a newspaper advert which invoked the final image of *Braveheart* in which Wallace's sword lies embedded in the ground. The highly sinister political ramifications of *Braveheart* in societies furth of Scotland will be examined in Chapter 9.

The Sporting Appropriation of *Braveheart*

It was principally after Mel Gibson had won the Oscar for Best Director and *Braveheart* the Oscar for Best Picture in 1996 that the enthusiasm for the film in Scotland became delirium. Ever since its dazzling European premiere in Stirling – complete with *son et lumière* effects on the castle esplanade, bagpipe music, the great and the good of Scottish society and the Wallace Clan in full regalia – *Braveheart* has enjoyed a rich intertextual life in Scottish culture. It became (unlike *Brigadoon)* a wholly benign reference point in press editorials, political cartoons and (particularly tabloid) journalistic discourse: for instance, a photograph of a baby who had been attacked in her pram was printed under the headline 'Braveheart'; an advertisement seeking staff for a Scottish public body was headed 'William Wallaces wanted'; and a newly-devised 'white-knuckle' ride in a funfair was named 'the Braveheart ride'. However, one of the most extensive appropriations of *Braveheart* was in sports journalism.

This began modestly with a prominent Scottish snooker player being described as 'the braveheart of the green baize', gathered pace when supporters of the national rugby team bore life-size cut-outs of Gibson as Wallace, and became positively demented with the arrival of the European football championship in London in the summer of 1996. Nor was the evoking of *Braveheart* in this context confined to solely to the British press. *Jyllands Posten* (Denmark), *Hamburger Morgenpost* (Germany), *Suddeutsche Zeitung* (Germany), *France Soir* (France), *Gazzetta dello Sport* (Italy) and *A Bola* (Portugal) all referred to *Braveheart* or Wallace in their reports on the Scottish team. The Scottish team were recurrently described in the British press as 'brave hearts' and every possible pun – a favourite rhetorical device of the British press – was extracted from the term. For example, Scotland's drawing with Holland, one of the top teams, was hailed as a 'brave start'. The journalists' description of the Scots players generated a curious, related description of the English team, whom the Scots were to face in the second round. Having constructed the Scots within the medieval discourse of *Braveheart*, the press felt compelled to construct a medieval counter-myth for the English. Thus the latter became 'lion hearts' – a reference to the twelfth-century English King, Richard the Lionheart. This myth – within which could be heard, from time to time, vague echoes of Shakespeare, another hegemonic discourse in British culture – became incarnated in the figure of Paul Gascoigne and several montages were published showing him in the accoutrements of Richard. One such coupled Gascoigne with Mel Gibson's Wallace, except that Gibson's face had been replaced with that of the Scottish captain, Gary McAllister. As it happened, Scotland lost 2–0 to England, after which the Scots team, supporters and journalists abandoned their *Braveheart* triumphalism and reverted to their more usual elegiac role of tearful, though gallant, losers.

Like its political counterpart, the sporting appropriation continued to resonate within Scottish culture with Scottish international teams reputedly psyching themselves up before fixtures with screenings of *Braveheart* and one newspaper – perhaps tongue in cheek – purporting to find a relationship between the date of the film's release and the moment when Scotland ceased to concede goals. However, to illustrate how mercurial and malleable intertextuality may be, during the 2002 World Cup a tv shot of two English supporters rigged out as medieval knights during the England v Argentina match elicited from the commentator the words 'we could do with some bravehearts now'.

The Touristic Appropriation of *Braveheart*

Somewhat coincidentally, four Hollywood films were shot wholly or partly in Scotland within a relatively short time span. They were *Highlander* (1985), *Rob Roy* (1995), *Braveheart* (1995) and *Loch Ness* (1995). They excited great interest within the Scottish tourist industry and its institutions such as the Scottish Tourist Board to the extent that a new concept appeared in their discourse – film tourism. The creation of the concept focused the industry's attention on the diverse ways in which film production, at its various stages, might generate substantial tourist income. This could range from the provision of accommodation, food, entertainment and transport for those scouting locations for a possible film, through the provision of the same services plus supplies and film extras when the film was being shot, through to the welcoming of those tourists from all over the world who had become entranced by the milieux they had seen in the completed movie. The folk wisdom of the Scottish tourist industry has it that *Braveheart* is the most important element in the development of film tourism in Scotland, to the extent that an image from the film graces the cover of the brochure produced by the STB on the topic of film tourism and images from the film have been deployed within the brochures emanating from Stirling, the area round which has come increasingly to be called '*Braveheart* country', a concept assiduously promoted by the local tourist industry.

The STB has also exploited the film in its campaigns outside the UK, particularly in Germany and France, and calculates that more than 26 per cent of visitors to Scotland in 1996 came to Scotland partly because they had seen *Braveheart* or one of the other 'kilt' movies. When *Braveheart* was released on video in 1996, the STB mounted a promotion with the video company, offering the possibility of winning a holiday in Scotland. *Braveheart*, and probably the other 'kilt' movies, has been key in drawing tourists to the most important site of the Wallace myth, the Wallace Monument at Stirling. In the year following the cinema release of *Braveheart*, visitors to the monument increased from 66,000 to 167,000. The tourist organisations have assessed the tourist implications of *Braveheart* and other movies very carefully, hiring consultants who have subjected tourists to a battery of questions designed to tease out their precise reasons for coming to Scotland. The main conclusion of the

15. Touristic appropriation: the cover of
a Scottish Tourist Board brochure.

consultants' report was that exposure to the films may not have been
the prime reason for coming to Scotland but that, once there, tourists
who had seen the films, particularly *Braveheart*, were keen to include
Stirling and the Wallace Monument in their itinerary (Costley 1997).
The report further established that the elements in *Braveheart* which
most attracted visitors were the scenery, the historical interest and the
characters. There is a strong suspicion that Scottish tourist
organisations and filmmakers have learned the lesson of *Braveheart*
too well and – though they are cagey about admitting this – have
become increasingly symbiotic. The television series *Monarch of the
Glen*, for example, carries landscape and castle shots disproportionate
– in their number and length – to their function in the narrative.

Clearly the touristic appropriation of *Braveheart* is joining with
another powerfully developing current in Western culture, the
marketing of *heritage*, an activity in which – because of its severely

retarded social formation – Britain excels. Virtually every Western society has embarked upon a frantic appropriation of the past (Füredi 1992). Formerly the prerogative of the right, the pursuit of the past is now as ardent on the left. Nor is academia immune from the syndrome, as the number of recent academic books with the word 'memory' in their titles attests. However, the subtlety and nuance of academic explorations of memory tend to be absent from filmic and touristic appropriations of the past, which invariably repress contradictions. The touristic appropriations of *Braveheart* and Wallace stress the qualities of heroism and patriotism. Few outside the small group of professional historians of Scotland would be aware, for example, that far from being a spontaneous outpouring of popular feeling, Wallace's army was raised by conscription, with those refusing to serve liable to be hanged, or that, far from resisting England to the death, Wallace attempted to sue for peace.

In short, precisely because of the operation of the Scottish Discursive Unconscious, *Braveheart* is perfectly tailored to function in touristic appropriations. Its success throughout the world, and in Scotland in particular, is a source of dismay to those Scots who feel that the pernicious historical discourses within which Scotland has been constructed ought to be interrogated rather than submitted to or appropriated for diverse purposes. That task has become infinitely more difficult due to the coming together of several factors, one of which is central. *Braveheart's* money-spinning qualities have strongly encouraged the setting up of a series of film commissions throughout Scotland. Their function is nakedly economic – to lure filmmakers to Scotland irrespective of the kinds of films they might make or how they might represent Scotland and the Scots. The tie-up between *Braveheart* and this phenomenon is neatly illustrated by the execrable *The Evil Beneath Loch Ness* (2000). A shoddy rip-off of *Jaws* (1975) and *Alien* (1979), it has a character who, setting out to hunt for the monster, dons a kilt and paints his face like Gibson in *Braveheart*. The officers of Scottish Screen who facilitated the making of this outrage are named (and hopefully shamed) in the film's credits.

The Vertigo of Appropriation

Graeme Morton concludes his book on Wallace with a chapter entitled 'Wallace.com' which, among other things, outlines the vertiginous experience of following up references to Wallace and *Braveheart* on the internet and he is rightly concerned about the extent to which this palimpsesting of fact, half-truth and myth proceeds largely in ignorance of what responsible academic historians have to say about original sources. It will be recalled that a search for 'Brigadoon' produced just under 50,000 results. Tapping in 'Braveheart' produces the astonishing figure of 210,000, and 'information about *Braveheart*' is among the most frequent requests on a site devoted to answering questions about Scotland. A far from comprehensive trawl of these sites has revealed that the name 'Braveheart' has engendered and/or become attached to a bewildering variety of objects, animals, services and activities including racehorses; a breed of cats; several breeds of dogs; dog kennels; an Australian cattery; flowers; swords; several electronic games; fireworks; yachts; shoes; wallpaper; videos; a motorbike (the Braveheart Valkyrie); a regatta; a form of wedding service; a cardiac arrest self-help group; a charity providing aid to Africa; an investment company; a cookbook; and a Portuguese rock band.

The Blindness of Appropriation

Tim Edensor (Edensor 1997 and 2002) has traversed some of the same ground as this chapter and gives a fuller account both of the touristic appropriation of *Brigadoon* and the disagreements over its political meaning for Scotland. He raises an important issue which helps explain the diversity of the film's appropriations and the vehemence of the disagreements. Analyses of the *Scotch Reels* type, deploying 'rigid categories' such as Tartanry and Kailyard, ignore, he suggests:

> the interpretations of audiences and the ways such [filmic] representations are reclaimed, recycled and used to express a wide range of meanings. Such analyses presume that films are unproblematically consumed by viewers, that they are encoded within dominant messages which are simply and consensually decoded. Although it is commonly attributed to popular films that they are formulaic, market-led and predictable, it is necessary to recognise that they are consumed in particular historical contexts and specific political cultures.
>
> *(Edensor 1997: 139)*

Edensor's point is a substantial one. Undoubtedly the *Scotch Reels* analysts tended to see the popular iconography of Scottishness as irretrievably tarnished by the ideological use to which they had been put. On the other hand, since its appearance in 1982 there have been persuasive arguments indicating that *Scotch Reels'* view may indeed have been too rigid and that this same iconography is more malleable than was supposed. Richard Giulianotti (Giulianotti 1991), exploring the behaviour and iconography of Scottish football supporters at the World Cup in Italy in 1990, suggests that their warm reception by local Italian people resulted from their having defined their identity dialectically as the binary opposite of the English supporters. The latter (or a substantial minority of them) had arrived in Italy with a fearsome reputation for aggressiveness, xenophobia and violence. In order to be discernibly un-English, therefore, says Giulianotti, the Scots constructed themselves as genial, internationalist and peaceable with the markers of their identity – the kilts, saltires and lions rampant – thereby becoming progressive rather than regressive signs.

Conflating Edensor's and Giulianotti's positions, they represent a growing tendency within cultural studies which operates under several rubrics: reader response criticism, ethnography, the shift from text to audience or, more straightforwardly, the idea that texts do not do things *to* people, people do things *with* texts. Henry Jenkins writes:

> In an essay about *Casablanca* (1942), Umberto Eco identifies what he sees as the defining characteristics of cult movies. Rather than being 'whole' and cohesive, a cult movie must be 'already ramshackle, rickety, unhinged in itself, the coming together of various archetypes and quotations, an unstable mixture of contradictions, gaps and irresolutions. Cult films such as *Casablanca* and *The Rocky Horror Picture Show* (1975) fall apart in our hands, a 'disconnected series of images' readily accessible as materials for our fantasies... Timothy Corrigan adopts the opposite perspective, arguing that films become cult objects not so much because their intrinsic properties as through the process of interpretation and appropriation... Eco stresses the properties of texts (their fragmentation, their excesses), whereas Corrigan emphasises the properties of audiences (their alienation, their appropriation). However, both describe an exchange of meanings

which is partially determined by the film text and partially by the filmgoer.

(Jenkins 2000: 167–8)

There is a very strong tendency, among certain reception theorists – a tendency aggravated by certain strands of postmodernism – to tip the balance so heavily in favour of the filmgoer that the text ceases to have any real substance, the focus of interest shifting from its aesthetic structures to what people say impressionistically about it rarely, if ever, with any detailed reference to its form. As the foregoing analysis of *Brigadoon* and its reception made clear, this study is alert to both sides of the binarism, the productivity of both text and audience. However, in the context of *Braveheart*, it is very much with Eco on insisting on the *textuality* of the film, that it was put together consciously (which does not preclude unconscious elements within it) by professional filmmakers with affective aims using the dramaturgical, stylistic, performative and technical resources of Hollywood cinema. The point of this insistence is to confront the appropriators of *Braveheart* with the detailed textual features of the film and demand of them that they justify their accounts of the film in the face of that evidence. That is the task of the succeeding chapters.

6

Braveheart:
A (Quasi-)Barthesian Reading
in Slow Motion

The bastard form of mass culture is humiliated repetition...
always new books, new programmes, new films, news items, but
always the same meaning.

Roland Barthes

The model for the following reading of *Braveheart* is *S/Z*, Barthes'
1970 study of Balzac's story *Sarassine*. *S/Z* has been seen – by
Terry Eagleton among others – as marking Barthes' transition from
structuralism to post-structuralism, from seeing written works
(Barthes' main sphere of activity) as closed, bounded structures each
with an unarguable beginning, middle and end, to seeing them as
sunbursts of signs, as having, in Eagleton's words:

> no determinate meaning, no settled signifieds, but [being] plural
> and diffuse, an inexhaustible galaxy or tissue of signifiers, a
> seamless weave of codes and fragments of codes through which
> the critic may cut his own errant path. There are no beginnings
> and no ends... All literary texts are woven out of all other literary
> texts, not in the conventional sense that they bear the traces of
> 'influence' but in the more radical sense that every word, phrase

or segment is a reworking of other writings and which precede or surround the individual work...

(Eagleton 1983: 138)

S/Z, and Barthes' subsequent work more generally, is notoriously elusive and playful – a factor heightened when it is approached by way of English translation from the French original. This produces the paradox – which Barthes himself surely would have enjoyed – that, while the precise meaning of his operational concepts is hard to pin down, taken together they constitute a remarkable armature with which to explore the density and diversity of meaning at play in any particular text and the extent to which it throws grappling hooks outwards to (virtually) every other text ever produced. Eagleton's version of Barthes' core concepts is as follows:

> Barthes' method [in *S/Z*] is to divide the Balzac story into a number of small units or 'lexies', and to apply to them five codes: the 'proiaretic' (or narrative) code, a 'hermeneutic' code concerned with the tale's unfolding enigmas, a 'cultural' code which examines the stock of social knowledge on which the work draws, a 'semic' code dealing with the connotations of persons, places and objects, and a 'symbolic' code charting the sexual and psychoanalytic relations set up in the text.

(Eagleton 1983: 138–139)

My understanding of the five codes is broadly in accord with Eagleton's although – while I see the symbolic code as certainly including the sexual and psychoanalytic – it seems to me that Barthes is here talking more generally about the great binary oppositions beloved of structuralism (Man v Woman, Country v City, Agrarian v Industrial). However, the emphasis on the psychoanalytic in relation to the symbolic code might be justified in seeing the symbolic code as the 'unconscious' of the text. It will be noted immediately that Barthes' five codes give access to both the 'inside' and the 'outside' of the text. The proairetic and hermeneutic codes give access to the internal workings of the text, the semic, cultural and symbolic codes to the text's appropriation of elements of the social world (in its widest sense) out of which the text has emerged. This is helpfully clarified in Mike Wayne's description of the proairetic and hermeneutic codes as 'sequencing' and the other three as 'enriching' and his designating the former thus → and the latter thus ↑, although it is equally helpful to think of the hermeneutic code being understood forward and the proairetic backward, the reader having constantly to survey the text retrospectively to understand the latter's functioning. Following Barthes' practice, I shall refer to the five codes as follows:

Proairetic	(ACT) – Barthes speaks of this code as the code of actions, what Eagleton calls the narrative code
Hermeneutic	(HER)
Semic	(SEM)
Cultural	(REF) – Barthes speaks of the cultural code as the reference code
Symbolic	(SYM)

Importantly, any individual element in a text may function in several codes simultaneously. Augmenting Barthes, I shall add two further codes, the cinematic code – rendered (CIN) – to engage primarily with those elements which have no existence outside of individual films, but which are nevertheless significatory, such as particular camera movements or technical processes such as cuts, fades, dissolves and wipes. My second augmentation is to propose a code of absence – rendered (ABS) – for those moments in the film when – usually for ideological reasons – something must remain unspoken or unvisualised. An example would be the flaying of the English commander Hugh de Cressingham after the Battle of Stirling Bridge and Wallace's using part of his skin as a belt or horse girth, a recurrent motif in stories about Wallace and an apparently natural event for inclusion in this most bloodthirsty of films. However, to have included this would have rendered Wallace as cruel rather than, as the film portrays him, righteously ferocious and would thereby have undermined the film's ideological project. The film makes some nice distinctions in this area, for example, that it is okay for Wallace to send to King Edward the severed head of his relative.

Why '(quasi-)Barthesian'? *S/Z* is itself reductive in the sense that it comes nowhere near comprehensiveness in teasing out all the threads which make up the weave of *Sarrasine* – an impossibility in any case since every text continues to generate new meanings – but, nevertheless, in its English edition it runs to upwards of 250 pages. The publishers of this book would have raised their eyebrows at a chapter on *Braveheart* of similar length to *S/Z*. That said, the *politics* of adopting, however reductively, Barthes' method are simple – to demonstrate that the meaning of *Braveheart* is much denser and more multi-dimensional than the utilitarian appropriations of it by, for example, opportunistic travel agents and those with diverse political axes to grind. The apparent paradox is that Braveheart is culturally rich (true of virtually every film) while being aesthetically indigent. One of the (on the face of it) most startling claims of Barthes, and of post-structuralism more generally, is that individual texts have no beginnings or ends, the corollary being that the critic might virtually toss a coin as to where to enter the text for analysis. If it does make sense to talk of *Braveheart* having a beginning, at what point should that be set? With writer Randall Wallace's first marks on his computer screen? With the first mentions of the project in the film trade press? When director Mel Gibson first called 'Action!' in a rain-sodden Scottish field? With true Barthesian arbitrariness, I have chosen to define the text of *Braveheart* as everything on the VHS cassette of the film purchasable or hireable for use in the domestic context. As will be seen, this choice will have consequences congenial to the analysis' ideological project of widening the meaning of *Braveheart* and *locating it in the world that produced it rather than the world it ostensibly represents.* Underlying this is the continuous question of why the ideological meaning of *Braveheart* is so urgently sought in its representations at the expense of its structure.

16. The vista revealed at the opening of *Braveheart*. The Scottish Discursive Unconscious decrees that the landscape must be highland.

A: Preliminaries

1. 14/09/96
   DNSN 518991 2
   01020333
   The date of the cassette's production and its numerical data distinguishing it from all other video titles. A highly organised electronics industry involved in the manufacture of hundreds of thousands of such titles (REF).
2. THX Letterbox
   A description of the cassette's technical format, distinguishing it from other possible technical choices (e.g. CinemaScope, standard ratio, scanned print), again locating it in a highly sophisticated technical armature (REF).
3. Copyright Assertion
   'The copyright proprietor has licensed this picture... for private home use only and prohibits other use...' Legality, prohibition, international copyright law, transnational capitalism (REF).
4. Logo: Twentieth Century Fox Home Video
   Brass fanfare, the Hollywood Hills, modernist buildings, (American) modernity, searchlights raking the sky. Specific associations: *Flash Gordon*, *Triumph of the Will* (REF).
5. Trailers
   The X Files, *Broken Arrow*, *Independence Day* and two separate trailers for *Braveheart*. What is being signified by the presence of trailers on the cassette? Twentieth Century Fox is selling not just *Braveheart* but *cinema*. What do the trailers have in common? The foregrounding of story (expressed in key lines of dialogue), spectacle/violent action, heterosexual romance and stars (REF).
6. Logo: Icon Productions
   Mel Gibson's production company. The star as entrepreneur (REF).

B: The opening of *Braveheart*

1. Mist
   Geographical location, 'Scotch mist', the Scottish Discursive Unconscious, the analogous openings of *Brigadoon*, *Scotch Myths* and *Local Hero* (REF).
   Temporal location, 'the mists of time', the margins of recorded history, the domain of myth (REF).

2. Helicopter shot
   Par excellence the cinematic mechanism of the tourist documentary (CIN). Scotland (and the Celtic world more generally) as 'picturesque', the site of tourism (REF).
3. The revelation of the vista
   The cinematic trope wherein indistinct music swells into a recognisable theme as the landscape vista is revealed. Specific references: *Lawrence of Arabia* (the transition from England to the Arabian Desert), *The Last of the Mohicans* (credits giving way to mountains and forests) (CIN).
4. The orgasmic gasps
   As well as being introduced by swelling music, the revelation of the vista is accompanied by a female voice gasping twice. Is this the ecstasy of the sublime (REF) and/or the first assertion of the film's association between nation and woman? (SYM)/(HER)
5. 'Scotland. 1280 A.D.'
   Time and space precisely recorded. History versus Myth (SYM).
6. 'I shall tell you of William Wallace...'
   The narration begins. But who speaks? A Scottish voice uttering anti-English sentiments, but whose voice? (HER) The voiceover as cinematic trope, one of a series of tropes (the scrolled written text is another) often associated with the genres of historical epic and biopic and with claims to truth (CIN). Specific references: *Buffalo Bill* (1944) and, more ironically, *Barry Lyndon* (1975).
7. The approach to the deserted farmhouse
   The approach is completed with the discovery of the bodies of the hanged lords and pages (ACT). Opening a film with the discovery of a massacre fulfils the classical dramaturgical move of the 'hook' – beginning with an arresting incident (REF). It is also a generic trope of the Western (REF). Specific references: *Major Dundee* (1965) and, more complexly, *Flaming Star* (1960).

C: The Child William

1. William's character
   The massacre of the lords, the pages and his family provides the initial psychological motivation for William's later life, but his character had earlier begun to be signalled by his eagerness to accompany his father and brother (SEM). In classic cinema, narrative proceeds by the acts of psychologically rounded characters (ACT).

2. William and Hamish play at fighting the English
   William is established as the leader, Hamish the follower, which will
   be reprised in their adult lives (HER). In classic (cinematic) narrative,
   the qualities of the adult are invariably discernible in the child (REF).
   Specific reference: Abel Gance's *Napoleon* (1927) in which the young
   Napoleon acts as general in a fight with snowballs (REF). William
   and Hamish fight each other, setting up the dangling parallelism
   which will be completed when they fight as adults (ACT)/(HER).

3. The gift of a thistle
   The thistle (the emblem of Scotland) is handed to the child William
   by the child Murron (his future wife), continuing the film's
   association between woman and nation (SYM). The importance of
   the gift (ACT) will not, at this stage of the film, be wholly
   understood. It is in the nature of the proairetic (and hermeneutic)
   codes that the importance of early acts is understood only
   retrospectively.

D: William's Uncle Argyle

1. Argyle's white, sightless left eye
   The discourse of Dark Ageism (the Dark Ages as site of squalor,
   religio-mysticism, cruelty and physical deformity). Specific reference:
   Kirk Douglas in *The Vikings* (1958) (REF).

2. Argyle as mentor
   This passing reference in Barthesian analysis would assume greater
   importance in Proppean analysis within which the narrative *functions*
   of characters are stressed.

3. 'Playing outlawed tunes on blood pipes'
   Argyle's answer to William's question about what his dead father's
   neighbours are doing. The reference is to the period following the
   failed Jacobite Uprising of 1745, it being widely, but erroneously,
   believed that the playing of bagpipes was among the prohibitions
   (such as the bearing of arms and the wearing of tartan) enacted by
   the victorious Hanoverian authorities. A potent trope in historical
   Scottish victimology, it is tailor-made to be mobilised into *Braveheart*
   (REF). Also the reference to 'blood pipes' reveals the traces of fascist
   ideology – blood and soil – which the film, probably unwittingly,
   subscribes to (see Chapter 9).

4. The backlighting of the mourning neighbours
   Backlighting – cinematic coding for romance and romantic memory
   (CIN).

5. Burning torches
Specific reference: the *Illustrated London News*' late-nineteenth-century representation of Highlanders paying homage to Queen Victoria at Balmoral (REF). Does it also speak subconsciously of the torchlight Nuremberg rally in *Triumph of the Will*? (ABS)

E: Edward I, his son Edward and the latter's marriage to Princess Isabelle of France

1. The introduction of these three figures completes the requirement of classic (cinematic) narrative that the central protagonist (Wallace), the central anatagonist (Edward) and the heterosexual romantic interest (Murron and Isabelle), be introduced early in the story (REF/HER).
2. 'Grant them *primae noctis*'
The film's foregrounding of the historically dubious concept of *jus primae noctis* (the right of the first night) – in keeping with the norms of classic cinematic narrative – elevates the sexual to equal status with the historical/political (REF). Specific reference: *Rob Roy* (1995).
3. The *mise-en-scène* of Edward's '*primae noctis*' speech
Edward's speech is delivered with intercut shots of him staring intently at Isabelle and her fearful return of his look, thereby meeting the classical dramaturgical requirement of *subtext* (REF)/(CIN). This is somewhat superfluous since the (still) mysterious off-screen narrator has already alluded to Edward's intention of impregnating Isabelle himself.
4. The homosexuality of Edward's son
This is conveyed in the *mise-en-scène* through a series of exchanged looks among Edward, his son and his son's lover. The film's construction of the son as weak and effete is generally in accord with the masculinism of the film as a whole and its transmission of the dominant societal view of homosexuality (REF)/(SYM).

F: The introduction of Robert the Bruce

1. It was dramaturgically necessary to introduce the Bruce at this early point since – within the narrative of the film and the version of Scottish history it subscribes to – he will take on the Wallace mantle after the latter's death (REF). The character of Bruce is constructed as Janus-like – uttering sentiments of political trimming, but darting hate-filled glances at the English soldiery to signal to the audience where his 'real' loyalty lies (SEM).

G: The return of Wallace the man

1. The return to the ruined croft
   Classic (cinematic) narrative delights in parallelisms. The last sight of the child William was of him looking backward to the family croft (so-called in the film, but a misnomer since the term was applied only in the Gaidhealteachd). His return must therefore parallel his departure (REF).

2. The presentation of Wallace/Gibson
   The *mise-en-scène* presents Wallace from behind as he rides into the croft and halts his horse. He is then shown from the front, but at a distance, not yet recognisable as Mel Gibson. He is being signified here as Wallace, the Man of Destiny returned to the home from which he was expelled (REF). As he begins to dismount there is a cut – the cut on movement marks the assertion of an orthodox cinematic code (CIN) and Wallace is revealed in close-up as Mel Gibson. The long duration of the close-up, and Gibson's isolation within the frame, mark the assertion of another cinematic code – the first appearance of the star (CIN). Such shots (as in this case) say implicitly to the audience 'Here is he/she whom you have come to see. Enjoy!' Specific comparison: the introduction of Humphrey Bogart in *The Harder They Fall* (1956).

3. The festivities
   Ring dancing, tumblers, jugglers, wrestlers, 'medieval' music. The brighter, reverse side of the Dark Ageism coin, medieval folk as bucolic simpletons (REF).

4. The first sight of the adult Murron
   Wallace enters on horseback and he and Murron exchange the kind of long looks which, in romantic cinema, signal that they are destined for each other (REF).

5. The retard and the contest
   Wallace's progress towards Murron is blocked by the massive frame of Hamish. The retard (*ritardando*) – the postponement of closure – is a recurrent trope of time-based classical arts such as music, theatre and cinema (REF). Hamish challenges William to a stone-heaving contest, the testing of the hero being a recurrent trope of classical narrative, again, very much foregrounded in function-based Proppian analysis (REF). William's recognition of Hamish comes about as a result of Hamish's punching him, by which act the dangling parallelism of their childhood encounter is completed (ACT)/(REF).

6. The character of Hamish
   The other sense of 'retard' is perhaps appropriate here, Hamish being

huge and rather slow on the uptake (SEM). He shares with his equally large father the structural role of Little John to Wallace's Robin Hood, exemplifying *Braveheart*'s multigeneric quality, specifically its relationship at this point to the historical epic (REF). Specific comparison: Alan Hale in *The Adventures of Robin Hood* (1938).

7. The trope of comic violence

Braveheart, at so many points, asserts its relationship to certain (particularly) Hollywood traditions, never more so than in the comic violence between Wallace and Hamish in this scene (REF)/(CIN). Specific comparisons: the male group films of John Ford and Howard Hawks, e.g. *Fort Apache* (1948), *Hatari!* (1962).

8. The interruption of festivities by hostile forces

Classical (cinematic) narrative loves abrupt reversals of tone, here the arrival of the English soldiery and the local lord to claim *jus primae noctis* of the bride (REF). Specific comparisons: Indians interrupting homesteaders' celebrations in *Canyon Passage* (1946) and *Wagonmaster* (1950). This exemplifies *Braveheart*'s marked affinity with the Western genre (an affinity more usually ascribed to *Rob Roy*).

9. The foreshadowing of Murron's sexual assault

Classical (Hollywoodean) dramaturgy is asserted once more in the mechanism of foreshadowing. As the English soldiers leave with the bride, one of them – who will later assault Murron – leers at her (REF).

H: The courtship

1. Images of romance

The horse ride in slow motion (CIN) – the classic cinematic trope for romance – Wallace's talking to Murron in French ('the language of romance') (REF), sunrise on the mountaintop (REF), reprise of the 'gift of a thistle' musical theme (REF). Specific comparisons: Mills and Boon novels, the paintings of Caspar David Friedrich.

2. The articulation of the talisman

Wallace returns to Murron, pressed in a cloth, the thistle she has given him as a child. Inflected in this scene as a romantic icon (REF), it nevertheless retains the symbolic charge of Woman and Nation (SYM).

I: The call to arms and the refusal of the call

1. Summoned by Campbell and others to a 'secret meeting', Wallace indicates that he wants to live in peace and raise a family (ACT).

17. Murron (Catherine McCormack) and Wallace (Mel Gibson)
in the slow-motion ride signifying romantic exultation.

The call and refusal would loom larger in Proppian than in Barthesian analysis. Specific comparison: *The Patriot* (2000).

J: The elopement and marriage

1. Images of romance: running hand in hand through the trees; lingering looks; a quasi-pagan ceremony, carried out by a priest, but in the open air in a glade by a stream; hands tied together in a wedding cloth embroidered with a thistle – the cloth a dangling trope the significance of which will be revealed later (REF)/(HER).
2. The consummation
   Backlighting, a cinematic code for romance (CIN).

K: The assault on and murder of Murron, Wallace's revenge and her burial

1. Murron assaulted by the leering soldier, thereby completing an action initiated in an earlier scene (ACT). Wallace engages the soldiers who have attacked her, manoeuvring acrobatically in the process (REF). Specific reference: the films of Douglas Fairbanks Snr. and the swashbuckling tradition more generally, further extending *Braveheart*'s range of generic reference. The violence being enacted

in slow motion is another cinematic reference (CIN). Specific references: *Bonnie and Clyde* (1967) and *The Wild Bunch* (1969).

2. Murron's throat cut by Heselrig, the English lord, narratively provoking Wallace's return, the mobilisation of the Scots against the English garrison (ACT) and Wallace's parallel cutting, on the spot where Murron was murdered, of Heselrig's throat (ACT).

The *mise-en-scène* of the two otherwise identical murders is different, much more explicit and bloody in the case of Heselrig. Why? Societal attitudes to the depiction of the murder of women? (REF) Dangling trope of the wedding cloth temporarily completed as Wallace retrieves it, bloodstained, from the spot on which Murron was murdered (HER).

3. Murron's murder marks the film's observation of a 'rule' of classic cinematic dramaturgy (fetishised in DIY books about screenwriting such as those by Syd Field) – fashioning a turning point, or plot point (defined by Field as 'an event that hooks into the story and spins it in a new direction') early in 'Act I' (REF)/(CIN).

4. Murron's burial (ACT), effecting narrative closure of the first half of the film. In the 1960s there was a brief fashion for long epics – *Lawrence of Arabia* (1962), *Dr Zhivago* (1965), *Khartoum* (1966) – which, because of their inordinate length, included an interval. *Braveheart*, half as long again as the average two-hour feature film, to some extent echoes this tradition (REF)/(CIN) but is short enough not to warrant an interval. If there had been one, however, this is where it would have occurred.

L: The mobilising of the Scots

1. The contemplation of the talisman. After the burial, in an encampment, Wallace contemplates the now talismanic wedding cloth. Reassertion of the Woman/Nation trope (SYM).

2. The removal of the arrowhead from Campbell's chest (ACT). This is an example of an action which seems narratively superfluous, apparently flowing from the kind of literalism which reasons that, Campbell having taken the arrow, it must be removed. The action's realisation – with Campbell drunk and punching his son Hamish for hurting him – reasserts the comic violence trope. The cauterising of the wound restates the Dark Ageism discourse (REF). Specific comparison: *The Vikings*.

3. Montage. The Scots forces gather. Images of men running through forests and down mountainsides (CIN).

M: The intercutting of Wallace's skirmishes
and Isabelle's learning about him (CIN)

1. Wallace's taking of Lanark

   The realisation of this capture – Wallace and his men riding into Lanark in captured uniforms – draws heavily on the Western (CIN). Specific reference: *The Wild Bunch*.

2. The murder of the Sheriff of Lanark

   The Sheriff is he who took the bride off to assert his *jus primae noctis* earlier in the film. He is murdered by the outraged husband of the bride (ACT). The proairetic code, the code of actions, is discernible by ranging back and forth across the text in its unfolding and perceiving actions and their (often delayed) consequences. The murder of the Sheriff in this scene effects closure on his earlier action. It is also at this point that the instability and plurality of Barthes' five codes become visible. We have talked about the *jus primae noctis* episode and the Sheriff's murder in terms of the proairetic code, an action started and its consequences realised. Although it is not strictly an enigma, one is tempted to talk about the two events in terms of the other code apprehended by traversing and re-traversing the text, the hermeneutic code. Locating the events in this code would be expressed as the Sheriff having violated the bride, when will he pay for it? (HER) The overall lesson to be drawn is that any incident, impulse or fragment of the text may be 'decipherable' within any number of codes.

3. Wallace's ambush of the English

   This too is realised in terms of a trope of the Western, more particularly that of a sub-genre, the Western set in Mexico. A small part of Wallace's force leads a larger English formation into a 'canyon' ambush. Once inside, the English commander's question 'Where is Wallace?' is answered by the appearance of Wallace and his larger force on the horizon of the 'canyon' rim (CIN). Specific comparison: *Viva Zapata!* (1952). A variation of this might be called 'the Custer syndrome' in which, at the Battle of the Little Big Horn, Custer's 7th Cavalry is lured into an ambush by the same ruse – see *They Died With Their Boots On* (1941) and other versions of the Custer story.

4. 'Now, that's love, no?'/ 'Love? I wouldn't know'

   This is the exchange between Princess Isabelle and her lady-in-waiting as the latter relates how Wallace 'fought for the love of a woman'. It marks the point at which the 'necessary' mechanism of heterosexual love is transferred from Murron to Isabelle. Her remark 'Love? I

18. The Western as template for *Braveheart*.
The canyon ambush of the English.

wouldn't know' brings to the surface the film's opposition between
the effete homosexual Prince Edward and the dashing heterosexual
Wallace, one of the most fundamental binarisms of the contemporary
social world within which *Braveheart* is constructed (SYM). It is worth
remembering Barthes' observation that *all* codes are cultural codes.

N: New recruits, strategy and betrayal

1. Messy eating
   Wallace, Campbell, Hamish and others eat noisily from a collective
   pot – Dark Ageism (REF). Specific comparisons: *The Private Life of
   Henry VIII* (1933), *The Virgin Spring* (1960).
2. 'We will build spears, long spears, spears as long as men'
   Discussing the invincibility of the heavy horse the English will deploy,
   Wallace says they will counter them with long spears, thereby
   delivering on the previous actions of his father and uncle who tapped
   the child William's forehead and urged him to think (ACT)/(HER?).
3. 'Some men are longer than others'
   The discussion of the spears gives rise to sexual banter. The Scots'
   military prowess is consistently linked to their sexual prowess and
   binarised against English sexual lack or perverse sexuality (REF)/
   (SYM).
4. 'Insane Irish'
   Two new recruits, one a Scot, Fodran, the other Irish, Stephen, a
   garrulous and eccentric figure. Anachronistic binarism of the
   convivial, if violent, Irish and the dour, taciturn Scots (REF)/(SYM).
5. The *mise-en-scène* of betrayal

Wallace, hunting in the forest, is attacked by Fodran, who is killed by Stephen. The *mise-en-scène* of this episode is constructed to suggest that it is Stephen who is threatening Wallace's life when, in fact, he is saving it, an example of the reversal beloved of classic cinematic narrative (REF)/(CIN). Specific reference: around the time *Braveheart* was being made, an advertisement was playing on British television in which a black man is seen running. Exploiting a widely-held stereotype of the black man as criminal, the advertisement then reveals that he is running to save someone's life. Both the tv commercial and this episode exploit the audience's (likely) prejudice against the Other.

O: The mountain-top mobilisation and the Battle of Stirling Bridge

1. 'Are you ready for a battle?'
   Wallace's question occurs on a mountain-top at sunrise, echoing an earlier scene with Murron (REF) and asserting the connection between mountains and 'freedom' (REF).
2. The political trimming of the Scots nobility (REF).
   The film, having referred previously to this historically well-documented fact (as in the scenes between Bruce and his father) here uses it for material for a dramatic reversal in...
3. Wallace's undermining of the Scots nobility's peace overtures
   The *mise-en-scène* – more accurately the dramaturgy – sets up one mood/purported action only to reverse it with another (REF).
4. Painted faces
   There being no historical evidence that the Scots painted their faces for battle in the medieval period (unlike the probability that they did so 1,000 years previously), this might be read as yet another intertextual reference to the Western (REF). In fact, Gibson has indicated that he got the idea from witnessing modern Scottish battle re-enactment groups; intertextuality still, but with a different text.
5. 'We didn't come here to fight for these bastards'
   The words are spoken by an anonymous Scottish foot soldier about the Scots nobility who are ostensibly directing the battle. Part of the dubious appeal of *Braveheart* was its mobilising of two of the most potent discourses of the modern world – nationalism and populism. The key (naturally undefined) terms of *Braveheart*'s rhetoric – 'Scotland', 'freedom' and 'the people' – are empty vessels into which can be poured the most noxious of contents (REF).
6. 'They can take our lives but they cannot take our FREEDOM'

Wallace addresses his troops before the battle, a specific trope of the historical epic (REF). Specific comparison: *Spartacus* (1960). The generative instance of this trope is probably Henry's address to his troops before Agincourt in Shakespeare's *Henry V*, which speech has certain resonances in Wallace's speech. The particular line beginning 'They can take our lives...' has had considerable intertextual life in, for example, newspaper cartoons and politicians' speeches (REF).

7. Wallace's sword, the long spears and the exposed genitals and backsides
It has been noted that the first mention of the long spears provoked sexual banter. Here also, at the battle, the Scots do not simply impugn English military prowess, but English manhood as well. This is reflected in the casting and playing of the English commanders as effete and connects with the already established opposition between Wallace's masculinity and Prince Edward's homosexuality (SYM). As indication of the continuing potency of the gesture, see Robbie Fowler's taunting of Graeme Le Saux by showing him his backside in a Liverpool versus Southampton football match. It seems that, within the macho culture of British professional football, Le Saux is regarded as effete and Other for, among other things, being seen reading the *Guardian* newspaper.

8. The cavalry charge in slow motion
Used very briefly here (but more attenuatedly in the earlier scene of Wallace's vengeance on the soldiers who attacked Murron) slow motion is a specifically cinematic way of choreographing action (contradictorily violence and romance) (CIN). Specific comparisons: *Seven Samurai* (1954), *Bonnie and Clyde*, *The Wild Bunch*.

9. The flaying of de Cressingham (ABS)
Widely circulated as the story of the skinning of the English commander was, and a 'natural' inclusion for this most gory of films, it was clearly 'unspeakable' for ideological reasons, being incompatible with modern conceptions of the hero who can, at most, be righteously ferocious, but not cruel.

P: Wallace's knighthood, his meeting with Bruce, the sack of York and Edward's response

1. The knighting
Wallace knighted, he strides from the room in disgust at the squabbling of the Scots lords over the succession to the throne (SEM). The Balliol and Bruce factions argue, but Bruce is constructed as being above faction (SEM).

2. Wallace and Bruce's first encounter
   Their characters are constructed as opposites (SEM), Wallace impetuous and open, Bruce cautious if not calculating, a classic opposition in narrative cinema (REF). Specific comparison: Michael Collins and Eamon DeValera in *Michael Collins* (1996). Bruce will eventually don Wallace's mantle (HER), so he must retain the sympathy of the audience despite his political trimming which is, anyway, ascribed to the malevolent influence of his father from which he frees himself. Audience sympathy is largely created and maintained by casting the engaging figure of Angus Macfadyen as Bruce (CIN) but also through the *focalising* of Bruce as a character, i.e. the degree of attention paid to him in the unfolding narrative. For instance, he is seen wrestling with the problem of his political commitment while the other lords are not (REF).

3. An army on the horizon
   In the introduction to the scene of Wallace's advance on York, his army is shown outlined against the horizon, a specifically cinematic tradition (CIN). Specific comparisons: the cavalry Westerns of John Ford.

4. The sack of York
   Boiling oil, burning bodies, the head of Edward's nephew sent to him in a basket – Dark Ageism (REF).

5. Edward's entry to his son's chamber
   The *mise-en-scène* of this sequence hinges on Prince Edward's fearful waiting for his father's arrival, heightened by intercut zooms towards the door through which his father will appear and images of the Prince's terrified face (CIN). The particular cinematic reference here is to the horror genre. Specific comparisons: *Jaws* (1975), the films of Alfred Hitchcock.

6. King Edward's soliloquy
   Deciding to parley with Wallace, Edward speaks his thoughts aloud about who he will send (REF). The model here is Shakespeare's plays, the hegemony of which in Anglophone culture ensures that virtually everyone in the audience will recognise the convention of the soliloquy. It is generally unacceptable in the cinema except in films set in the distant past.

7. King Edward's cough
   During the soliloquy, Edward begins to cough, the first sign of the illness which will bring him to his deathbed at the end of the film. In classical (cinematic) narrative events must have causes, hence the early preparation for his death (REF).

Q: Wallace's dream, his first encounter with Isabelle, her aid and Bruce's oath

1. The dream
   Wallace dreams of Murron. She bids him wake, but he wants to remain in the dream with her. This scene, strategically placed before his first encounter with Isabelle, has two functions: firstly, to signal Wallace's continuing loyalty to Murron (SEM), and secondly and paradoxically, to mark the transfer of heterosexual interest from Murron to Isabelle (REF).
2. The encounter
   Ostensibly about conveying King Edward's terms to Wallace, the scene as played – principally through the looks and glances of Isabelle and Wallace – is about their as yet unspoken sexual attraction (CIN).
3. Isabelle's aid to Wallace
   Learning from the King that, while she has been parleying with Wallace, he has sent forces to Scotland, the Princess informs Wallace. Readable as her irritation at Edward's treachery or her growing sexual interest in Wallace (SEM).
4. Bruce's oath
   At a meeting of the Scottish council, Wallace enters and upbraids the nobles for their hesitation in joining him (REF), shaming Bruce into a declaration of loyalty (SEM). Bruce's father re-convinces him to think strategically.
5. The leprosy of Bruce's father
   Readable as Dark Ageism (REF) and/or as an outward sign of his inner turpitude, a familiar trope in classical narrative (REF).

R: The Battle of Falkirk, two reversals and the transfer of the talisman

1. The Irish levies
   Central to classic (cinematic) narrative, the battle is structured in terms of opposing moods – repose and action (REF)/(CIN). The two armies drawn up facing each other, Edward sends forward his Irish levies and the Scots and Irish run towards each other as though to do battle. The expectation is that they will clash (ACT) but the first reversal is delivered when they halt within yards of each other (reversion to repose) then embrace each other, completing an action, but in an unexpected way (ACT). Specific comparisons: *Orphans of the Storm* (1921), *A Tale of Two Cities* (1935). There is also the

ideological suggestion that the Irish and the Scots are 'natural' allies because of the contempt the English have for them both (REF), Edward having sent the Irish in first because they were expendable.

2. The anonymous knight
   Edward is flanked by a knight visored to be anonymous. The question posed is who is this knight? (HER) This is answered in the second reversal (REF). The anonymous knight turns out to be Bruce, following his father's instructions to take the field on Edward's side. The wounded Wallace is dismayed, but not wholly surprised, that the other Scottish nobles – Lauchlan, Mornay and Craig – have fled the field, bought with Edward's favours. Totally disheartened by Bruce's 'treachery', he lies down to die as the English soldiers approach. Bruce saves his life (SEM).

3. The transfer of the talisman
   Depositing Wallace with one of his captains, Bruce picks up the wedding cloth adorned with the thistle which Wallace has dropped. The talisman has been transferred, the charisma ceded (REF), setting Bruce up for his later victory against the English at Bannockburn (HER).

4. Bruce among the fallen at Falkirk
   Bruce, traumatised at what he 'had' to do, wanders among the dead and dying. It is a moment of resolution for him (SEM). No film about Scottish history would be complete without a wailing lament following a lost battle (REF). Specific references: Flodden, Glencoe, Culloden.

5. The death of Campbell
   The death of close comrades is a recurrent trope of epic literature and popular cinema (REF)/(CIN). Specific references: the films of Howard Hawks and, particularly, Cecil B De Mille.

S: Wallace's revenge and the growth of his legend

1. The murder of Mornay
   Wallace is first glimpsed as a figure in Mornay's nightmare, a Fury riding out of Hell (REF). Specific reference: the guilty dreams of the Macbeths in Shakespeare's play. Wallace, having ridden into Mornay's bedchamber and smashed his skull, escapes Mornay's retainers by riding his horse off the castle's heights into the moat, the action being attenuated by slow motion (CIN). General reference: the Western. Specific reference: *Butch Cassidy and the Sundance Kid* (1969) (REF).

2. The murder of Lauchlan

At a banquet in Craig's castle, Craig and Bruce discuss Mornay's murder and who might be next. Blood drops from the ceiling onto Craig's hand, followed by Lauchlan's body, the throat cut, crashing onto the table. General reference: the horror movie. Specific reference: *Rio Bravo* (1959) (REF).

3. Montage of figures relaying the Wallace legend... (CIN)
   ... while Wallace himself is seen racing along a mountain ridge before pausing, eagle-like, on a mountain top. There is an association within the film of love and freedom with mountain tops (ACT), connecting with a more general cultural association (REF). General reference: Romantic painting. Specific reference: the paintings of Caspar David Friedrich but without their unsettling, mysterious quality.

19. Mountains, freedom, Caspar David Friedrich.
Wallace (Mel Gibson) atop the mountain.

T: Edward's trap, the impregnation of Isabelle, and the betrayal of Wallace

1. The trap
   Edward uses Isabelle as bait to lure Wallace into a trap, but her lady-in-waiting overhears the plan and Isabelle warns Wallace. In classical (cinematic) narrative, psychological motivation, however tenuous, must be provided to 'explain' characters' actions. Thus, Edward's treachery and his willingness to put her life at risk are Isabelle's 'motivation' for informing Wallace of the plan (SEM). Likewise, Wallace's burning alive of those sent to take him is 'justified' as their getting their just deserts, explicable again as Wallace's righteous ferocity (SEM).

2. 'Because of the way you are looking at me now'
   Isabelle's answer to Wallace's question 'Why do you help me?'. Their sexual coupling is the inevitable act to which the narrative has been moving (ACT) and her body language will later indicate that she has become pregnant by the encounter, another muted reference to the binary opposition between the virile Wallace and the 'barren' Prince Edward (SYM). However, Wallace's copulation with Isabelle poses something of an ideological problem for the film given its fetishising of Murron and of Wallace's love for her. The contradiction is elided in two ways: by making the sex brief, discreet and reticent in terms of its *mise-en-scène* (CIN) and by suggesting – the framing and lighting of their parting – the identification of Murron with Isabelle (CIN).
3. The betrayal and capture of Wallace
   Organised by Craig, with the connivance of Bruce's father, the betrayal is structured to exculpate Bruce himself, who thinks Wallace has come to Edinburgh simply for a meeting. The talismanic wedding cloth figures in this sequence, Bruce having sent it back to Wallace as a token of his good faith (ACT).

U: Wallace's trial and execution, Bruce at Bannockburn and narrative closure

1. The dwarves and the torture implements
   Prior to the execution, two dwarves enact in dumb show the hanging, drawing and quartering of Wallace – Dark Ageism (REF).
2. Wallace as Christ
   At various points in the execution process the *mise-en-scène* presents Wallace as the crucified Christ (REF).
3. The narrative's problem is how to make Wallace's fate seem like a victory – the usual outcome for a central protagonist who dies at the end of a classical narrative movie (CIN). Specific comparison: *The Eddy Duchin Story* (1956). The problem is resolved partly by Wallace's refusal to bend the knee to Edward (SEM), but more particularly, by having Isabelle inform the dying King Edward that the child she is carrying is not of his line (SYM).
4. Narrative closure
   It is an axiom of classic (cinematic) narrative that all the narrative threads be drawn together and tied in a knot. This is achieved during the execution by locating many of the leading characters within it: Hamish and Stephen witness the execution; Isabelle and King Edward are intercut with it, as is an image of Bruce praying; and Wallace

20. Charisma ceded. The Bruce (Angus MacFadyen)
comtemplates the talismanic cloth at Bannockburn.

hallucinates that he sees Murron in the crowd (REF)/(CIN). The final image of the execution scene, after the headsman's axe has fallen, is the fluttering to the ground, from his now lifeless hand, of the talismanic cloth (REF)/(CIN). This cloth has already, of course, become associated with Bruce, a fact reasserted in the dissolve from the cloth to the field of Bannockburn (CIN).

5. Bannockburn

The enigma at the start of the film of whose voice narrates (HER) is resolved when Bruce reveals that he is the narrator. This lends a (very likely unintended) irony to the third sentence of Bruce's opening narration 'But history is written by those who hang heroes'. It is an axiom of narrative theory that the veracity of the narrator cannot be guaranteed. This raises an acute question with regard to *Braveheart*: if Bruce is indeed the narrator of what we see, what is the status of the highly flattering portrait of himself? Bruce takes the talismanic cloth, now handled like a religious relic, from inside his armour and articulates in words what the film has already established in images, the charismatic succession – 'You have bled with Wallace, now bleed with me' (REF). Specific reference: Robert Burns' song 'Scots Wha Hae Wi' Wallace Bled'. Reinforcing the narrative closure (REF), as in the execution scene several of the main characters are present: Stephen, Craig the trimmer (aghast to the last that Bruce should be mentioning Wallace), and Hamish, bearing Wallace's massive broadsword. To the recurrent cry of 'Wallace! Wallace!' Hamish hurls the sword in the air where it twirls in slow motion (CIN) before plunging into the ground.

V: End credits

1. Cinema as a business bound by contractual hierarchies (REF). Although the foregoing analysis refers to most of the major sequences of *Braveheart*, it deals with only a miniscule amount of its overall coding. For instance, despite its wish to assert the connection between *Braveheart* and scores of other films, the analysis is light on cinematic coding especially that relating to sound design and music. To some extent the musical dimension of that lack is made good in the next chapter. *Braveheart* has been widely perceived and appropriated as unambiguously 'about' Scotland and its history. On the contrary, the foregoing analysis reveals that its 'Scottish' elements are entirely secondary to its enmeshment in the history of Hollywood narrative, generic and performative protocols, but it connects with Scotland sufficiently to make it a kind of *The Name of the Thistle*, albeit considerably less erudite, playful and, certainly, politically progressive than Umberto Eco's *The Name of the Rose*. Those who have appropriated *Braveheart* to advance diverse 'Scottish' agenda have done so by ignoring its manifest textual features. These features are, of course, created *partly* to be ignored. That is, classic narrative fiction films operate in a contradictory way. Their makers on the one hand solicit consciousness of some of cinema's aesthetic features: for instance the spectacle of *Braveheart*'s battle sequences has often been a source of favourable comment. On the other hand, as David Bordwell and others have pointed out, classic narrative cinema has evolved a way of telling stories whereby, by putting technical procedures – eyeline matching, shot reverse shot cutting, framing and camera movement, etc – at the service of character representation and development, these procedures are, to all intents and purposes, rendered invisible to audiences. The same is true of narrative structures. The hope is that, once the techno-aesthetic procedures of *Braveheart* have been spelled out, as in the foregoing analysis, those who would claim that it is primarily 'about' Scotland and its history will be required to measure that claim against the counterclaim of this chapter that *Braveheart* is primarily 'about' Hollywood cinema and, secondarily, about the discourses and states of feeling of the contemporary world. This is an argument which underpins the next chapter as well.

7

'No' a Fuckin' Dry Eye in the Hoose': *Braveheart*'s 'Gift of a Thistle' Sequence

If you don't cry during this film there is something wrong with your heart.

Alex Salmond

When crocodiles fully extend their jaws to swallow a victim [their] lacrimal ducts are squeezed and… tears are produced. Real crocodiles' tears are in fact meaningless in emotional terms.

Tom Lutz

The vernacular quotation in the title of this chapter was the punchline, in an account by a West of Scotland screenwriter, of a script he had written about a Scottish regiment in the American Civil War. It came at the end of his graphic description of how the bodies of the dead Scots, slain at Gettysburg, would be shipped in coffins back to the Hebrides to be met by weeping and keening widows 'wi' black shawls on their heids'. There are two interesting aspects to the account: that the screenwriter was setting out deliberately to move the audience to tears (somewhat cynically as the punch line indicates) and, that, in order to mount this scene 'reality' would have to be tampered with in the sense that public

21. Woman and Nation. The child William
is handed the emblem of Scotland

health considerations (not to mention cost) would decree that the
slain be buried where they fell. Additionally, the Scots killed in the
American Civil War were largely migrants to the USA and so unlikely
to be 'repatriated' in death. The account, and the questions it poses,
bring irresistibly to mind *Braveheart* as a whole and, in particular,
the much remarked-upon sequence in which, at the burial of his
father and brother, the child William is handed a thistle by the child
Murron, causing one tear to fall from his eye.

What is the function of this scene in the overall structure of
Braveheart? In the preceding scene, William has witnessed the bodies
of his dead kin and is traumatised, so the funeral scene is certainly
not meant to establish his trauma. It 'advances' the narrative in two
ways: it brings together Wallace and Murron at an early stage of the
plot and it introduces William's Uncle Argyle who will become his
guardian. But how structurally necessary are these plot elements?
This can be answered by a commutation test. If this early meeting
of William and Murron, and the figure of Argyle, were removed,
would this fundamentally affect the structure and meaning of the
film? The answer is emphatically no, so why is the scene there? Its
raison d'être is precisely that of the Gettysburg coffins arriving in
the Hebrides – to move the audience to tears.

James Horner's score is central to the emotional impact of
Braveheart as a whole and perhaps particularly to the sequence in
question. The main musical motif of the film – described on the
CD of the soundtrack as 'The Gift of a Thistle' – is a slow, wailing

melody played mainly on Uillean pipes. Particularly associated with the romance between Wallace and Murron – it figures on the CD in 'Wallace Courts Murron' and 'The Secret Wedding' – it is used also to signify 'romance' in 'The Love of a Princess' (Wallace's romantic interlude with Isabelle) and 'pathos' in 'Betrayal and Desolation' and 'The Princess Pleads for Wallace's Life'. It also reappears over the end credits. A formal, academic account of this musical motif has described it as follows:

> The 'B' theme tune appears frequently throughout the film, but is not stated until 00:11:22 – 00:12:18 [i.e. about eleven and a half minutes into the film] with a simple chordal accompaniment by the harp. The 'B' theme is in common time, and is played mostly by the Uillean pipes and is then repeated by legato strings with a steady bpm [beats per minute] of 72. This theme first enters when Wallace and Murron are shown together for the first time as children, as Murron presents Wallace with a thistle. The theme represents hope and freedom for Scotland, and is often played to love scenes between the couple. The theme gives hopeful but sad tone to the execution scene of Wallace when played by the Violins and Cello (02:31:08–02:32:52) at 63 bpm.
>
> *(Whitfield and Tagg 2002: 10)*

Being purely a formal description of the motif, this offers no aesthetic or moral judgement, unlike several other critiques. Horner's music is extremely controversial among musicians, composers of film music and, to some extent, the musically-educated public. The debate surfaced initially – and has consistently rumbled on – in the pages of *Film Score Monthly*, which might be termed the *Sight and Sound* of film music. An editorial referred to Horner's 'relentless creation of pastiche *without* form' and the critique was developed in another piece which, despite appearances, is admiring of Horner's work:

> There are few composers in film music today as controversial as James Horner. Heralded as a great new talent when he burst onto the scene in the early 1980s – a wunderkind capable of brilliant technical and artistic music composition – his reputation became blotted when it emerged that he had a predilection for re-quoting large sections of his own material in subsequent scores, as well as leaning heavily on the classical repertoire for thematic inspiration,

notably Russian greats such as Prokofiev and Dmitri Shostakovich, and American fixture Aaron Copland.

(Broxton 2001: 24)

Horner's specific 'borrowings', and the films in which they are deployed, include Schumann's *Third Synphony* (*Willow*), Prokofiev's *Cantata for the Russian Revolution* (*Red Heat*), Copland's *Rodeo* (*An American Tail: Fievel Goes West*), Khachaturian's *Gayanne Ballet* (*Aliens*), Orff's *Carmina Burana* (*Glory*), Arvo Pärt's *Fratres* (*Sneakers*), Charles Ives' *The Unanswered Question* (*Wolfen*) and Mahler's *Eighth Symphony* (*Enemy at the Gates*). Several reviews of Horner's soundtracks and articles on him come close to accusing him of plagiarising the work of a wide range of artists from Leonard Bernstein to the Irish vocalist Enya and the estate of the late Nino Rota successfully sued on the basis that Horner's score for *Honey, I Shrunk the Kids* (1989) used elements from Rota's score for the Fellini film *Amarcord* (1973). It would seem that *Braveheart* inaugurated a 'Celtic' phase in Horner's work, in which Uillean pipes and bodhran drums were foregrounded and which was particularly prominent in *The Devil's Own* (1997) and culminated in *Titanic* (1997), for which Horner won two Oscars, two Golden Globes and many other awards. Quite apart from the epistemological status of Celticism in music or any other field (Chapman 1978 and 1992), what is puzzling about Horner is that, as a former academic – he taught composition and music theory at UCLA – who had studied with the Hungarian avant-garde composer Ligeti, he should so comprehensively abandon the cerebral dimension of the European (particularly the modernist) tradition and opt so ostentatiously for an uncomplicated emotion-ality. Doug Adams, author of the most substantial essay on Horner's work, puts the issue starkly:

> In *Titanic*, as in most of his recent work, Horner uses music strictly for emotion... Every musical element in *Titanic*'s score has been heard before. Each has been chosen for its individual emotional effect, and each has been placed in order to trigger the proper emotion at the proper time... He is not a composer, he is an 'emotionalist'. As an 'emotionalist' he doesn't need to be innovative. He may repeat certain licks in every score, he may even steal a riff from other composers, but his particular assemblages and his individual timings are always emotionally effective and affective in

the scenes at hand. To him he has never copied himself, since he has never used the same piece of music for exactly the same scene in the same movie... Horner's score [for *Titanic*] provides the film with everything, but does so without any musical substance.

(Adams 1998: 39–41)

If Horner's music is at all times apt for the simplified, unambiguous states of feeling which the movies advance, there is an ethical problem discerned by Adams which connects with Horner's abandonment of intellect and is particularly acute with regard to 'historical' films such as *Apollo 13* (1995), *Titanic* and *Braveheart*:

Then there's the issue of Horner's use of this totally headstrong, unambiguous music. Is it right to use these kinds of constructed moralities in historically-based films... or is it a misappropriation of power? Should filmmakers and composers really be painting the past in shades of pure black and white? Should any grown-up films be portrayed as such, or should they be truer to the ambiguous nature of reality?

(Adams 1998: 41)

There is substantial agreement, then, that Horner's music is designed wholly to produce emotion in the audience, which inevitably means that much of it will be coldly calculated to elicit *tears*.

Regrettably, despite Alex Salmond's injunction at the head of this chapter, we do not have a detailed account of the relationship between *Braveheart* and weeping, but some work exists on the role of tears in relation to *Titanic*. Tom Lutz, in his *Crying: The Natural and Cultural History of Tears*, examines, as the title indicates, the history of crying, in what times and places tears were encouraged or discouraged and for what reasons. He reminds us that at certain moments – the late eighteenth and early to mid-nineteenth centuries in Europe for example – giving way to tears was not only a duty but a pleasure and that, having been repressed, certainly in some Euro-American cultures over the next century and a half, tears now seem to be returning with a vengeance. Citing examples such as Pentecostal Christian prayer meetings, and (some) late-twentieth-century psychotherapies (he might have added the death and burial of Princess Diana and England's eviction from World Cup 2002), he zooms in on *Titanic*:

The teenagers who are helping to make *Titanic* one of the few top-grossing films of all time clearly understand the relation between tears and pleasure. Journalist Deirdre Dolan interviewed teenagers in New York who had seen the film ten or more times, weeping voluminously each time… These adolescents go to the film knowing that they are going to witness a horrible and melodramatic tragedy, and this, Dolan writes, is why they go… 'so *that* they can weep'… Some of the teenagers understood their own crying in terms of release – the letting go of pent-up emotion. But others were clear that crying was important for the pleasure it afforded. As one girl explained, 'It's so much better to cry because it makes the movie so much more enjoyable'.

(Lutz 99: 42–43)

Lutz and Dolan are much more interested in the fact that *Titanic* elicits tears than in the specific aesthetic triggers it deploys to do so. Consequently, they do not explore the role of Horner's music in producing the tears, but it would be a safe bet that his keening, Celticist licks – not to mention Céline Dion's wailing rendition of the Horner-composed theme song, 'My Heart Will Go On' (note Horner's relationship with the word 'heart', popularly opposed to 'head' as the site of emotion) – has a central role. There is, among the astonishing 87,000 sites garnered on the web by tapping in Horner's name, an intriguing extract from the journal *Entertainment Weekly* which ties together *Braveheart, Titanic*, Céline Dion and the theme of this chapter:

After reading *Titanic*'s script with wet eyes, Horner contacted Cameron [the director]. The filmmaker, who at the time was enamoured with Horner's *Braveheart* score, screened 36 hours of *Titanic* footage for the composer. Horner wrote the movie's main theme in one night… [and] called in a favour from friend Celine Dion, who laid down the vocal for 'My Heart Will Go On'. 'She was singing the song,' Horner recalls, eyes welling up, 'and 20 people in the studio started crying. Celine had to stop to compose herself'.

(Snierson 1998: 1)

The making of *Titanic* – never mind its reception – seems to have involved a veritable orgy of weeping.

If Lutz does not raise the question of structuration in relation to Dolan's *Titanic* research, he does raise it elsewhere in his book by reference to psychologist John Sloboda's research (Sloboda 1991) which is an account of an experiment in which 83 music listeners, mostly professional musicians, filled in a questionnaire relating to their physical reactions – spinal shivers, tears, lumps in the throat, laughter – to particular pieces of music. Sloboda's most interesting finding, as summarised by Lutz, is that:

> Tears were most reliably evoked by melodic appoggiaturas, or grace notes, in which a note above or below the main tone precedes it, creating a certain amount of tension, which is then released when the main note is sounded. (Tears were also caused, to a lesser extent, by sequences and harmonic movements that resolve tension by returning to the tonic, or the first note of the scale of the song's key.)

> *(Lutz, 1999: 258)*

The 'Gift of a Thistle' theme follows very closely Sloboda's account of which musical forms most elicit tears in the sense that it is replete with appoggiaturas and grace notes and is structured within the tonic. However, the tear-generating elements go beyond the technical elements of musical form. The wailing quality of the Uillean pipes – plus the fact that they are activated by human breath – and the simple, *volkisch* character of the melody are important. The lachrymose quality may even be boosted by the widespread acceptance of a highly questionable category. Gerry Smyth, reviewing a guide to 'Celtic' music, observes:

> the opening pages introduce a rhetoric that pervades the entire volume:
>
> > When all the techniques are checked off, the element that the music of the Celtic lands most commonly shares is *something* a lot more intangible and certainly less quantifiable – a feeling or quality that evokes emotions of sadness or joy, sorrow or delight. All share, for want of a better word, a Celtic spirit, a unique bond with one another that transcends time, distance, and political units (reviewer's emphasis added).
>
> Some academics go through a whole career without finding a passage so ripe for deconstruction. For [the writer] this 'something' (wonderful mystificatory term) animates the culture not only of the disparate 'Celtic' nations of Europe, but also of the Celtic

diaspora, whether it surfaces in Nova Scotia, Chicago or Sydney. The notion that there is a trans-historical 'feeling', 'quality', 'spark', or 'spirit' infusing an arbitrarily defined body of music would not pass muster in a first-year media seminar. Here it underpins an entire world-view.

(Smyth 2002: 243)

The same trenchant critique of the epistemological status of the category 'Celtic' is carried out at greater length and depth by Malcolm Chapman (Chapman 1992) and the same headlong rush to embrace the category in the American South has further accelerated post-*Braveheart* (see Chapter 9). Clearly the book reviewed by Smyth is formulated within a wider 'Celtic' version of the Scottish Discursive Unconscious.

However, the clincher, as far as tear-inducement is concerned, is the abandonment of the simple melody played on a 'folk' instrument and its replacement by the same melody lushly orchestrated in the late Romantic style. Not accidentally, the transition from one version of the melody to the other occurs precisely at the moment of the transfer of the thistle and the appearance of the tear in William's eye. By ushering in the swelling strings at this point the filmmakers are effectively signalling the moment for the sobs to burst forth in the audience. By returning once more to the Uillean pipes, the film, having taken the audience to a pitch of emotion, lets it down gently.

If Horner's tearful Celticism is read as a reaching out for a 'land of lost content', as nostalgia for a Celtic dream world – an idea wholly in accord with *Braveheart*'s xenophobia and exclusivist conception of the nation – it is also congenial to *Braveheart*'s proto-fascism (see Chapter 9). Jeremy Tambling, in his *Opera and the Culture of Fascism*, suggests that such musical nostalgia:

may be associated as regressiveness with militarism itself and the death wish in battle and with sexuality as inseparable from death.

(Tambling, 1996: 22–23)

Tambling finds this association in much nineteenth-century opera, including parts of Puccini's *Turandot* and *La Fanciulla del West*, Verdi's *Aida* and Wagner's *Tannhäuser* and *Tristran and Isolde*, a tradition Horner is not averse to drawing on. If it is accepted that Horner's conception of film music is reductive, simplistic and strictly emotionalist, it might be thought that this is par for the course, reflecting what 'background' music in popular cinema is principally about. As with other artistic fields, however, the situation is more complex, with many of Horner's film composer contemporaries taking a more complex view of their work. Thus, David Shire, who did the music for *The Conversation* (1974) and *All the President's Men* (1976) – the former, in particular, exemplary in the complexity of its soundtrack – is at a far remove from Horner's one dimensional perspective:

> Film music is so often an art of juxtaposition. When the music is more about subtext – adding an element that isn't on the screen – that's the most satisfying. The most simple-minded scoring is what you get in most B-movies and bad television, where they want happy scenes made as happy as possible, love scenes made as loving as possible.
>
> *(Quoted in Morgan 2000: 1)*

Shire might have added, vis-à-vis the 'Gift of a Thistle' sequence, sad scenes made as sad as possible, to the point of drawing tears from the audience. What then is at stake in the, on the face of it, solely aesthetic decisions film composers make, and film directors make use of? Another of Horner's contemporaries, Carter Burwell – who did the scores for *Blood Simple* (1985) and *Miller's Crossing* (1990) – begins to make clear that what a film composer does is not simply aesthetic, but *moral* as well:

> I prefer doing romantic music, like *Miller's Crossing*, when the music's put up against something *unromantic*. I feel comfortable doing it in these situations because I know it's not exploitative of the emotions of the audience. I'm not pushing anyone's buttons because you're hearing romantic or sentimental music, but you're seeing very cold-blooded people acting on screen...
>
> *(Quoted in Morgan 2000: 5)*

'Exploitative of the emotions of the audience' and 'pushing anyone's buttons' are phrases which might have been fashioned to describe what James Horner's music does, arguably most grossly in the 'Gift of a Thistle' sequence. The cold calculation of this is heightened if it is recalled – as everyone is, of course, aware – that film music is

22. 'Jump-starting tears': William (James Robinson)
after he has been handed the thistle.

added at the post-production stage. That is, at some point in the
post-production of *Braveheart*, director Mel Gibson and composer
James Horner met in a sound studio and decided not only that the
'Gift of a Thistle' theme be added to this scene, but at what point it
would enter and at what decibel level. Is it not bizarre to think of
two highly-paid, respected, not stupid and not insensitive men
focused solely on the task of what Tom Lutz has described as 'jump-
starting tears'? One wonders if, at any point, the *morality* of this
enterprise was discussed.

Clearly it is not just the music which is 'working on' the
audience's feelings in this scene. The casting of a large-eyed,
'beautiful' boy as the young Wallace is crucial to the emotional
effect of the scene, as is what narratologists call *focalisation*, the
process within the unfolding of the narrative whereby the child
Wallace has already become the centre of our attention and
sympathy. The tradition of representing wide-eyed, weeping
children survives today – outside of certain Third World charity
commercials – primarily in what has been called, by Wayne
Hemingway, 'mass-market masterpieces'. To demonstrate the extent
to which the universe evoked in this kind of art connects with
Braveheart and its more demented internet outcrops, the following
is Hemingway's account of the 'crying boy' tradition:

> It is not clear when [sic] and who painted the first crying child, but
> mass-market artists such as Dallas Simpson, Anna Zinkieser and

Irene Spencer all grasped the concept that sad eyes cry. I'm not clear why tens of thousands should want something as sorrowful as a child in distress peering down from the living room wall, but there is no doubting the haunting quality of some of the works. Eventually, however, the 'haunting' was interpreted as a curse. In the early 1980s a series of house fires were attributed to what *The Sun* called 'the curse of the Crying Boys'. National panic was fanned by the tabloids. *The Sun* reported that 'many' homes were destroyed by fire while a Crying Boy picture survived untouched! Some said they had been dogged by ill-luck since buying a Crying Boy and in the words of *The Sun*, 'people who have tried to burn their own prints deliberately have found them indestructible'. *The Sun* offered to burn Crying Boys for their readers...

(Hemingway 2000: 78)

This, it will be recalled, is happening in late-twentieth-century Britain and not sixteenth-century Spain! The discussion of the 'Crying Boy' phenomenon may seem to be taking us far afield from *Braveheart*, but the suggestion is that they inhabit the same aesthetic and emotional universe.

The carefully constructed emotional purpose of the 'Gift of a Thistle' scene would appear to be doing its work only too well. Neal Ascherson, a distinguished Scots journalist who has not only written illuminatingly about the theoretical aspects of nationalism but, as a correspondent in Central Europe, has seen at first hand some of its more monstrous forms, writes:

Seeking heroes, I went the other day to see *Braveheart*. As an account of the real William Wallace, or of late 13th-century Scotland, it is a joke. The list of cultural howlers and historical distortions rolls on forever. As in the similar *Rob Roy*, the English feature as degenerate, upper-class sadists... You go to scoff... and yet there are moments when this shilling schlocker takes you unawares. One strong-minded, progressive friend found herself in tears. Another Scottish colleague reacted with a furious attack on the film for reducing his country's struggles to crude anti-English racism. Both went to the film certain they were immune to its allure – but neither was. They saw a child give a flower to a boy standing at his murdered father's grave, and the flower was a thistle. They heard a man speak easily of his country's 'freedom' without seeking a lesser word. Suddenly, they were undone. Wallace is a real hero, which means that he lives on in the shadows at the back of people's heads.

(Ascherson 1995: 20)

The piece from which this comes was an argument, from the left, that popular heroes are necessary, made at the moment when the right seemed to have had a monopoly on them, so it reads as if Ascherson was prepared, at that time at any rate, to accord the 'Gift of a Thistle' scene greater house room than the present writer, evidence that even the best-armed can be seduced by this scene.

Chapter 5 alluded to the marked shift in academic film studies in recent years from concern with the operations of the text – what films do *to* people – to concern with filmgoers' responses – what people do *with* films. A late development within this tendency is the exploration of the emotions filmgoers experience when confronted with films. Broadly speaking, this tendency is pro-emotion, much of its polemical energy coming from its hostility to Brechtian and psychoanalytic theories of cinema, both – in their different ways – distrustful of emotion. Part of the usefulness of this tendency is its ground-clearing function, its attempt to clarify the vocabulary of emotion in relation to cinema. A passage in an essay by Carl Plantinga could have been written with the 'Gift of a Thistle' scene – and, indeed, *Braveheart* more generally – in mind:

> False or unearned sentiment has been maligned as not only distasteful but immoral. 'Being sentimental', Mary Midgley writes, 'is misrepresenting the world in order to indulge our feelings'. It is a 'howling self-deception', she goes on, and a 'distortion of the world'. Mark Jefferson adds that sentimentality is grounded in a fiction of innocence, emphasising the 'sweetness, dearness, littleness, blamelessness, and vulnerability of the emotion's objects'. And as Anthony Saville writes, sentimentality not only requires the idealisation of the object but also contributes to self-righteousness or self-deception in encouraging a 'gratifying image of the self as compassionate, righteous or just'. If we grant that sentimentality idealises its object, we still must know why that makes it immoral and ideologically dangerous. Jefferson claims that sentimentality impairs one's moral vision, especially when the objects of sentimentality are persons or countries... Moreover, as both Midgley and Jefferson claim, sentimentality is implicated

in a brutality stemming from vilification rather than idealisation. As Jefferson writes, the 'unlikely creature and moral caricature that is someone unambiguously worthy of sympathetic response has its natural counterpart in a moral caricature of something un-ambiguously worthy of hatred'. Thus sentimentality may contribute to an emotional culture that also produces animosity towards a vilified other.

(Plantinga 1997: 385–386)

As Plantinga's question about why sentimentality should be viewed as immoral and ideologically dangerous makes clear, he is setting out positions rather than necessarily endorsing them. Quite rightly, he goes on to suggest that the validity of these arguments has to be tested against specific films and, within them, specific scenes. That said, there is an uncanny homology between the sentimentality/brutality dyad Plantinga reveals in those writers he cites and the specific charges that can be levelled at *Braveheart*: the sentimentality of the 'Gift of a Thistle' scene and the xenophobia of the film as a whole, its construction of, precisely, 'animosity towards a vilified other' (see Chapter 9).

This chapter has dealt sketchily with an issue of some complexity, the (doubtless diverse) responses we make to (particularly) music in the cinema. Its harsh judgement on Horner and, especially, the 'Gift of a Thistle' theme should not be taken as a general condemnation of music in the cinema, or even its use to evoke emotion. As Plantinga suggests, the issue is always one of context. This is best illustrated by the concrete example of David Lynch's use of Samuel Barber's *Adagio* in the scene in *The Elephant Man* (1980) in which the title figure, Merrick, deliberately falls asleep in a position he knows will result in his death. This is discussed by Jeff Smith in an article, 'Movie Music as Moving Music', highly relevant to this chapter. Smith writes:

Viewed as an expression of Merrick's point of view, Samuel Barber's music conveys the character's feelings of resignation and muted regret. However, the mood the scene evokes, at least in me, is sadness. This may seem like a subtle distinction, but it arises from a judgement that my own emotional response is somewhat different from that signified by the character. Merrick does not weep, sob, or display any of the other behaviours we associate with overt expressions of sadness... [W]hile the simple epithet 'sadness' seems adequate to describe my emotional state, it is inadequate for the emotions depicted within Merrick, whose situation within the film's narrative is quite a bit different from my position as a spectator. On this view, Merrick's emotional expression is a good deal more complex than my own, since it is bound up with the character's deeply held beliefs about spirituality, corporeality, dignity and morality. My own response, on the other hand, is largely an effect of the text and rests on my sympathy with the character's unhappy predicament. These judgements in turn produce a change in my physiological state (the welling of tears, a lump in the throat) that I experience as sadness.

(Smith 1999: 155)

Though this scene from *The Elephant Man* is liable to have the same tear-inducing effect as the 'Gift of a Thistle' scene, there is no compulsion to bring a charge of sentimentality against it for a number of reasons: the greater emotional complexity of the Lynch scene, the greater formal and emotional complexity of Barber's (as opposed to Horner's) music and, not least, the ideological relationship between the event and the tears it induces. A Russian writer – was it Turgenev? – has a story about a countess who weeps copious tears at a sentimental play in a warm theatre while, waiting outside for her in the bitter Russian winter, her coachman freezes to death. We all know, or ought to, the difference between appropriate and inappropriate tears. The tears we shed for a teenage Palestinian suicide bomber and her innocent Israeli victims seem appropriate (though no substitute for whatever political action we can take) while the one-dimensional, coldly manufactured tears of *Braveheart* seem more akin to those of the Russian countess.

As might be expected by the turn to feeling in the culture at large, the reawakening of interest in emotion is evident in academic fields outwith Film Studies. It is on the rise in art history, to judge by James Elkins' book *Pictures and Tears*, a work preoccupied with the loss of art works' capacity to elicit tears. In a chapter entitled 'False tears over a dead bird', Elkins discusses at length a mid-eighteenth-century painting by Jean-Baptiste Greuze, *Young Woman Who Weeps Over Her Dead Bird*, delivering an apparently harsh judgment on it:

I don't know anyone who has cried over this painting... [b]ut in the eighteenth century... people were deeply moved. At the time it seemed to be wonderfully pure and true to a child's heart. It had real innocence. People said that it had genuine affect – real emotional force – and true sentiment. We wouldn't use the same words today. What they called affect we might call affectation. What they called sentiment we would call sentimentality. What they thought was sweet, we would say is saccharine. To them, this painting was pure loveliness; to us, I'd say, it has unpleasant undertones of perversion.

(Elkins 2001: 110)

Elkins had earlier cited Anita Brookner's view that Greuze's girls are always 'on the verge of orgasm'. Nevertheless, underneath his laser-like modern sensibility there is a yearning for something he feels has been lost in the intervening two and a half centuries:

These days we resist Greuze's brand of coercion. We do not want to feel manipulated and we resent being tricked by a little girl's false tears. Greuze's eighteenth century, it seems, is very far away. We fancy ourselves more honest and sober, and less naïve. We say Greuze is maudlin… To me this is a desperate situation… We regard [eighteenth-century painting] with all the condescension of scholarship: not because we are too mature to be swayed by histrionics and melodrama (the movies prove otherwise!), but because we have stopped believing that a painting's value depends on its power to affect us. I find that sad and largely inexplicable. How did we become so callous, so full of airy sophistication and false refinement? How did we lose the desire to cry openly?

(Elkins 2001: 124–5)

As this quotation implies, Elkins tends to be harsher on cinema than on eighteenth-century art and – despite his interest in rehabilitating crying – he would probably find the 'Gift of a Thistle' sequence as maudlin as he now finds the Greuze painting. That said, a beady eye needs to be kept on the return of crying to art discourse lest key questions – such as the ideological tendency of particular works – be swept away in a flood of tears. Needless to say, however, there are works (e.g. Smith 1995) which deal sophisticatedly with both emotion and ideology.

Falsity, lack of genuineness, is at the heart of the 'Gift of a Thistle' scene, not only at the level of Horner's music, and the glycerine tears of the child William, but also in an important dimension of the pro-filmic event, the action staged for the camera. Despite the extensive discussion of *Braveheart*'s (mainly historical) falsifications, no one has seen fit to point out that the central action of this scene – Murron's plucking a thistle in order to hand it to William – would be, if not a physical impossibility, at least a highly painful activity. An enquiry to botanists at the Science Museum in London and the Royal Botanic Gardens in Edinburgh as to whether there existed a thistle that could, with impunity, be plucked produced the reply that there is a member of the thistle family that could be, but it is unrecognisable as a thistle. The thistle plucked by Murron is unambiguously a standard, spiky Scots thistle: indeed, it had to be for ideological reasons since it is this thistle which is the emblem of Scotland. A further enquiry from a member of the *Braveheart* cast who had appeared in the scene in question revealed that the thistle Murron plucked was indeed a non-spiky prop specially made for this scene. One would not wish to fetishise reality and become one of those figures who calls the BBC angrily with a single response to a complex drama – that the particular regiment depicted had five buttons rather than four on their tunics – but the principle of adherence to reality is a good one which should be set aside only for a very good reason. The reason the makers of *Braveheart* set it aside in this scene was to elicit tears and create an ideological symbol. It is worth noting that this act sets them apart from certain honourable traditions in film history.

The kind of purism which recoils from manipulating the 'real' world is to be expected from documentary traditions such as French *cinéma vérité* and American direct cinema and one would not wish to hold *Braveheart* to this standard. But, interestingly, the same concerns have been voiced in relation to fictive cinema as well. Two instances will suffice: the practice of the French critic André Bazin and of the Danish *Dogme* group of filmmakers. Bazin was an influential critic often called the father of the *Nouvelle Vogue* on account of his mentoring relationship, within the journal *Cahiers du Cinéma*, with figures such as Truffaut and Godard. Although his reputation rests equally on the massive reassessment of the American cinema, his general theory of the cinema is what is relevant here. Always tending to broach theoretical questions in terms of particular directors, Bazin divided them into two camps: those, such as DW Griffith, SM Eisenstein and Alfred Hitchcock, whose principle cinematic tool was montage, and those, such as Erich von Stroheim, Orson Welles and Jean Renoir, who left the world intact, who did not 'cut it up into pieces' but set up the camera and let the action unfold in front of it. The contradictions of Bazin's position – he had a fondness for certain kind of cinematic artifice – can be set aside in this context, the main point being his view that the central purpose of cinema was to respect the wholeness and integrity of the 'real' world. As always with Bazin, he is most interesting when discussing particular films and filmmakers, for example the films of the Italian Neo-Realists in general and those of Roberto Rossellini in particular. It was in the context of Rossellini's work that Bazin formulated the metaphor which is so much at odds with the fake thistle in *Braveheart*. In finding all the means for his art within the 'real' world, Rossellini was 'someone who crossed rivers on stepping stones provided by nature rather than by constructing an artificial bridge of bricks' (quoted in Nowell-Smith 1996: 438).

More playful, though probably no less serious, than Bazin are the Danish filmmakers who, in 1995, outraged at the economically and technologically inflated nature of, primarily Hollywood, cinema, formulated their 'Vow of Chastity' to which each agreed to adhere in his own filmmaking. Their 'manifesto' read:

1. Shooting must be done on location. Props and sets must not be brought in (if a particular prop is necessary for the story, a location must be chosen where this prop is to be found).

2. The sound must never be produced apart from the images or vice versa. (Music must not be used unless it occurs where the scene is shot.)

3. The camera must be hand-held. Any movement or immobility attainable in the hand is permitted. (The film must not take place where the camera is standing; shooting must take place where the film takes place.)

4. The film must be in colour. Special lighting is not acceptable. (If there is too little light for exposure the scene must be cut or a single lamp be attached to the camera.)

5. Optical work or filters are forbidden.

6. The film must not contain superficial action. (Murders, weapons, etc. must not occur.)

7. Temporal and geographical alienation are forbidden. (That is to say that the film takes place here and now.)

8. Genre movies are not acceptable.

9. The film format must be Academy 35mm.

10. The director must not be credited.

Furthermore, I swear as a director to refrain from creating a 'work', as I regard the instant as more important than the whole. My supreme goal is to force the truth out of my characters and settings. I swear to do so by all the means available and at the cost of any good taste and aesthetic considerations.

Thus I make my VOW OF CHASTITY.

(cited in Wood 1998: 47)

The 'vow' carries the signatures of Lars von Trier and Thomas Vinterberg, both of whom were involved in arresting films made more or less within these rules. The narratives are often strong, even melodramatic. *Festen* (1998), for example, concerns an upper-middle-class Danish family assembling to celebrate the birthday of the paterfamilias and his being accused by one of his sons of sexually abusing his children and driving one to suicide. The experience of watching *Festen* is rather like watching the script of Luchino Visconti's *The Damned* (1969) as filmed by Ken Loach. As with Bazin, the contradictions of the *Dogme* position can be set aside in this context. Clearly all the rules are the very antithesis of how *Braveheart* was made, but the first two in particular highlight the very defects in the 'Gift of a Thistle' scene discussed above.

This does not amount to a general critique of artifice in the cinema or to the suggestion that all films should be made within the aesthetics of Bazin or *Dogme*, but it does raise questions about the morality of the 'Gift of a Thistle' scene. Up to now, accusations of falsity have been made only against *Braveheart*'s handling of history. The charge needs to be extended to its aesthetics as well. In addition to 'falsity' the conception of 'sentimentality' has been central to the argument of this chapter. In the light of the charges made against *Braveheart* in Chapter 9, it is fitting to recall the words of Carl Gustav Jung – 'sentimentality is the superstructure erected on brutality'.

8

'That's Show Business!' The 'What' and 'Why' of *Braveheart*'s Historical Distortions

As soon as histories are properly told there is no more need of
romances
Walt Whitman

Much of the derision *Braveheart* has elicited relates to the
grossness of its historical distortions, for instance its giving
Wallace a sexual liaison with Princess Isabelle, in which he
impregnates her with the future King Edward III, when it is known
that she came to England from France three years after Wallace's
death and that her child was born seven years after that again.
Scrutiny of reviews and features about the film reveals a curiously
recurrent trope relating to its handling of history:

> [T]he film includes 'a lovely French Princess of Wales… who in
> reality probably didn't have the opportunity for clandestine kiss-
> ups with Wallace… but that's showbusiness'.
>
> *(Premiere)*

> [T]his is a Hollywood epic and not a documentary about
> revolution; and William Wallace owes more to Errol Flynn than

he does to Che Guevara.... It might be a dodgy history lesson, but it's riveting cinema.

(Film West)

Edward II's lover is thrown to his death from a window by... Edward I. This never actually happened... but then who expects a historical epic to be gospel?

(Village Voice)

Historians will no doubt tear *Braveheart* apart... But it is not intended as a history lesson, any more than Shakespeare's *Macbeth* was.

(Scotsman)

[Y]ou could quibble for a century about Gibson's view of the past... He is out to make a movie that will sell.

(Guardian)

The film's inaccuracies have inflamed the usual bevy of historians... To be honest, the historians can keep their history... In this film, history boils down to just one thing, hunkiness. *Braveheart* is all about Gibson.

(Sunday Times)

What I find most wearismome, however, is the bellyaching of those who are upset over the film's lack of historical accuracy... What do they expect? This is Hollywood, not a BBC documentary.

(Scotland on Sunday)

One presumes that the writers of these lines – for the most part professional (often film) journalists – would not approve of consciously relaying falsity or, to put it more bluntly, *lying*, in 'real' life. How then have they come to accept that facts which are generally known or, at least, relatively easily ascertainable, may be wantonly flouted in films dealing with history? The answer they offer in the above quotations – 'it's show business' or 'it's Hollywood' – is often delivered indignantly as if 'the usual bevy of historians' were being unreasonable in pointing out the lies. The position of these writers is both ethically and intellectually suspect, ethically for its endorsement of lying and intellectually for its failure to make itself aware of the protocols which have been fashioned by historians for dealing with the interface between film and history.

Robert Rosenstone is a professional historian who has reflected at some length on the question, having himself acted as historical consultant on a documentary film, *The Good Fight* (1984) – about the Abraham Lincoln Battalion of the International Brigade during the Spanish Civil War – and on a fiction film, *Reds* (1981), Warren Beatty's biopic about John Reed, American communist and author of *Ten Days That Shook The World*. His account of his experience with both these projects is contained in his book *Visions of the Past: The Challenge of Film to Our Idea of History*, which also enunciates a protocol which the makers of *Braveheart* – and their diverse apologists cited above – might have benefited from. Rosenstone reserves his warmest approbation for those films – for example, Chris Marker's *Sans Soleil* (1982) and Alex Cox's *Walker* (1987) – which he describes as displaying some at least of what he calls a 'postmodern' view of history and historiography. Rosenstone writes:

> What do those 'real' postmodern films do to the past? Lots of things: (1) Tell the past self-reflexively, in terms of how it means to the filmmaker historian. (2) Recount it from a multiplicity of viewpoints. (3) Eschew traditional narrative, with its beginning, middle and end – or, following Jean-Luc Godard, insist that these three elements need not necessarily be in that order. (4) Forsake normal story development, or tell stories but refuse to take the telling seriously. (5) Approach the past with humour, parody, and absurdist, surrealist, dadaesque and other irreverent attitudes. (6) Intermix contradictory elements – past and present, drama and documentary – and indulge in creative anachronism. (7) Accept, even glory in, their own selectivity, partialism, partisanship, and rhetorical character. (8) Refuse to focus or sum up the meaning of past events, but instead make sense of them in a partial and open-ended, rather than totalised manner. (9) Alter and invent incident and character. (10) Utilise fragmentary or poetic knowledge. (11) Never forget that the present is the site of all past representation and knowing.
>
> *(Rosenstone 1995: 206–207)*

Clearly, by celebrating those features, Rosenstone is implicitly attacking 'illusionist' historical films, those films – like *Braveheart* – which, in their own form, conceal the fact that they are offering a representation of the past from the standpoint of the present by evacuating all signs of the present from the film or rendering them 'invisible' by subordinating them to character and narrative.

That said, Rosenstone is not wholly censorious of mainline historical narrative films such as *Braveheart*. However, he does subject them to rigorous historical protocols without forgetting that they are not primarily acts of historiography. In particular, he makes the crucial distinction between 'false invention' and 'true invention', the difference between them being that the former 'ignores the discourse of history' and the latter 'engages the discourse of history'. He illustrates this by reference to two contrasting films: *Mississippi Burning* (1988) – about the FBI investigation into the murder of three civil rights workers in the American South in the 1960s – and *Glory* (1989) – about a regiment of black Union Army soldiers in the American Civil War. Rosenstone points out that *Mississippi Burning*:

> Taking for its heroes two FBI men… marginalises blacks and insists though they are victims of racism, they had in fact little to do with their own voting rights drive. The resulting message is that the government protected African Americans and played a major role in the voter registration drive of Freedom Summer. Yet this is palpably untrue. This story simply excludes too much of what we already know about Mississippi Freedom Summer and the rather belated actions of the FBI to solve the murder of the three civil rights workers. [Rosenstone cites in a footnote several historical works which bear out his argument.] The central message of that summer, as responsible historians have shown, was not simply that blacks were oppressed, but that they worked as a community to alleviate their own oppression. This is the theme that the film chooses to ignore. By focusing on the actions of fictional FBI agents, the film engages in 'false invention' and must be judged as bad history. Indeed, by marginalising African Americans in the story of their own struggle, the film seems to reinforce the racism it ostensibly combats.
>
> *(Rosenstone 1995: 72–73)*

So indulgent has the wider community – particularly those who make and write about films – become in relation to historical lying in the cinema that the director of *Mississippi Burning*, Alan Parker – challenged in a tv discussion about the kind of argument Rosenstone was making (an argument widely articulated in the black community in Britain as well as in the USA) – appeared not to understand what was at stake. It should be perfectly acceptable to make Rosenstone's kind of criticism of the film and at the same time celebrate its considerable pleasures, most notably the sharpness of the writing and the excellence of the playing, particularly of the actors who play the FBI agents, Gene Hackman and Willem Dafoe, their characters brilliantly conceived to be dramatic opposites: Hackman's a laid-back Southern ex-sheriff who knows the terrain and handles racial questions with discretion, and Dafoe's a tight-arsed, Bobby Kennedy-type Yankee who charges in and makes things worse for the blacks he is so intent on helping. It is precisely those kinds of nuanced responses that the quotations at the start of this chapter close off.

Contrasting *Glory* with *Mississippi Burning*, Rosenstone outlines how the former alters, compresses and invents history but in such a way that does not contradict what is already known by historians. For instance, *Glory* suggests that the 54th Massachusetts Regiment – the actual historical unit represented in the film – were ex-slaves when, as is known, they had been freemen before the war began. Rosenstone feels this alteration to have been historically justifiable since 'it serves to bring the particular experience of this unit into line with larger experience of African-Americans in the Civil War'. With regard to historical compression, Rosenstone describes how *Glory*, instead of deriving its characters from existing regimental histories, concentrates on four invented characters – Rosenstone calls them 'stereotypes', but without the usual negative connotation that term carries – the country boy, the wise older man, the angry black nationalist and the Northern intellectual. He regards this compression as also historically justifiable since:

> these four men stand for the various possible positions that blacks could take towards the Civil War and the larger issues of racism and black-white relations, topics that are not solely 'historical' – or that, like all historical topics, involve an interpenetration of past and present.
>
> *(Rosenstone 1995: 74)*

With regard to direct invention, Rosenstone discusses an incident in the film in which the black troops are refused boots by a racist Union Army quartermaster, ostensibly on the grounds that the regiment will not be used in battle, but really because he hates blacks and does not think them fit for combat. As Rosenstone indicates, there is no evidence that such an incident ever took place, but he does see the invention as entirely in accord with the Northern racism well documented in other sources, a good example of the 'true invention' he regards as historiographically warrantable.

In his discussion of *Glory*'s concentration on the four invented characters, Rosenstone speaks of them as '[creating] a range of possibilities for tension and conflict that will reveal character and change'. By making this point, he indicates that, unlike many historians, he understands the workings of classical narrative cinema, which he does not see as wholly incompatible with a responsible attitude to history. As it happens, those historians who have most forcefully denounced *Braveheart*'s historical shortcomings have tended to be rather less appreciative of what cinema might bring to the understanding of history. The American medieval historian, Sharon L Krossa, referring to *Braveheart* as 'That Film Whose Name Shall Not Be Uttered', writes:

> Basically, as a historian, my opinion of *Braveheart* is that it is a work of fantasy, not history. Any resemblance to actual persons or events, in other words to real history, appears to be purely accidental. My best advice, for anyone interested in the real story of William Wallace, Robert Bruce, and the Scottish Wars of Independence, is not to believe *anything,* whether major or minor, depicted in the film, but instead read some reliable history books about the period.
>
> *(Krossa 1997)*

A considerable debt of gratitude is due to those historians who have brought their knowledge and insights to bear on *Braveheart* and revealed its historical shortcomings. In a sense, however, they are, like Dr Krossa, telling only half the story. To go back to the quotations which opened this chapter, it was suggested that they amount more or less to an endorsement of lying. Without letting the writers wholly off the hook on this point, one can offer a more charitable reading to the effect that the quotations reflect the exasperation of one group of professionals, concerned with the economic and aesthetic structures of cinema, at the apparent blindness of another set of professionals, the historians, to the existence and force of these structures. Undoubtedly they have a point. To run together rather crudely questions of economic organisation, narrative structure and audience composition, it might be said that anyone producing a mainline, Hollywood-style, classical narrative film is required to emerge with a product which delivers on several fronts. Virtually *every* such film is built to the following structure: in the main plot – there are usually several sub-plots and there may be a prologue and epilogue – an initial state of affairs is disrupted when a drastic change occurs in the life of the central protagonist creating thereby in him or her an intense need which often has both internal and external dimensions (for example, catching the man who killed a relative and overcoming a personal shortcoming such as alcoholism). The protagonist's need(s) are blocked by a powerful antagonist with whom the protagonist will struggle, sometimes gaining, sometimes losing, the advantage until a new state of affairs, a new equilibrium, is reached with the closure of the narrative and (usually) the triumph of the protagonist. This is the basic narrative template from which all mainline narrative films, irrespective of genre, from horror movies through to romantic comedies, are constructed.

Holding this template against *Braveheart*, there is a prologue (Wallace's childhood) and an epilogue (Bruce at Bannockburn), a central protagonist (Wallace), an initial equilibrium (Wallace's return to Scotland and his marriage to Murron), a disruption of this equilibrium (Murron's murder and the assault on Scotland) creating intense needs in Wallace, an internal need (to avenge Murron's murder) and an external one (to rid Scotland of the English), a powerful antagonist (King Edward) against whom the protagonist struggles, sometimes gaining the advantage (the Battle of Stirling Bridge), sometimes losing it (the Battle of Falkirk) and eventually triumphing (symbolically rather than actually, since Wallace dies) with narrative closure after the epilogue (the Battle of Bannockburn) which will seal Scotland's independence. The several subplots include Wallace's relationships with Isabelle, with Bruce and with the Scottish lords. Within this basic narrative structure common to all genres, the question of genre specificity comes into play. Posing as a historical epic – or possibly a historical biopic – *Braveheart* is required to deliver *spectacle*, which it does primarily in the battle scenes. But the stability/ disruption/new stability – traced through the protagonist/antagonist opposition – is not the only required element that a mainline Hollywoodean movie must deliver. It has been estimated that between 80 and 90 per cent of such films involve heterosexual love relationships, sometimes the 'meat' of the film, as in romantic comedies, sometimes more secondary. In *Braveheart* this is carried initially in the Wallace/ Murron relationship and, when she dies, in the Wallace/Isabelle coupling. The third absolute requirement that films of this type must deliver is an ideological position congenial to its primary audience, the (mainly 17–25 age group) filmgoers in the USA and the 'western democracies', which means variants of populism. It is no accident that the keyword of *Braveheart* is 'freedom' and of *Rob Roy* 'honour' – who could dissent from these! These three features – classic narrative, heterosexual love and congenial ideology – are the base requirements of (virtually) every classical Hollywoodean narrative film. They have been separated out here for analytic reasons, for they are very much interpenetrated in particular films. For instance, the first two categories carry ideological implications as well. To construct a narrative round a single main protagonist is to suggest not only that personal identities are whole and unfractured (an idea increasingly questioned), but that history is made primarily by individuals rather than by, say, classes and institutions. Similarly, to insist on the centrality of heterosexual love is to imply that celibacy or same-sex love is non-normative. *Braveheart*, of course, goes very much further than this, constructing homosexual love as aberrant, which caused the film to be picketed in several American cities by the Gay and Lesbian Alliance Against Defamation.

To the exasperation of the journalists cited at the start of this chapter, it is the above three requirements – pristinely embodied in *Braveheart* – that many professional historians are either blind to or accord minimal importance. Sharon Krossa, for example, has produced an analysis of the first two and a half minutes of *Braveheart* in which she lists no fewer than 18 historical errors with, it has to be said, little indication that what she is analysing is a classic, Hollywoodean narrative-fiction film pitched at a popular audience rather than a historical monograph aimed at professional historians. Needless to say, this is not to *excuse Braveheart*'s historical distortions (as some journalists are wont to do), rather to *explain* them. Historians need to ask themselves what there is in the Hollywood production and consumption milieux which virtually *requires* its films to manipulate history, not always irresponsibly, as Robert Rosenstone has demonstrated. By drawing on the above outline of the structural nature of the Hollywood fiction film and Rosenstone's concepts of 'true invention' and 'false invention', it should be possible to identify the likely causes of *Braveheart*'s historical 'errors' and to judge which are permissible and which impermissible in a more nuanced way than has been the practice hereto. As Jeffrey Richards (Richards 1998) has pointed out, there is an additional factor connected with *Braveheart* which further impels it to historical distortion – its script having leaned heavily on the 1470s poem *Wallace* by the minstrel Blind Harry. Richards mentions the Bruce's participation on the English side at the Battle of Falkirk and Wallace's sack of York as but two of Blind Harry's inventions which found their way into Randall Wallace's script. However, even Blind Harry's inventions can be subject to Rosenstone's protocols, being acceptable if not contradicted by existing, source-related historiography.

23. The necessity of Hollywood dramaturgy.
The liaison between Wallace (Mel Gibson) and
Princess Isabelle (Sophie Marceau). FALSE INVENTION. Backlighting,
the cinematic code for romance.

DISTORTION	REASON	COMMENT
1. Setting the opening of the film – and therefore implying its action takes place – in the West Highlands and not the Central Lowlands.	The Scottish Discursive Unconscious. The filmmakers (and their primary audiences) live within the dominant narrative of Scotland as highland. Mountains and lochs are part of the international iconography of 'Scottishness'.	It would be optimistic to expect the lay audience (including filmmakers) to give a damn about the highland/lowland distinction. This is a a less serious 'error' than the manipulation of historically verified dates.
2. Title: 'Scotland 1280 A.D.' Narrator: 'I shall tell you of William Wallace... The King of Scotland had died without a son and the King of England, a cruel pagan known as Edward the Longshanks, claimed the throne for himself'.	The filmmakers' structural priority is to begin the construction of Wallace's anatagonist, Edward I, as unremittingly evil, by suggesting a lengthy, though non-existent, period of English oppression, incarnated in Edward.	Some form of simplification of the very complex Scots polity of the 1280s and 1290s was obviously necessary, but the film seriously distorts events to demonise Edward and the English generally. King Alexander III of Scotland, and his two sons, were alive in 1280. It was 1286 before all were dead. Edward, who was Christian, not pagan, claimed the throne only in 1296, and then only after a period of complex *political*, not military instability. FALSE INVENTION.
3. The Scots are clad in tartan kilts despite there being no evidence that (particularly Lowland) Scots wore tartan or kilts in the 13th century.	Scottish Discursive Unconscious. Kilts and tartan are part of what the filmmakers and their primary audiences would think of as Scottish.	Again, it would be optimistic to expect this to concern non-Scots.
4. Wallace's family are shown as poor subsistence farmers despite his father being a land-holding knight and are clad, almost literally, in rags.	The reason is ideological. As well as operating in terms of the binary opposition English/Scots – the national opposition – it operates in terms of upper/lower – the class opposition.	Unlike many historical films, *Braveheart* had no historical adviser, a serious omission which aggravated the the question of historical distortion and might suggest that the filmmakers were aware that their

ideological project
was incompatible
with historical
accuracy.

5. Edward's hanging of the Scots knights and their pages, having called them for a truce, in the the 1280s and William's catching sight of the dangling bodies.

Classical narrative cinema often operates in terms of a 'hook', a dramatic, often violent incident. It also provides psychological motivation – another important feature of this kind of cinema – for Wallace's struggle.

Apart from the date of this event, it might be argued that this is precisely the kind of incident (a Blind Harry invention) which might have occurred post-1296. TRUE INVENTION.

6. The construction of the English and the Scots nobility as fundamentally different – Scots in animal skins, English in fine cloth, London as stone city, Edinburgh as wooden fort – despite all the evidence pointing to their similarity, interpenetration and common Anglo-Norman heritage.

The reason is both ideological and drama-turgical. The Scots must be shown as underdogs and must therefore be visibly different from the English. Lurking beneath this is another ideology that the Scots are 'Celtic'.

It would be difficult to invoke 'true invention' regarding particularly the representation of medieval Edinburgh when so much is known about its similarity to medieval London.

7. The deployment of the concept of *jus primae noctis*, despite its never having been established as existing.

The reason is dramaturgical. By making this an explicit policy of Edward's, the sexual harassment of Scots women by English soldiers can be presented as his calculating villainy.

If the term *'prima nocte'* (as the film calls it) were not used the individual acts of sexual harassment might plausibly be TRUE INVENTION.

8. The evacuation from the film of Wallace's co-Guardian of Scotland – Sir Andrew Moray.

The cause is ideological and dramaturgical. Moray's being a knight might have been problematic for the film's populism and its traducing of the spineless Scots nobility. Also, in dramaturgical terms, Wallace could not share 'top billing' with another character.

Omissions tend to escape attention, unlike visible distortions. FALSE INVENTION.

9. The evacuation from the film of the flaying of the body of the English commander, Hugh de Cressingham, after the Battle of Stirling Bridge, and Wallace's wearing of the skin – alluded to in several sources.

The reason is ideological. Wallace's ferocity is constructed as the product of righteous anger, difficult to square with the skinning of a dead enemy.

The omission suggests that the film's ideologies may be in conflict. Bathed in 'Dark Ageist' cruelty and gore elsewhere, the film had to draw the line here to allow free passage to the dominant discourse

		of Wallace as honourable hero.
10. The creation of an Irish fighter, Stephen, as one of Wallace's senior aides and the prominence given to the Irish at the Battle of Falkirk.	Two separate ideologies are at play here. The first is Celticism which sees the Irish and the Scots as virtually identical and relates to making the film easier to understand in America. The colonial confrontation between Britain and Ireland is better understood there than the less unambiguously colonialist English/Scottish relationship.	Perhaps more than any other feature of the film, this reminds us that *Braveheart* is more about the world it is made in than the world it represents. In fact, the Welsh were more important in this battle than the Irish. Although, like the Irish, they are Celts, there is no significant Welsh diaspora in the primary market for the film, the USA.
11. The leprosy of Bruce's father.	This has two functions, one ideological, the other dramaturgical. It renders visible the 'Dark Ageism' discourse, since disfiguring disease is one of its tropes. Its dramaturgical function is as a metaphor for the father's moral decay.	This seems like an acceptable piece of TRUE INVENTION, since it is not contradicted by the sources.
12. Bruce's political trimming and his presence at the Battle of Falkirk.	The main reason is dramaturgical. In order to emerge as Wallace's 'heir' – the meaning of the epilogue – Bruce must begin here to be constructed as loyal to Wallace.	The film's account of Bruce's political weathervaning is one of the few historical accuracies of the film and hence, in its various instances, constitutes TRUE INVENTION. However, having him actually present at the battle is wanton since the sources confirm that he was elsewhere on that day.
13. Evacuation from the film of the known fact that Wallace's levies were raised by conscription with the hanging of resisters.	This is suppressed for ideological reasons, forced enlistment being incompatible with the film's construction of Wallace as 'man of the people'.	By omitting this, the filmmakers missed the chance to make Wallace's character more complex.
14. Evacuation from the film of the known fact of Wallace's having	This too is suppressed for ideological reasons as	The film's showing Wallace as having no

sued for peace.

being incompatible with the 'true to the death' construction of Wallace.

strategy after Falkirk contradicts the earlier indications – dinned into him by his father and uncle – that 'it's our wits that make us men'.

15. Dwarves amusing the crowd before the execution by miming Wallace's castration and drawing.

The physical grotesquerie of the dwarves expreses the Dark Ages discourse.

This should be seen as TRUE INVENTION since it confirms what is known from other sources about the carnivalesque quality of (medieval) public executions.

16. Rendering the deaths of Wallace and Edward as contemporaneous, despite Edward's dying two years after Wallace.

This is enacted solely for dramaturgical reasons, classical Hollywood narrative demanding that all 'loose' ends are tied up to arrive at a new stability and narrative closure.

The general problem remains for *Braveheart* that – since the lives of prominent historical figures are well documented – moving around the dates of their deaths (and other important facts about lives) inevitably is exposed as FALSE INVENTION.

24. The dwarves mime Wallace's execution.
TRUE INVENTION.

As indicated above, this is not a comprehensive attack on *Braveheart*'s historical errors and omissions, still less an attempt to excuse them. It is an attempt to explain how the systemic pressures of the Hollywood milieu – pressures relating to economic targets, aesthetic and ideological norms and audience expectations – combine to produce the mindset wherein accuracy to known historical facts becomes secondary to delivering the normative product. That said, not every departure from fact is of the same degree of seriousness and some may, indeed, dramatically intensify in a wholly responsible way the known facts. A protocol such as Rosenstone's false invention/ true invention binary, fair to both historians and filmmakers, could produce a more nuanced response to historical films but it is probably optimistic to expect an early ceasefire between these groups. As the example of Alan Parker – confronted with the response of historians and the black community to *Mississippi Burning* – makes clear, filmmakers may be unconscious of the ideological implications of their own films. *Braveheart* embodies this in a particularly lethal form, as the final chapter demonstrates.

9

It Takes One To Know One: *Braveheart*'s Appeal to the Proto-Fascist Psyche

> In every mythology the hero is an exceptional being, but in the Ur-Fascist ideology heroism is the norm. This cult of heroism is closely connected to the cult of death: there is nothing accidental about the fact that the motto of the Falangists was 'Viva la muerte!'
>
> *Umberto Eco*

Although *Braveheart* has been reported as inspirational to genuinely oppressed groups resisting control from outside their own self-defined formations – the Chechens in their struggle against the Russian Federation being perhaps the most dramatic example – a much more widespread phenomenon is the extent to which it has become talismanic for the extreme Right, often groups who, being historically privileged, now imagine themselves victims defending the citadel of 'civilisation' against rampaging hordes of leftists, liberals, feminists, Jews, homosexuals, Muslims and diverse people of colour. References to *Braveheart* abound in the speeches of Umberto Bossi, leader of the Italian Northern League, the main political aim of which is to secede from Italy and set up the state of Padania which would exclude, in particular, southern Italians whom leaguers see as 'Africans' retarding the energetic 'European' north. *Braveheart* also circulates extensively in the rhetoric of Pat Buchanan, extreme rightwing candidate for the United States presidency, and in that of his supporters such as televangelist Pat Robertson, and has been described by a southern anti-racist organisation as having 'risen to the status of mythology in the minds of America's [Ku Klux] Klansmen'. Hitler has been described on a neo-Nazi website as 'a twentieth century Braveheart' and one of the 50 or so German neo-Nazi rock bands, *Landser* (whose members have been arrested by the German authorities on account of their membership of the banned neo-fascist organisation Blood and Honour) has incorporated part of James Horner's score for *Braveheart* into its album *Rebell* and speaks of itself as wishing 'to provide the soundtrack for the Aryan revolution'. References to the film crop up in the utterances of some anti-immigrant groups in the Republic of Ireland and *Apologetics* – a mainline Christian website which, among other things, monitors the lunatic fringes of Christianity – has noted that 'the secular movie *Braveheart* has been embraced by many within the Toronto Blessing Movement – as they claim – illustrative of the spiritual warfare they feel called to'. It has even been suggested that one of the practices of the Movement – warrior anointing – may derive from *Braveheart* and:

> is said to bring 'deliverance from your enemies'. The visible effects of the receiving of this 'anointing' include roaring, shouting and grasping the hands above the head, then swinging them up and down as if one was actually holding a sword and attacking an enemy... Interestingly, many in the renewal and revival movements embraced the movie *Braveheart* in which they claimed to see spiritual significance.

All of the foregoing provides anecdotal evidence that *Braveheart* has proved to be most congenial to (neo-)fascist and other groups on the extreme right of the political spectrum. Can it therefore justly be called a fascist film? The answer is, of course, it depends what is meant by 'fascist'. Despite possible flickers of recognition relating to *some* aspects of fascism, *Braveheart* could scarcely be said to display consistently what Noël O'Sullivan has described as 'the fascist *weltanschaung*':

National aggrandisement, the concept of corporatism [roughly, the attempted elision of contradictions between the major forces in the social formation], the idea of permanent revolution, the cult of despotic leadership, and an ideal of self-sufficiency leading inevitably to a programme of world conquest.

(O'Sullivan 1983: back cover)

However, the term 'fascist' might reasonably be applied to *Braveheart* if given a psychological rather than a political/sociological meaning. Its psychological closeness to fascism is evident in what within that movement attracted Robert Brasillach, a French journalist and film historian turned German collaborator who was executed by the French after the Second World War:

poetic images of young men camping around fires at night, of mass meetings, of heroic exploits of the past.

(cited in O'Sullivan 1983: 5)

Traditional, including Marxist, analyses of fascism have tended to stress social and economic rather than psychological factors: economic collapse, the impoverishment of formerly comfortable bourgeois citizens, some of whom then joined the resentful cadres of rightwing militias; and the forsaking of democratic parties by the immiserated bourgeoisie and by other groups similarly affected, such as the petit-bourgeoisie and the peasant farmers. The overall situation was aggravated by the collapse of profits and by capitalism's ensuring that the working class bore the brunt of the collapse in terms of reduced wages and benefits and unemployment. To be sure, there had been Marxist attempts – most notably by Adorno and others of the Frankfurt School in their exploration of 'the authoritarian personality' – to address the psychology of fascism, work which is still relevant today, but it is only relatively recently that close attention has been paid to the centrality of the kind of 'poetic images' Brasillach refers to and their productivity in the manufacture of the fascist personality.

The most substantial work in this tradition is Klaus Theweleit's *Male Fantasies*. It is impossible adequately to summarise a work of such scope, density and allusiveness, but the core of Theweleit's method was to search for the contours of the proto-fascist personality primarily in the letters, diaries and novels (read and sometimes written) by members of the *Freikorps*, a body consisting mainly of rural and gentrified ex-soldiers who, burning with anger, humiliation and resentment, returned to Germany from the First World War fit for nothing but waging war and continued to do just that, against other fierce nationalisms in Central Europe, against communists on the same terrain and against the German working class on their own soil. These were the men who would go on to play the most active roles within National Socialist formations such as the SA and the SS. Obersturmbannfuhrer Rudolf Höss, commandant of Auschwitz and a leading architect in the destruction of the Jews, was an archetypal *Freikorps* figure. The *Freikorps* men were effectively making war from 1914 to 1945, a warrior caste who saw themselves as precisely that. What Theweleit found most centrally in the utterances and fantasies of the *Freikorps* men was a dread of psychic disintegration, which they associated particularly with the *feminine*. Their male self-image had therefore to be armoured (sometimes literally) with fanatical discipline against 'feminine' qualities such as softness, weakness, intimacy and sensuality. Some psychoanalytic and feminist traditions would see this simply as a totally unbridled version of 'normal' masculinity. For the *Freikorps* men, the only permissible joy and union with other bodies was in waging war. Needless to say, such an anti-feminine psychic orientation was in no way incompatible with the distant veneration of certain kinds of women: 'virginal' mothers, wives, sisters and the 'white nurses' who tended their wounds. As Theweleit reveals, however, a particular form of *Freikorps* dread was of 'red women', exemplified by the brutal murder by *Freikorps* soldiers of Rosa Luxemburg, who was both communist and Jewish. It might plausibly be argued that unfettered masculinity is at the very core of *all* fascisms. It is hinted at in the flags, the parades, the disciplined phalanxes of men, the uniforms, the leather boots and belts and, often, the steel of helmets and weapons. It becomes more explicit in the puffed-out chest and jutting jaw of Mussolini and in the somewhat more restrained body language of Hitler: the spring in the step, the clutched belt buckle and, above all, the snatching of the air at the end of his Nazi salute, especially when reviewing parades. It is not just for rhetorical effect that Barbara Spackman entitles her study of aspects of Italian fascism *Fascist Virilities*. There is a newsreel of a parade in Nazi Germany and among the foreign formations is a single Spanish Falangist whose feet, when he goosesteps, reach eye level. It is an image of exultant masculinity which provokes laughter and shudders simultaneously.

While Klaus Theweleit probes deeply into one aspect of (proto-) fascism, Umberto Eco's essay 'Ur-Fascism' is a more general account of the elements which underpin diverse fascisms, although he draws many of his examples from the Italian fascism he was brought up within. Interestingly, in the context of this chapter, Eco points to a fascination with Celtic mythology as being, if not part of 'official' fascism, certainly a preoccupation of some of its ideologues. Among the features of Ur-Fascism – though these may be characteristic of other kinds of despotisms and tyrannies as well – Eco identifies the cult of tradition, the toleration of contradictions, a commitment to irrationalism (and a consequent suspicion of intellectual activity), a hatred of dissent, fear of difference, xenophobia, an obsession with conspiracies, scorn for the weak, the cult of heroism and martyrdom, *machismo*, and a recurrent address to 'the people'. In the light of both Theweleit and Eco, *Braveheart* might be seen as a kind of modern analogue of the *Freikorps* texts, a farrago of partial, contradictory proto-fascist impulses largely below the consciousness of the film's makers, a source of immediate appeal to neo- and crypto-fascists and a focus for the energy of testosterone-fuelled young men in many societies who, given the correct socio-economic conditions, such as are described by the classic analysts, would provide the foot soldiers of any neo-fascist movement.

But surely, it might be countered, the dread of the feminine Theweleit focuses on is immediately contradicted by the importance of heterosexual love in *Braveheart*, to the extent of its manufacturing a historically impossible liaison between Wallace and Isabelle. However, the *Freikorps* texts – unlike Hollywood movies – were under no obligation to include and valorise heterosexual love. When it is argued that *Braveheart*'s proto-fascism is partial and contradictory, articulated with other elements deriving from narrative protocols and audience expectations, it is in the full awareness and expectation that heterosexual love will figure in it, as it does in 80 per cent plus of other Hollywood movies. But is heterosexual love or, putting it in wider terms, the *feminine* quite so central to *Braveheart*? William Luhr has pointed out the curious absence of *mothers* from the film, the only one being that of Murron. All the major male characters who might be reasonably expected, given their ages, to have had

25. *Braveheart*'s motherless warriors: Stephen (David O'Hara),
Wallace (Mel Gibson) and Hamish (Brendan Gleeson).

mothers are, in fact, motherless: Wallace himself, even as a child;
Hamish, Wallace's childhood friend and, as adult, his key lieutenant;
Robert Bruce; and the future King Edward II. Theweleit also
describes his *Freikorps* men as 'not being fully born', a condition in
which the mother (or her absence) is central, the condition being
produced by the 'extremes' of mothering, that is by the withdrawal
of nurturing or the son's pathological attachment to the mother,
there being no necessary incompatibility between the two. Elsewhere,
Theweleit describes his *Freikorps* men as – in a phrase that fits the
males of *Braveheart* like a glove – 'motherless children'. Theweleit
raises the question that, for the rigid, emotionally-armoured *Freikorps*
warriors, threatened by maternal warmth and tenderness, 'are the
only good mothers dead mothers?'. All the motherless *Braveheart*
males, on the other hand, not only have on-screen *fathers*, but have
intense relationships with them. It is these fathers who harden, or
attempt to harden, their sons, to 'make men' of them – a phrase
which recurs in the film. The world of *Braveheart*, then, is a male
world: a world of warriors. What then of the heterosexual love which
is so widely taken to be so manifestly 'there' on the screen. In a film
lasting nearly two and three quarter hours, Wallace's screen time
with Murron amounts to under 15 minutes and with Isabelle, under
six minutes. As Luhr puts it, 'the few women visible in the film…

really exist as implements by which men inflict pain on other men' (Luhr 1999: 244). The great bulk of the remaining screen time shows males talking politics with each other, plotting against each other and humiliating, torturing and killing each other. A male warrior world indeed, homosocial if not homoerotic. Though not manifestly apparent in *Braveheart*, the linking of violence to homoeroticism is another recurrent trope of Theweleit's *Freikorps* texts. However, anyone who doubts the phallic nature of *Braveheart*'s warriorism should look at the function of 'the long spears' in the Battle of Falkirk sequence, at the sexual banter which surrounds them, and at how the provocation of the English enemy is sexualised by the Scots displaying their genitalia and buttocks. Wallace's immense, two-handed sword has a similar, if less explicit, function in the film. The original recently fetched £277,000 at auction and replicas of it can be bought. Is it too far-fetched to speculate that this may represent a desperate attempt to sustain the film's phallicism by, literally, inheriting the Phallus.

What is it then that the proto-fascist most dreads? If, again following Theweleit, it is psychic and physical disintegration and, to make explicit Theweleit's psychoanalytic paradigm, *castration*, is it entirely coincidental that this is what happens to Wallace (as, indeed, to his

26. *Braveheart*'s phallicism: the long spears.

real historical counterpart) at the end of *Braveheart*? Scots schoolboys learn, with morbid relish, that Wallace – with Robert Bruce the principal national hero – was taken by the dastardly English and was hanged, drawn and quartered (the castration bit tends to be omitted) and his various body pieces displayed on the battlements of towns up and down the realm. Psychic and physical disintegration? If what happened to Wallace is not the re-enactment of the *Freikorps* nightmare, what is? *Braveheart* certainly makes a meal of the execution (the sequence lasts for 11 minutes), even to the extent of performing a striptease with the ghastly implements used, although even *Braveheart* draws the line at representing the quartering. William Luhr explains the extent and nature of the execution sequence in terms of the conservative masculinity which he rightly sees as underpinning the film and how that impulse is rendered in terms of the tradition of Christian masochism (the clear references to the Crucifixion and the relentless concentration on Wallace's suffering in the *mise-en-scène*) which he relates to other Gibson pictures such as *The Man Without a Face* (1993) and to Gibson's own well-documented Christian conservatism. Without discounting Luhr's reading, one might see the masochism of the execution scene as the necessary binary opposite of the sadism implicit in the film's phallicism, the acting out of the nightmare of what it means literally to lose control of one's body. This view, which is operating at the level of the film's (and the filmmakers') unconscious, is in no way contradicted by the film's conscious construction of Wallace's torment as the price that has to be paid for the creation of the exclusive, bounded body of the nation. This is a price which Theweleit's *Freikorps* men would certainly have regarded as worth paying. *Braveheart*'s Rottweiler masculinity has been noted by several critics, including James R Keller in his 'Masculinity and Marginality in *Rob Roy* and *Braveheart*'. Keller's piece is simultaneously a persuasive analysis of the heterosexual/homosexual binarism of both films and an object lesson in the limitations of identity politics. Preoccupied exclusively with the homophobia of *Rob Roy* and *Braveheart*, Keller misses the chance to relate resistance to homophobia to wider questions, specifically the anti-fascist struggle.

Up to this point, *Braveheart*'s embodiment of and appeal to the proto-fascist psyche has largely been asserted rather than demonstrated. The most substantial evidence for this is its appropriation by rightwing political formations in the USA, but retaining the connection with Scotland in the extent to which many of these formations have an imaginary relationship with Scotland or with Celticism more generally. Just as one of the major groups to have embraced *Braveheart* within Scotland, the Wallace Clan Trust, has done so within a vocabulary of battle, war and warriorism, so too have these North American formations operated within the same terms. When a number of press reports appeared in the period 1997–98 outlining the extent to which *Braveheart* had been appropriated by extreme (sometimes illegal) rightwing groups, particularly in the USA, and how the film had re-energised the mythic connections many such groups make with Scotland, many erstwhile enthusiasts for *Braveheart* expressed surprise and horror and were quick to argue that it was not *Braveheart*'s fault that it had been put to such uses. The argument of this chapter is that it is *precisely* the fault of the film that it has been so appropriated, its proto-fascism being woven (largely unconsciously) into the warp and woof of the project. Despite the account which must be taken of the concept of 'active audience', constructing rather than passively ingesting films, that construction must be made out of *something*. The building blocks with which to erect the fascist redoubt are scattered throughout *Braveheart*. Senior figures in the Scottish National Party will confess off the record that the party's relentless exploitation of the film was a tactical error, quite apart from being morally and aesthetically blind. Like many decent, pragmatic nationalists before them, they have learned that they are riding a tiger. A modicum of European history might have told them that before the fact, and a passing acquaintance with American history might have alerted them to the poisonous brew distilled when Scotland is mixed with things American, particularly relating to the American South. This is exemplified by accounts of the death of William Pierce, the extreme rightwing American ideologue, whose writings are widely felt to have encouraged the Oklahoma bombing and other hate crimes. One obituary reads:

> His best-known product was *The Turner Diaries*, a self-published book he wrote under the pseudonym Andrew Macdonald. In this he displayed a predilection for Scottish myths and heritage shared by others in extreme right-wing politics.
>
> *(Reed 2002: 20)*

The Scots' inability to make good object choices in relation to the American South continues to be embarassingly revealed. The ridiculous Tartan Day (McArthur 1998: 13) was shepherded through Congress by none other than Trent Lott, Senior Senator from Mississippi and Republican majority leader, who was forced to resign that role when, having lauded the 1948 presidential bid (on a separation of the races ticket) of Strom Thurmond, he was revealed as a closet segregationist. His ushering of Tartan Day through the congressional machinery suggests that he subscribes to the mystical union of Scotland and the American South so important in the appropriation of *Braveheart*.

There can be little doubt that *Braveheart* is the energising focus of many rightwing, often Southern, groups. As Kirsty Scott reported:

> While many extremist groups were already using Scottish history as part of their doctrine, the release of the film *Braveheart* in 1995 marked a turning point for the Celtic connection. At the Radio for Peace International monitoring station in Costa Rica, which keeps a check on the movement's short-wave radio broadcasts in the United States, operators were used to Scottish heritage, but noticed a dramatic increase following the film's release. 'It was being mentioned to such an extent that we had to go and watch it to see what all their excitement was about' said RPI director James Latham. 'They still talk about it a lot and now it's being used as a tool to recruit people into the groups. We hear them telling people: if you have friends who aren't in the movement and you are trying to convince them, make them watch this film, use it as an entry point'. The Ku Klux Klan has also pounced on the film as an endorsement of its stance. 'This movie may well become a movement piece de resistance for Christian Patriots', Texas Klan leader Louis Beam was recently quoted as saying.
>
> *(Scott 1997: 12)*

Such reports may have a tendency to over-dramatise the American appropriation of *Braveheart* by concentrating on its being embraced by the most extreme of the Southern groups. Such oversimplification may indeed underlie the earlier remark that the conjoining of Scotland and the South distils a 'poisonous brew'. What tends to be elided is the diversity of the 'real' South. Certainly, Celeste Ray's *Southern Heritage on Display* – with its account of Mexican fiestas, New Orleans jazz funerals, Native American powwows, not to mention Scottish-African-Americans and Scottish-Native-Americans who, replete in tartan, compete in highland dancing and athletic events in American-based highland games – suggests a density and hybridity to the American South not often appreciated by those outside the region. Just as there is a Scottish Discursive Unconscious within which the hegemonic narratives are Tartanry and Kailyard, there may well be a Southern Discursive Unconscious – like the Scottish one, ardently subscribed to by the 'natives' themselves – in which the dominant tropes are *Gone With the Wind*-style defeated grandeur, Tennessee Williams-inspired dementia and *Deliverance*-style redneckery, all subsumable within HL Mencken's notorious and influential concept of 'the benighted South'. That said, however, there does remain a peculiarly intense quality about the conjoining of Scotland and the South. What historical factors, then, brought this about?

As with other European groups, there had been extensive, uneven and diversely-motivated influxes of Scots to North America from the early seventeenth century well into the twentieth century. As well as expressing itself in the material culture of Scots-owned and staffed enterprises, church buildings and forms of worship, under the influence of the Scottish Discursive Unconscious it had often expressed itself in St Andrew's Societies, named clan societies and the maintenance of highland games, pipe bands and 'clan gatherings'. While this would be true of Scottish enclaves from Canada to Florida and from Massachusetts to California (as the earlier discussion of *Brigadoon* has indicated), the Scots 'inheritance' took a particular form in the South, as American anthropologist Celeste Ray explains:

> American celebrations of Scottish heritage drew on romantic, nineteenth century interpretations of Highland manners and Scottish identity – a mythic Scottish past that in the South blends harmoniously with nostalgic visions of antebellum southern society and the Lost Cause. Celebratory and commemorative reflections on ancestral experience commonly merge historical realities, religious inheritance, and folk memories with selected (and often invented) traditions to interpret the past in a form meaningful for the present. Southerners take to the Scottish heritage movement so well because its present form draws on parallel mythologies,

rather than actual cultural continuities, that underlie the construction of both Scottish and southern identities. Both derive from perceived historical injuries, strong attachments to place and kin, and links between militarism and religious faith... In heritage lore, the southern experience and identity unfold in continuous tradition from Scottish culture and history, rather than a relationship to slavery or Jim Crow. Members of the Southern Scottish American community are of the generation that experienced desegregation and the reinvention of the new South. By attributing southern distinctiveness to Scottish roots, a post-Civil Rights movement celebration of 'southerness' takes on an uncontroversial, multicultural dimension focused on ethnic identity rather than race relations. The 'new southerner' is no longer just a white, Anglo southerner, but an ethnically Celtic southerner with other reasons for being different and unassailable justification for celebrating that difference.

(Ray 1998: 28–29)

In the original essay by Celeste Ray from which this quotation comes, the two traditions are bizarrely conjoined in the photograph of an attendee at the Biloxi, Mississippi Highland Games and Celtic Festival. From head to waist he is attired in Confederate uniform, from waist to toe in tartan kilt, sporran and hose. In retrospect, it seems far from coincidental that Jefferson Davis, former President of the defeated Confederacy in the American Civil War, should visit the site of the Battle of Culloden in 1869. What a meeting of (what were to become) two lachrymose *weltanschaungen*! As Ray indicates, both the vanquished Jacobites and the defeated Confederates would be transformed into saintly martyrs by their 'descendants', the more unsavoury elements of their social systems – adherence to absolute monarchy in the former and to slavery in the latter – airbrushed out or 'explained' as the myths of the 'noble' highlanders and the 'gracious' antebellum South were progressively elaborated, within a long ideological manoeuvre culminating, in *Braveheart*, in a moist-eyed, ill-defined Celticism. As Celeste Ray indicates in a later work (Ray 2001), the Battle of Culloden looms disproportionately large in the memorialising and heritage building of even 'normal' Scots-Americans.

How Southern Celtic consciousness looks from the inside, as it were, can be gauged by consulting the website of the League of the South, an organisation dedicated to the re-secession of the former

Confederacy from the United States of America. Members may post their musings on the site, as in the following by Barry Reid McCain:

> The South received a unique migration of Celts from the years 1715 to 1815... By 1830 Anglo-Celtic people and culture dominated from the Virginia Piedmont, throughout the Carolinas and into Northern Florida, westward into Alabama, Mississippi and west Tennessee. They were already pushing into Louisiana, Arkansas and east Texas and their longhunters were a common sight in Taos and Santa Fe. By the early twentieth century successive generations of Anglo-Celts, in their varied roles as frontiersmen, settlers, mountain men, cowboys and family farmers, had extended their people and culture across the Spanish southwest into southern California... Other Celtic traits live in the South as well, elements of a cultural continuum that reaches back to ancient Europe. The warrior culture continues with the normal Southern male (and female) equating being armed to being free... A 'coalition' of groups exists today that would prefer that the Southerner not have any concept of an ethnic identity. Frankly, they are trying to socially-engineer the Southerner out of existence (a cultural genocide)... The coalition (the usual suspects: various leftists, Europhobic academics, Feminists, the media, etc) aggressively works to deconstruct the ethnicity of the indigenous Southerner.
>
> *(McCain 1995)*

Reading this piece symptomatically, is it too far-fetched to hear in its thrusting geographical phallicism, its warriorism and its paranoia, the not too distant echoes of Theweleit's *Freikorps* men? One wonders about the degree of self-consciousness of these 'symptoms' since the League of the South protests its constitutionalism and anti-racism.

On another part of the League's website one can have a curious experience. Between two fluttering standards – the Stars and Bars of the Confederacy and the Scottish Saltire – there appear images of Mel Gibson and Sophie Marceau in their *Braveheart* roles. As Horner's 'Gift of a Thistle' theme rises on one's tinny computer sound system, the following text emerges:

> The League of the South highly recommends Mel Gibson's movie *Braveheart*, the story of Scottish hero William Wallace. Wallace led a popular uprising against the tyrannical Edward I of England,

handing superior forces humiliating defeat at Stirling Bridge in 1297. Wallace kept alive the flame of militant Scottish nationalism until it burst into a conflagration under Robert the Bruce and consumed Edward II's army at Bannockburn in 1314. Scotland thus won her independence. *Braveheart* is immediate and powerful (and violent). Good and evil are clearly delineated (rare in Hollywood these days). Unreconstructed Southerners will find it difficult to miss the parallels between the Scots and our Confederate forebears.

(Hill 1995: unpaginated)

It is probably not coincidental that *Braveheart* was released in 1995 and the first Southern Celtic conference, under the auspices of the League, was held in 1996. The above endorsement of *Braveheart* was penned by the President of the League of the South, Dr Michael Hill, who is in the somewhat paradoxical position of teaching history at a Southern university, the student body of which is over 90 per cent African American. He is described in the online Archives for the Study of Academic Racism as:

greatly influenced by one of his teachers [at the University of Alabama], Grady McWhiney, a well-known historian whose book *Cracker Culture* attributes the character of white Southerners to their origins as freedom-loving Celts in the British Isles. Hill made Celtic Studies his speciality; he has written two books on Celtic history and counts *Braveheart* as one of his favourite films.

In the context of the warriorism motif, it might be added that McWhiney is co-author of *Attack and Die* which attributes the Confederacy's defeat partly to its 'Celtic' military tactic of the headlong charge, and Hill is himself the author of a book entitled *Celtic Warfare*. Celeste Ray mentions the significant presence in Scottish-American clan and other societies not only of serving and ex-military men, but the Special Services sector of the military such as the Green Berets and Navy Seals. In her conversations with such figures, they often spoke of being sustained by their sense of their 'Scottish warrior past' and, with others in the community, frequently alluded to *Braveheart* without prompting. This, and other themes of this chapter, were strikingly condensed in a single moment of a CBS news bulletin during the US build-up of forces in the Persian Gulf.

An image of Mel Gibson as Wallace gave way to an interview with General Scott Wallace, introduced as 'distantly related to William Wallace'.

To some extent, this indicates that *Braveheart* is making inroads into the 'normal' American psyche as well as its lunatic fringe. Cultural geographer Euan Hague has done extensive work, much of it interview-based, in both Scotland and the USA on the perception of Scotland. Much of that work overlaps with the ideas rehearsed in Chapter 5 and in this chapter, and it certainly demonstrates the international hegemony of the Scottish Discursive Unconscious, particularly in its Tartanry dimension. Its interest in this context, however, is in its demonstration of the extent to which *Braveheart*, as emblematic of Scotland, is percolating into the psyches of ordinary Americans, both adults and children, in a much more general and, probably, less politically active way. Thus, with regard to his questioning of American adults about their 'knowledge' of Scotland, Hague writes:

> To assess how an international audience conceived of 'Scotland' in 1997 I conducted 'semi-structured' 'informal interviews' in New York State… Although as the interviewer I had a general selection of questions and issues to address, I did not ask any direct questions about *Braveheart* or film in general. Yet during the interviews respondents often chose to discuss *Braveheart*.
>
> *(Hague 1999: 6)*

Also, in a comparative study involving schoolchildren in Edinburgh and Syracuse, New York State who were asked to draw a picture of 'Scotland', Hague notes:

> In Syracuse it is likely that broadcast media is a significant source of information about Scotland. For example [seven year-old] Jim was one of three Syracuse children to ask if *Braveheart* was Scottish. When I replied that it was he said 'Scotland has special sports where people throw logs' and drew 'a man from *Braveheart*' tossing the caber.
>
> *(Hague 2001: 93)*

This general filtering of *Braveheart* into American consciousness is borne out by many of the US-based websites alluded to in Chapter 5 and, while regrettable in terms of the Scottish Discursive Unconscious becoming even more deeply embedded, is less worrying than the film's appropriation by more politically active groups. Examples of the celebration of *Braveheart* in ultra-rightwing discourse could be laid out *ad infinitum* and, often quite literally, *ad nauseam*. Perhaps the penultimate word should go to the 'White Nationalist' website, Yggdrasil:

> *Braveheart* is THE white nationalist masterwork... [I]t dramatises the very central dilemma of Western Civilisation... *Braveheart* shows us a peasant revolt. A revolt of a nationalist White underclass... [E]very male descendant of European Christendom would immediately understand its modern relevance... [T]he dilemma faced by William Wallace is unchanged to this day. We have an inner party composed primarily of aliens who have taken over all positions of power in the electronic media, the universities and the government in the United States. They have mounted a massive cultural attack on the descendants of European Christendom throughout the Western world... with the objective of de-racinating and de-nationalising them... Gibson's *Braveheart* uses the word 'freedom' as modern code for something else... [T]he word 'freedom' has come to have two meanings. Primarily the word 'freedom' has come to mean what the inner party wishes it to mean, namely the ability to indulge in individual vices such as adultery, abortion, drug use and homosexual sodomy... [I]t becomes clear that Wallace is using the term 'freedom' in exactly the same way that a modern member of a dissident militia group uses the term. It is a code word meaning independence of the group and control over its evolutionary destiny... But the real wonder was that *Braveheart* was released to critical acclaim rather than massive protest... For us that is wildly optimistic news, for it intimates that our movement can, if we are smart, propagate itself without much resistance.

It is comforting to learn that, after the coming Aryan triumph, *heterosexual* sodomy will remain unproscribed.

The position articulated in this chapter is very close to that of Christopher Whyte's conclusion to his essay on Neil Gunn's *The Silver Darlings*, 'Fishy Masculinities':

> There can be little doubt that Gunn's gender ideology, with its strict separation of domains, its women trapped in the domestic sphere while men go forth to fight, explore and hunt, its young men who attain maturity by disowning the feminine and distancing

themselves from it, was closer to that of European fascism than to any other contemporary ideological conformation. This is not to say that Gunn was a fascist. But it does mean that the time has come to look honestly, with the perhaps wiser eyes of the 1990s, at the political implications of his seductive rhetoric of blood, ethnicity and gender stereotypes, and to find it an appropriate place among the range of cultural nationalisms, both progressive and reactionary, practised and preached in Scotland in the course of this century.

(*Whyte 1995: 66*)

Indeed, with the names of Mel Gibson and Randall Wallace – *Braveheart*'s screenwriter – substituted for that of Gunn, this passage might make a suitable epilogue for the chapter, were its conclusion not so even-handed and did it not appear to lay the charge of fascism at the door of the artist rather than at the specific aesthetic forms he used. Not to mince words, it is *Braveheart,* as the modern 'Ur-Fascist' text *par excellence,* and not its makers which is profoundly dangerous and which must be confronted with analysis and rational argument at every opportunity.

It remains to offer those (particularly my fellow Scots) who admire *Braveheart* a slogan for their banner – 'Ur-Fascism is Oor Fascism'.

Epilogue

All writers, film historians included, like to end their books with a rhetorical flourish – amusing and apt or fatuously smart-arsed, according to the reader's taste – such as that which ended Chapter 9. In this respect we are not much different from the makers of Broadway musicals or Hollywood movies. However, to have closed the book on the slogan which ended that chapter would have implied that *Braveheart* is a problem only for Scotland and the Scots. It is certainly that but it is much more. The insidiousness of *Braveheart* must be seen in the context of the worldwide political, economic and ideological framework which emerged unevenly throughout the twentieth century (and arguably before that) but the outlines of which have become clearer only since the collapse of communism in the last decade. The most salient features of that framework are: United States dominance in military, diplomatic and (less extremely) economic terms; the acceleration of globalisation and the move to awesome, barely restrainable power of transnational corporations, many (but by no means all) of them American; and – what connects most directly with *Braveheart* – the proliferation of lethal (sometimes, but not always, national) identity blocs, often in reaction to the first two factors. It would be possible to 'sieve' *Braveheart* through all these factors to demonstrate how closely it follows the contours of each. Widely, and largely justifiably, thought of as an American film, it is nevertheless tied in at various levels with Twentieth Century Fox which, while in itself an American company, is part of Rupert Murdoch's transnational News Corporation. At the ideological level, *Braveheart*'s xenophobia is absolutely prototypical of those modern politico-military identity formations – discernible from South America, through the British Isles, the Iberian peninsula, the Balkans, the Middle East, the Indian subcontinent to the Philippines – characterised by utter indifference to the pain of their own 'vilified Others'. These blocs are as likely to be recognised states as minorities who oppose them.

The dense framework within which there might be a relationship – however attenuated – between the dominance of the USA and *Braveheart*'s relaying of xenophobic ideology is not easily penetrable. A possible route, however, might be by way of an examination of the ruthlessness with which the USA pursues its own interests on *every* front, through *every* ostensibly international organisation, opportunistically abrogating agreements when it perceives its interests to be threatened. If the jobs of American steelworkers are at risk – especially in the run-up to domestic mid-term elections – slap tariffs on foreign steel, American rhetoric about 'free trade' notwithstanding; if the Kyoto protocol on carbon emissions is awkward for US industry, don't ratify it; if a particular figure heading an international organisation seeks to take an independent line, block the renewal of his contract; if a proposed International Criminal Court might be imagined a threat to US military personnel, demand that the USA be exempt from its provisions; and so on. Precisely this kind of iron-heeled 'negotiation' is apparent in the furthering of the interests of its entertainment – and within that its film – industry which, after aerospace, is its top foreign dollar earner. The key body here is the Motion Picture Association of America, under its powerful president, Jack Valenti, who has been right at the centre of the US political establishment since the Kennedy administration of the 1960s. It is far from insignificant that Brazilian film director Arnaldo Jabor, deploring both the commercial and aesthetic hegemony of Hollywood over Brazilian cinema, should express his feelings in a poem entitled 'Jack Valenti's Brazilian Agenda'. In pursuit of American entertainment interests Valenti works hand-in-glove with those institutions whose top personnel he has been close to for decades, the US diplomatic and security services. The measure of Valenti's success is that upwards of 90 per cent of the films shown on European screens (not to mention those of the rest of the world) are American (variously defined) while only 2 per cent of films shown on American screens are foreign. A trade deficit of that order in any other branch of 'commerce' would have national governments tearing out their hair, but it is treated almost casually by EU governments, with the partial exception of France. To the extent that politicians have a strategy to deal with US dominance in this area – the creation of the Film Council under Alan Parker in the UK, for example – the plan has been to produce images of Britain which will sell in the USA, which effectively means regressive, heritage-based images or inane comedies with a Hollywood star to guarantee 'marquee value' in America.

All of this may seem a long way from, and of doubtful relevance to, *Braveheart*'s relaying of its insidious ideologies in Scotland and throughout the world, but the connection is that until diverse national governments uncouple cinema from commerce and formulate individual and cooperative film cultural policies – which ensure that, among other things, diverse filmic accounts of history are not only made but distributed, exhibited and critically discussed – there is no hope of countering the pernicious influence of films like *Braveheart*. In the very broadest terms, the same argument applies to *Brigadoon*, though one would have to be aesthetically and ideologically purblind not to perceive the differences between the two films and the level of threat they pose. To be sure, *Brigadoon*'s relaying of the Scottish Discursive Unconscious needs to be understood and countered, as does *Braveheart*'s, but what must be most immediately grappled with is the latter's proto-fascist elements. At a very deep, attenuated level there is a relationship between the two in which *Braveheart* might be seen as a completely unhinged, demented version of *Brigadoon*. As I write, the United States of America – shamefully abetted by the Blair government in the UK – seems to be embarking on a course of reckless military adventurism in the Middle East. What is being enacted is 'the tragedy of a great country, with noble impulses, successful institutions, magnificent historical achievements and immense energies, which has become a menace to itself and to mankind' (Lieven 2002: 11). Films of the ideological orientation of *Braveheart* partly reflect and partly construct the will to act out this tragedy.

With regard to the likelihood of any early change in American dominance of the world (including its cinema screens) this epilogue is written with a particular phrase in mind, a phrase associated with, if not actually coined by, Antonio Gramsci – 'Optimism of the Will, Pessimism of the Intellect'.

Bibliography

Adams, Doug (1998). 'A score to remember? James Horner's technique critiqued', *Film Score Monthly* March/April, pp 39–41

Adorno, Theodor W *et al* (1950). *The Authoritarian Personality* (New York, Norton)

Ascherson, Neal (1995). 'Now is the time for official heroes to come to the aid of the party', *Independent on Sunday* 24 September, p 20

Barrie, JM (1889). *A Window in Thrums* (London, Hodder and Stoughton)

Barrie, JM (1892). *Auld Licht Idylls* (London, Hodder and Stoughton)

Barrie, JM (1925). *Mary Rose* (London, Hodder and Stoughton)

Barthes, Roland (1975). *S/Z* (London, Cape)

Barthes, Roland (1976). *The Pleasure of the Text* (London, Cape)

Behlmer, Rudy (ed) (1993). *Memo from Darryl F. Zanuck: the Golden Years at Twentieth Century Fox* (New York, Grove Press)

Birse, Graham (1996). Film Tourism Presentation for *Putting Scotland in the Picture* (Edinburgh, Scottish Tourist Board)

Black, Gregory D (1994). *Hollywood Censored: Morality Codes, Catholics and the Movies* (Cambridge, Cambridge University Press)

Block, Geoffrey (1993). 'The Broadway canon from *Show Boat* to *West Side Story* and the European operatic ideal', *Journal of Musicology* No 4, Fall, pp 525-544

Block, Geoffrey (2001). 'Frederick Loewe' in Stanley Sadie (ed) *The New Grove Dictionary of Music and Musicians* (London, Macmillan)

Bodnar, James (1992). *Remaking America: Public Memory, Commemoration and Patriotism in the Twentieth Century* (Princeton, Princeton University Press)

Bordwell, David, Kristin Thompson and Janet Staiger (1985). *The Classical Hollywood Cinema: Film Style and Mode of Production to 1960* (London, Routledge)

Broxton, Jonathan (2001). 'King of the world: the James Horner buyer's guide, Part 1', *Film Score Monthly* April/May, p 24

Byatt, Tony (1978). *Picture Postcards and Their Publishers* (Malvern, Golden Age Postcard Books)

Calder, Angus (1994). *Revolving Culture: Notes from the Scottish Republic* (London, I.B.Tauris)

Cameron, Kenneth (1997). *America on Film: Hollywood and American History* (New York, Continuum)

Casper, Joseph Andrew (1977). *Vincente Minnelli and the Film Musical* (London, Tantivy Press)

Chapman, Malcolm (1978). *The Gaelic Vision in Scottish Culture* (London, Croom Helm)

Chapman, Malcolm (1992). *The Celts* (London, Macmillan)

Clark, Arthur Melville (1981). *Murder Under Trust or The Topical Macbeth and Other Jacobean Matters* (Edinburgh, Scottish Academic Press)

Corrigan, Tim (1986). 'Film and the culture of cult', *Wide Angle* 8 (3/4), pp 91–100

Costley, Tom (1997). '*Braveheart* versus *Rob Roy*: How Stirling won the tourist battle', *Researchplus* June, pp 14–15

Craig, Cairns (1982). 'Myths against history: tartanry and kailyard in nineteenth century Scottish literature' in C McArthur (ed) *Scotch Reels: Scotland in Cinema and Television* (London, British Film Institute)

Craig, Cairns (1996). *Out of History: Narrative Paradigms in Scottish and English Culture* (Edinburgh, Polygon)

Crawford, Cheryl (1977). *One Naked Individual: My Fifty Years in the Theatre* (Indianapolis, Bobbs Merrill)

Daiches, David (ed) (1993). *The New Companion to Scottish Culture* (Edinburgh, Polygon)

Delameter, Jerome (1981). *Dance in the Hollywood Musical* (Ann Arbor, UMI Research Press)

De Mille, Agnes (1952). *Dance to the Piper* (Boston, Little Brown)

Domarchi, Jean (1956). Review of *Brigadoon*, *Cahiers du Cinéma* No. 63, October, pp 44–47

Eagleton, Terry (1983). *Literary Theory: An Introduction* (Oxford, Blackwell)

Easton, Carol (1996). *No Intermissions: The Life of Agnes De Mille* (New York, Da Capo Press)

Eco, Umberto (1983). '*Casablanca*, cult movies and intertextual collage' in *Faith in Fakes: Travels in Hyperreality* (London, Vintage, 1998)

Eco, Umberto (2001). 'Ur-Fascism' in *Five Moral Pieces* (London, Secker and Warburg)

Edensor, Tim (1997). 'Reading *Braveheart*: representing and contesting Scottish identity', *Scottish Affairs* 21 (Autumn), pp 135-158

Edensor, Tim (2002). *National Identity, Popular Culture and Everyday Life* (Oxford, Berg)

Elkins, James (2001). *Pictures and Tears* (New York and London, Routledge)

Ewan, Elizabeth (1995). 'Film reviews: Europe', *American Historical Review* 100, pp 1219–1221

Fanon, Frantz (1968). *Black Skin, White Masks* (London, Paladin)

Fiske, Roger (1983). *Scotland in Music: A European Enthusiasm* (Cambridge, Cambridge University Press)

Foley, Malcolm and J John Lennon (1996). 'Editorial: Heart of Darkness', *International Journal of Heritage Studies* 2/4, pp 194–197

Fried, Albert (1997). *McCarthyism, the Great American Red Scare: A Documentary History* (Oxford, Oxford University Press)

Füredi, Frank (1992). *Mythical Past, Elusive Future: History and Society in an Anxious Age* (London, Pluto)

Gerstäcker, Friedrich Wilhelm (1958). *Germelshausen* (New York, Barron's Educational Series)

Giulianotti, Richard (1991). 'Scotland's tartan army in Italy: the case for the carnivalesque', *Sociological Review* Vol 39, No 3, pp 503–527

Hague, Euan (1999). 'Scotland on film: attitudes and opinions about *Braveheart*', *Etudes Ecossaises* No 6, pp 75–89

Hague, Euan (2001). 'Nationality and children's drawings – pictures 'about Scotland' by primary school children in Edinburgh, Scotland and Syracuse, New York State', *Scottish Geographical Journal* 117 (2), pp 77–99

Harvey, Stephen (1989). *Directed by Vincente Minnelli* (New York, Harper and Row)

Hay, Peter (1990). *Movie Anecdotes* (Oxford, Oxford University Press)

Hemingway, Wayne (2000). *Just Above the Mantelpiece: Mass Market Masterpieces* (London, Booth Clibborn Editions)

Hill, Michael (1986). *Celtic Warfare: 1595–1763* (Edinburgh, John Donald)

Hill, Michael (1995). 'Statement on *Braveheart*', http://www.dixienet.org//spatriot/vol3no3

Hilton, James (1933). *Lost Horizon* (London, Macmillan)

Hobsbawm, Eric and Terence Ranger (eds) (1983). *The Invention of Tradition* (Cambridge, Cambridge University Press)

Hogg, James (1992). *Confessions of a Justified Sinner* (London, David Campbell)

Hutchison, David (1987). *The Modern Scottish Theatre* (Glasgow, Molendinar Press)

Jabor, Arnaldo (1995). 'Jack Valenti's Brazilian Agenda' in Randal Johnson and Robert Stam (eds) *Brazilian Cinema* (New York, Columbia University Press), pp 110–114

Jenkins, Henry (2000). 'Reception theory and audience research: the mystery of the vampire's kiss' in Christine Gledhill and Linda Williams (eds) *Reinventing Film Studies* (London, Arnold), pp 165–182

Keller, James R (1997). 'Masculinity and Marginality in *Rob Roy* and *Braveheart*', *Journal of Popular Film and Television* Vol 24, No 4, Winter, pp 146–151

Kislan, Richard (1980). *The Musical: A Look at the American Musical Theatre* (New York and London, Applause)

Krossa, Sharon (1997–2000). 'Regarding the film *Braveheart*', http://www.medievalscotland.org/scotbiblio/braveheart.shtml

Krossa, Sharon (2000). '*Braveheart*'s errors: an illustration of scale', http://www.medievalscotland.org/scotbiblio/bravehearterrors.shtml

Lauder, Sir Harry (1928). *Roamin' in the Gloamin'* (London, Hutchinson)

Lees, Gene (1991). *The Musical World of Lerner and Loewe* (London, Robson)

Lerner, Alan Jay and Frederick Loewe (1947). *Brigadoon* (London, Chappell)

Lerner, Alan Jay (1978). *The Street Where I Live* (London, Columbus Books)

Lewis, Robert (1980). *Advice to the Players* (New York, Theatre Communications Group)

Lewis, Robert (1984). *Slings and Arrows: Theatre in My Life* (New York, Stein and Day)

Lieven, Anatol (2002). 'The Push for War', *London Review of Books* Vol 24, No 19, 3 October, pp8–11

Limond, David (1994). '"Scottish second-in-command seeking approval": the Celtic nationalists and the academic profession in Scotland', *Proceedings of the Association for Postgraduate and Postdoctoral Historical Studies Conference: Core and Periphery*, pp 1–8

Luhr, William (1999). 'Mutilating Mel: Martyrdom and masculinity in *Braveheart*' in Christopher Sharret (ed) *Mythologies of Violence in Postmodern Media* (Detroit, Wayne State University Press), pp 227–246

Lutz, Tom (1999). *Crying: the Natural and Cultural history of Tears* (London, WW Norton)

Lyon, James K (1982). *Bertolt Brecht in America* (London, Methuen)

Massie, Allan (1995). 'Pride, prejudice and the birth of a hero figure', *Scotland on Sunday*, 3 September, p 12

McArthur, Colin (1982). 'Scotland and cinema: the iniquity of the fathers' in C McArthur (ed) *Scotch Reels: Scotland in Cinema and Television* (London, British Film Institute), pp 40–69

McArthur, Colin (1994a). 'Culloden: a pre-emptive strike', *Scottish Affairs*, No 9, pp 97–126

McArthur, Colin (1994b). 'The cultural necessity of a poor Celtic cinema' in John Hill, Martin McLoone and Paul Hainsworth (eds) *Border Crossing: Film in Ireland, Britain and Europe* (Belfast and London, Institute of Irish Studies in association with the British Film Institute), pp 112–125

McArthur, Colin (1995). Review of *Braveheart*, *Sight and Sound*, September, p 45

McArthur, Colin (1996). 'A travesty of history', *Scotland on Sunday*, 25 February, p 13

McArthur, Colin (1997). 'Chinese boxes and Russian dolls: tracking the elusive cinematic city' in David B Clarke (ed) *The Cinematic City* (London, Routledge)

McArthur, Colin (1998). 'Scotland may rue the day', *Scotland on Sunday*, 5 April, p 13

McArthur, Colin (2001). 'Caledonianising *Macbeth*', *Scottish Affairs* No 36, pp 12–39

McArthur, Colin (2003). *Whisky Galore! and The Maggie* (London, I.B. Tauris)

McBain, Janet (1990). 'Scotland in feature film: a filmography' in Eddie Dick (ed) *From Limelight to Satellite: A Scottish Film Book* (London and Glasgow, British Film Institute/Scottish Film Council)

McCain, Barry Reid (1995). 'The Anglo-Celts', http://www.dixienet.org//spatriot/vol3no3/member13.html

McConnell, Tom (1995). 'Battlers under the bridge', *Herald Weekender Magazine*, 2 September

McCrone, David (1992). *Understanding Scotland: The Sociology of a Stateless Nation* (London, Routledge)

McWhiney, Grady (1988). *Cracker Culture: Celtic Ways in the Old South* (Tuscaloosa, University of Alabama Press)

McWhiney, Grady and Perry D Jameson (1982). *Attack and Die: Civil War Military Tactics and the Southern Heritage* (Tuscaloosa, University of Alabama Press)

Morgan, David (2000). *Knowing the Score: Film Composers Talk About the Blood, Sweat and Tears of Writing for Cinema* (New York, Harper Entertainment)

Morrden, Ethan (1998). *Coming Up Roses: The Broadway Musical in the 1950s* (Oxford, Oxford University Press)

Morrden, Ethan (1999). *Beautiful Mornin': The Broadway Musical in the 1940s* (Oxford, Oxford University Press)

Morton, Graeme (2001). *William Wallace: Man and Myth* (Stroud, Sutton)

Morton, HV (1929). *In Search of Scotland* (London, Methuen)

Nairn, Tom (1977). *The Break-Up of Britain* (London, Verso)

Naremore, James (1993). *The Films of Vincente Minnelli* (Cambridge, Cambridge University Press)

Neale, Steve (2000). *Genre and Hollywood* (London, Routledge)

Nowell-Smith, Geoffrey (1996). 'Roberto Rossellini' in Geoffrey Nowell-Smith (ed) *The Oxford History of World Cinema* (Oxford, Clarendon Press), p 438

Oates, Jennifer Lynn (undated). 'The musical guises of Lerner and Loewe: *Brigadoon, My Fair Lady* and *Camelot*' (unpublished paper)

O'Sullivan, Noël (1983). *Fascism* (London, Dent)

Petrie, Duncan (2000). *Screening Scotland* (London, British Film Institute)

Plantinga, Carl (1997). 'Notes on spectator emotion and ideological film criticism' in Richard Allan and Murray Smith (eds) *Film Theory and Philosophy* (Oxford, Oxford University Press), pp 372–393

Ray, Celeste (1998). 'Scottish heritage southern style', *Southern Cultures* 4 (2), pp 24–45

Ray, Celeste (2001). *Highland Heritage: Scottish Americans in the American South* (Chapel Hill, NC, University of North Carolina Press)

Reed, Christopher (2002). 'Obituary: William Pierce', *Guardian*, 25 July, p 20

Richards, Jeffrey (1998). 'Popular Memory and the Construction of English History' – The Ninth Annual Bindoff Lecture (London, Queen Mary and Westfield College, University of London)

Rosenstone, Robert (1995). *Visions of the Past: The Challenge of Film to Our Idea of History* (Cambridge, MA, Harvard University Press)

Rousso, Henry (1991). *The Vichy Syndrome: History and Memory in France Since 1944*, trans. Arthur Goldhammer (Cambridge, MA, Harvard University Press)

Said, Edward (1978). *Orientalism* (London, Routledge and Kegan Paul)

Salmond, Alex (1995). 'National convener's address, SNP national conference, Perth' (Edinburgh, Scottish National Party)

Schatz, Thomas (1988). *The Genius of the System* (London, Simon and Schuster)

Scott, Kirsty (1997). 'The fatal attraction', *Herald*, 6 August, p 12

Seenan, Gerard (1999). 'Klansmen take their lead from Scots', *Guardian*, 30 January, p 12

Siegel, Marcia B (1979). *The Shapes of Change: Images of American Dance* (Boston, Houghton Mifflin)

Sloboda, John (1991). 'Music structure and emotional response: some empirical findings', *Psychology of Music*, Vol 19, No 2, pp 110–120

Smith, Henry Nash (1950). *Virgin Land: the American West as Symbol and Myth* (New York, Vintage Books)

Smith, Jeff (1999). 'Movie music as moving music: emotion, cognition and the film score' in Carl Plantinga and Greg M Smith (eds) *Passionate Views: Film, Cognition and Emotion* (Baltimore, Johns Hopkins University Press), pp 146–167

Smith, Murray (1995). *Engaging Characters: Fiction, Emotion and the Cinema* (Oxford, Oxford University Press)

Smith, Wendy (1990). *Real Life Drama: The Group Theater and America, 1931–1940* (New York, Alfred A Knopf Inc)

Smyth, Gerry (2002). Review of June Skinner Sawyer's *The Complete Guide to Celtic Music: From the Highland Bagpipe and Riverdance to U2 and Enya* in *Popular Music*, 21/2, May 2002, pp 242–244

Spackman, Barbara (1996). *Fascist Virilities* (Minneapolis, University of Minnesota Press)

Staiger, Janet (1992). *Interpreting Films: Studies in the Historical Reception of American Cinema* (Princeton, Princeton University Press)

Stein, Charles W (1984). *American Vaudeville As Seen By Its Contemporaries* (New York, Alfred A Knopf Inc)

Stevenson, Robert Louis (1886). *Dr Jekyll and Mr Hyde* (London, Longmans Green)

Stowe, David W (1994). *Swing Changes: Big Band Jazz in New Deal America* (Cambridge, MA, Harvard University Press)

Tambling, Jeremy (1996). *Opera and the Culture of Fascism* (Oxford, Clarendon Press)

Taylor, Ronald (1991). *Kurt Weill: Composer in a Divided World* (London, Simon and Schuster)

Theweleit, Klaus (1989). *Male Fantasies*, 2 vols, (London, Polity Press)

Tinkcom, Matthew (1996). 'Working like a homosexual: camp visual codes and the labour of gay subjects in the MGM Freed Unit', *Cinema Journal*, Winter, pp 24–42

Traubner, Richard (1983). *Operetta: A Theatrical History* (Oxford, Oxford University Press)

Walker, Alexander (1995). 'How Hollywood hates the English', *Evening Standard*, 7 September, p 27

Wallace, Mike (1996). *Mickey Mouse History and Other Essays on American Memory* (Philadelphia, Temple University Press)

Wayne, Mike (1997). *Theorizing Video Practice* (London, Lawrence and Wishart)

Whitfield, J and P Tagg (2002). '*Braveheart*: film music analysis', http://www.the blackbook.net/papers/tag/article.html, paragraph 10

Whitman, Walt (1855). *Leaves of Grass* (London, Secker and Warburg, 1960)

Whyte, Christopher (1995). 'Fishy masculinities: Neil Gunn's *The Silver Darlings*' in Christopher Whyte (ed) *Gendering the Nation: Studies in Modern Scottish Literature* (Edinburgh, Edinburgh University Press), pp 49–68

Williams, Martin (1992). *Hidden in Plain Sight: An Examination of the American Arts* (Oxford, Oxford University Press)

Womack, Peter (1989). *Improvement and Romance: Constructing the Myth of the Highlands* (London, Macmillan)

Wood, Robin (1998). 'Humble guests at the celebration: an interview with Thomas Vinterberg and Ulrich Thomsen', *Cineaction* 48, December, pp 47–54

Yggdrasil (1995). '*Braveheart*: a nationalist classic', http://www.ddc.net/ygg/cwar/brvhrt.htm

Young, James E (1993). *The Texture of Memory: Holocaust Memorials and Meaning* (New Haven and London, Yale University Press)

Yudkoff, Alvin (1999). *Gene Kelly: A Life of Dance and Dreams* (New York, Backstage Books)

Index of Films

General Index